RIGHTS
of the Public
Employee

RIGHTS
of the Public
Employee

Robert P. Dwoskin

American Library Association

Chicago 1978

Library of Congress Cataloging in Publication Data

Dwoskin, Robert P
  Rights of the public employee.

  Includes bibliographical references and index.
  1. Civil service—United States. I. American
Library Association. II. Title.
KF5337.D87   342′.73′068   78–1658
  ISBN 0–8389–0257–X

Printed in the United States of America

Contents

Introduction

This book had its origins in my involvement in the case of Ellis Hodgin, a public librarian in Martinsville, Virginia, who was dismissed from his job ostensibly because of his participation as a plaintiff in a lawsuit to eliminate a religious education program from his city's public school system.

Because this case brought up the issue of intellectual freedom for librarians, the American Library Association became extremely interested. Though the litigation itself was not successful, members of the association urged me to write a book on the constitutional aspects of public employment, since such cases as Hodgin's indicated that the whole area of the rights of the public employee constitutes a legal mine field; that common sense notions of legal rights serve no useful purpose; and that a decision of whether or not to take certain actions, if based upon a "seat of the pants" approach to the law, may have catastrophic repercussions for a public employee. In truth, the questions of constitutional rights of public employees are part of a larger issue, that of the exact nature of the legal relationship between the public employer and the public employee.

Public employment is different from private employment, if only because every act that a public employee does and every act done to a public employee constitutes, to a greater or lesser degree, an act of government, and the mere classification of something as an act of government brings into play a whole series of legal concepts which have no counterpart in the private sector. On a constitutional level such ideas as freedom of speech and assembly are strictly rights of a citizen against a government, not against other private individuals. Likewise, concepts of due process of law are strictly protections of the citizens against the government. This book is intended to elucidate these concepts and apply them to the relation between the government employee and his employer. Their relevance has not always been perceived. In discussing private employment and law, such ideas have no role whatsoever since, barring any specific contract limitation, a private employer can dismiss or discipline its employees for any or no cause, provided only that the dismissal or discipline is not for reasons of racial, sexual, or religious discrimination.

Government employment, of course, does not work in this way. Any personnel decision made by a public employer concerning the public employee must, at least in a conceptual sense, be weighed against these concepts of due process or, on an even lesser degree, ideas of just cause and lack of arbitrariness. This does not mean, contrary to popular belief, that no government employee can be fired except in the most serious cases; it does mean, however, that a certain level of formality has to enter into all personnel decisions and, ironically, the lower the level of employment, the greater the degree of formality that is required.

The legal concepts discussed in this book, while technical and in some cases speculative, are nevertheless realistic. In every area I have either had a case in court, have examined the possibilities of bringing a case for a public employee, or am aware of a case in which the legal issue and the legal right of the employee was determined by a technical and, I hope, sophisticated analysis of a particular concept. As an example, I have represented teachers who have suffered job actions because they ran for Congress, organized a faculty senate, or tried to introduce a progressive education program in a traditional school; prison guards who were dismissed for cooperating with a state police investigation; and employees who were fired while in the hospital after being assaulted by another employee. These are just a few examples of cases I have been personally involved in, and I mention them strictly to show that the theoretical ideas that will be discussed in this book have a direct relationship to actual incidents, not only in major metropolitan areas such as the District of Columbia, but also in numerous small cities and towns around the country.

The book itself is divided into three parts, with each part based on the general theme of public employment's legal relationship, with emphasis on the problems and rights which a single public employee must face or can assert concerning his legal job relationship. The first part deals with the concept of public employment in two chapters. The first discusses the historic relationship between the public employee and the employer, including concepts of the so-called right-privilege doctrine and how this evolved. While this might sound unnecessarily technical, these basic theoretical concepts must be understood for the reader to realize why a public employee, in many circumstances, cannot assert certain rights. The second chapter deals with the various grounds available to public employers to dismiss or exclude persons from public service without specifically violating their constitutional rights, as well as the limitations on such power of exclusion and dismissal in terms of the special interests the employee may have without asserting a specific constitutional right.

The second part of the book concerns the employee and the First Amendment, a constitutional problem limited exclusively to public employees in the area of job rights. This discussion is divided into three chapters. The first is naturally concerned with the right of free speech, the limitations which may be placed on the First Amendment rights of a public employee, and how, in many circumstances, those rights or limitations are not applicable to a private citizen in dealing with a nonemployment matter with the government. The second is the right, or limitations placed on it, of employee political activities which, as most people recognize, constitutes a totally unique limitation on First Amendment rights, one with no counterpart elsewhere in our society. Finally, the question of limitations on belief and association is discussed, including such matters as the loyalty oath.

The final part covers the area of nonjudicial remedies for public employees. Since other parts of the book are predicated upon the employee going to court to assert his rights, especially in the area of the First Amendment, what remedies are available to a public employee, short of actually suing his employer?* First, the employee's right of procedural due process, or the right to be given certain information and/or a hearing by the employer either before or subsequent to a job action, is discussed. This is, of course, a matter of extreme concern to public employees and, as in many other areas, the legal realities are far more complicated than often supposed and cannot be understood without an examination of the technical questions involved. Finally, the right of employee organization, namely unionization of public employees, is touched on. This area of law, a major new legal battlefield, will be discussed only in context of the individual employee-union relationship, including both the right of an individual employee to belong to a union, and the rights the individual employee may possess against the public employee labor union.

This book is not, of course, intended to be a definitive study; such a study would involve numerous volumes and continuous updating. It is,

---

*Here and in the chapters that follow, the masculine pronoun has been used for succinctness and should be understood to refer to both sexes.

instead, intended to provide the public employee with an idea of the legal framework of his employment. Too often the public employee gets into irreversible trouble by assuming a right to take a certain action or challenge a certain action of his governmental employer which, in fact, he does not possess. While I will discuss what I think the law should be, I will not lose sight of what the law actually is. The public employee reading this book should, if nothing else, derive from it a concept of the vast gap between what many people, including the author, would like the law to be with regard to public employees and their rights, and what the law is in reality.

Chapter 1

Historical Background

Although the main thrust of this study concerns those rights guaranteed by the Constitution, the concept of the rights of public employees is broader than constitutional rights per se. In fact, the actual topic under discussion here is the legal relationship between the government employee and his employer from the perspective of the individual employee. This relationship can be split into two major aspects. The first involves the employee's legal rights with respect to obtaining and retaining his job; the second involves the degree to which the conditions of employment can affect his legal rights as a citizen, especially rights guaranteed by the Constitution.

This focus avoids matters of public administration, the ways in which the business of government is administered. Instead it is concentrated exclusively on the legal relationships between the governmental employer and the employee, and the ways in which this relationship is defined by means of either statutory enactment, executive order or, of most concern, judicial decision.

The Courts and the Constitution

Before any further discussion of substantive issues is attempted, one important question that should be answered is that of the legal basis used by the courts to make decisions concerning governmental employers and their employees. As this book progresses, the reader should realize that any decision reached by a governmental agency with regard to personnel constitutes an act of government and, as such, can be reviewed on its merits by a court to determine whether or not it contravenes some kind of right, either statutory, constitutional, or otherwise. This is diametrically opposed to private employment where, in the absence of specific statutory authority prohibiting a private employer from taking some action against its employees, such as discrimination on the basis of racial, sexual, religious, or national origin, the private employer has full rights to dismiss or otherwise punish any of its employees for any reason, including such matters as the employee's political beliefs, his appearance, and so on.[1] Likewise, a private employer sets all terms of employment unless limited by a private contract with an individual employee or a union situation and a subsequent collective bargaining agreement.

Thus, while a great deal of this book is concerned with actions the government employer can take against its employees, note that the court decisions under examination are based on the premise that courts do have jurisdiction over these acts against governmental employees because they are acts of government. The courts, in short, define and control the powers of government. All this, of course, is an oversimplification of the problems of jurisdiction, but should, nevertheless, provide a basic framework for the more sophisticated questions of how a court determines the validity of a government's act against one of its employees.

In the context of this book, the term *constitutional* refers to two distinct types of legal relationships. The first such constitutional relationship evolves from the fact that differences between branches of the federal government and state governments are based upon the Constitution of the United States. The fact that the formation of the employing bodies is based on constitutional precedent is the reason why special legal situations develop which are not present in private employment; nonetheless, this aspect of constitutional law does not deal directly with the question of the right of the individual as such.

The second constitutional relationship develops from those parts of the Constitution, primarily the Bill of Rights, which guarantee to individuals

---

1. The primary areas of federally prohibited private discrimination are: public accommodation—prohibited by Title II of the Civil Rights Act of 1964, 42 United States Code (hereafter U.S.C.) §§2000a–2000(a)(6); employment—Title VIII of the Civil Rights Act of 1964, 42 U.S.C. §§2000e et seq.; housing—Fair Housing Act of 1964, 42 U.S.C. §§3601–19 and §3631; and age—Age Discrimination in Employment Act of 1967, 29 U.S.C. §§621–34. These statutes provide for injunctive relief, that is, reinstatement and back pay. However, one may possibly sue for actual and

certain basic rights or freedoms. A major portion of this book is concerned with trying to understand how these constitutional rights fit within the context of the public employment relationship.

In studying the historical background of the formulation of legal theory concerning the rights of public employees in relation to the governmental employer, the record shows that courts have very often failed to differentiate between the two types of constitutional relationships, that they have not understood that individual rights are really a variant of governmental action, thus severely weakening the ability of public employees to maintain their individual rights in the context of the employment relationship. This relationship is based on the concept that any action taken by a government is governmental action, and the act of a government in firing or punishing one of its employees is no less an act of the government than the act of seizing evidence for a criminal trial. This does not mean that governmental action is wrong; just as police agencies have wide latitude to seize evidence with or without a search warrant, governmental agencies have wide latitude to discipline their employees. But it does not make the action any less a governmental action, and to the degree that the action is based on the assertion of a constitutional right or what would be considered to be a completely arbitrary action, the employee would have an increased opportunity to challenge the action precisely because it was a governmental action. The courts have too often failed to understand that the governmental action is a part of the employment relationship and so judged the issue in the context of the rightness of the governmental action, not as if the matter was one of private employment.

This theory was originally based on a combination of constitutional law and common law, constitutional in the sense that the rights of public employees, as a class, were to be determined by an attempt to fix them into a system of intergovernmental relationships. When problems devolved to the level of one employee versus his employer, however, the special nature of the public employer was not perceived, and issues were often resolved by references to the common law of the day concerning labor-management relations which, of course, held that the employee had no rights in his job, but served at the will of his employer.

The decisions of the courts, one in particular, in deciding questions concerning rights of public employees as straight labor-management problems without making reference to the special status of the employer, severely limited the rights of public employees, both constitutional and

puntative damages under the Civil Rights Act of 1870, 42 U.S.C. §1981. See Jones v. Alfred H. Mayer Co., 392 U.S. 409 (1968); Runyon v. McCrary, 427 U.S. 160 (1976); McDonald v. Santa Fe Trail Transportation Co., 427 U.S. 273 (1976).

otherwise, for an unnecessarily long time.[2] In an important case in 1900, the United States Supreme Court described this theory very distinctly when it said:

> The appointment to an official position in the government, even if it be simply a clerical position, is not a mere ministerial act but involves the exercise of judgment. The appointing power must determine the fitness of the applicant, whether or not he is the proper one to discharge the duties of the position. Therefore it is one of those acts of which courts have no general supervisory power.[3]

Thomas Reed Powell, the famous commentator, in 1916 put his finger on the fallacy of the prevailing legal theory which viewed public employee-management relations problems in the same light as the problems of private labor relations. He stated:

> A significant difference between the individual employer and the state at once suggests itself. The federal Constitution does not require individuals to accord equal treatment to all. It does not forbid individuals to discriminate against individuals. It does, however, expressly declare that no state shall deny to any person within its jurisdiction the equal protection of the laws, thus state action is prohibited by the Constitution where individual action is not prohibited.
> Another reason why the effects of the Constitution on state actions differs from its effect on individual action is that unequal treatment by individuals is not the result of the passage of the law. Discrimination imposed by the state through legislation is opposed by law and the Constitution forbids denial of equal protection accomplished without intervention of law. The state, therefore, when it attempts discrimination through legislation lacks the freedom enjoyed by individuals, because the Constitution limits the state where it does not limit individuals, and limits legislative action where it does not limit action which is not legislative.[4]

While the special character of the public employee-employer relationship as perceived by Powell has been recognized by leading courts of the country with a concomitant expansion of the individual rights of public employees, vestiges of the old doctrine concerning public employees are

2. McAuliffe v. Mayor and Board of Aldermen of New Bedford, 155 Mass. 216, 29 N.E. 517 (1892), in which the right-privilege doctrine was formulated by Oliver Wendell Holmes, then chief judge of the Massachusetts Supreme Court.

3. Keim v. United States, 177 U.S. 290 (1900). See also Heim v. McCall, 239 U.S. 175 (1915); Traux v. Raich, 239 U.S. 35 (1915).

4. *The Right to Work for the State*, 16 COLUMBIA L. REV. 99, 105, 106 (1916).

still law. Often courts decide that a public employee serves at the will of the public employer and can be dismissed for good cause or for no cause at all. The old theory that public employees have no rights in the job is so ingrained in the minds of many judges that, despite advances in terms of individual rights by most other groups, in many ways the public employee still lags behind.[5]

Because vestiges of the old laws still remain and can still become incorporated in new decisions, an examination of the historical background on which the theory of public employment has been based is absolutely imperative. Of special concern is an examination of the 1900 doctrine, holding that the public employee serves at the absolute whim of his employer, to discover if it is in fact based upon a proper understanding of the nature of the public employment relationship as originally conceived. If a misreading of basic constitutional principles by courts around the turn of the century can be established, those attorneys seeking to vindicate the rights of public employees will gain a valuable weapon.

Employees and Officials

During the formation of the United States and the enactment of its Constitution, public employees as such did not exist. In fact, Thomas Jefferson, the first secretary of state, was able to conduct the foreign affairs of the country with only four employees.

At the outset of this country government departments were, of course, small in size. In addition, two other important facts should be recognized. First, those persons intimately involved with government at the nation's founding were often categorized as officers, rather than employees. Second, the eighteenth-century American concept of a public official was based on the English model, and many of the early fears concerning public servants were based on problems which developed in the English system. To better understand how American laws developed with respect to the rights of public employees, then, a brief overview of these two areas and their effects on the development of the law is necessary.

Article II, section 2, clause 2 of the Constitution provides:

5. Since much of this work is devoted to showing how the law has changed, no specific citations need be given here except to note that in one of the most recent cases by the Supreme Court concerning public employees, some of the old ideas may have been subtly reintroduced in the guise of limits of federal jurisdiction and lack of procedural due process. Since this case is discussed throughout the book, any greater detail at this time is unnecessary.

> [The President] shall nominate, and by and with the advice and consent of the Senate, shall appoint Ambassadors, other public Ministers and Consuls, Judges of the Supreme Court, and all other Officers of the United States, whose appointments are not herein otherwise provided for, and which shall be established by law, but the Congress may by law vest the Appointment of such inferior Officers, as they deem proper, in the President alone, in the Courts of Law, or in the Heads of Departments.

Clearly the Constitution differentiated between officers and inferior officers, but the public employee is not mentioned.

This poses the question: Is the inferior officer mentioned in the Constitution another term for a public employee? The answer is in the negative, but unfortunately legal doctrine has developed as if the two were synonymous. This has worked to the detriment of the employee, because real differences exist between the officer and the employee with respect to their responsibilities and obligations. Standards of conduct for an officer are higher than those for an employee, with the officer legitimately subject to increased restrictions on his personal life and less security in position than the employee. Failure to recognize these differences has constituted a great problem to the employee.

For the sake of clarification, any person who holds a government job by virtue of election is a public official. As such, his tenure in his job is subject only to further ratification by the voters, expiration of fixed terms of office without right of reelection, or impeachment and conviction according to strict terms of law.

However, with appointed officials the distinction becomes murky. All employees are appointed in one form or another, yet the differences between public officials and public employees can clearly be made. Mere rank is not a sufficient criterion for differentiation. Some very high members of the Civil Service could possibly have the attributes of officials, while some actual public officials perform exceedingly unimportant, functionary work, such as elected dog wardens.

A good definition of the public official is found in the case of *Pope* v. *Commissioner*, decided by the District of Columbia Court of Appeals in 1943.[6] The court stated that a person in government service is a public official if the following criteria are met:

> (1) His job is created by Constitution or the Legislature or by a municipality or other body conferred by the Legislature.
> (2) There must be a delegation of a portion of the sovereign powers of government to be exercised for the benefit of the public.

6. 138 F.2d 1006 (D.C. Cir. 1943).

(3) The powers conferred and duties to be discharged must be defined either directly or indirectly by the Legislature or through legislative authority.

(4) The duties must be performed independently or without control of a supervisory power other than the law.

(5) The office must have some permanency and continuity and the officer must take an official oath.

In common practice, the officer must also be appointed by the president, department head, or equivalent state or local officials, not by a general merit test or by officials inferior to the department head.

The key paragraph in terms of differentiating public officials from public employees is paragraph 4. In legal or functional terms, the other provisions could apply equally as well to public employees. All public positions, whether held by officials or employees, are created by law in one form or the other. An examination of each item on the list will provide the reasons.

Paragraph 1 is self-evident because if the job is not created by the Constitution or by a duly organized governmental body, it is not a public job or office. A special situation arises with quasi-public bodies, such as community action agencies. However, for the purposes of this book, once an individual is determined to be working in the public sector, all rights or lack of rights associated with government employment apply.

Paragraph 2 implies that the power of government is exercised by a delegation of functions. In the creation of a public job, a portion of the sovereign powers of the government is being delegated to the holder of the job. Legislatures are continually authorizing public jobs to be held by employees in much the same manner as they authorized new official posts. The only difference is that the legislature does not have to approve the individual holding the job in the same way it does public officials. However, approval by the legislative body is not a critical factor in determining the rights in the job of employees and officials, save in those jurisdictions where there is no clear difference between the legislative and executive branches of government (usually small municipalities and counties). This is because once an official is approved by the legislature, the legislature no longer has the power to affect his tenure in office, save through the elimination of the office or impeachment.

As paragraph 3 points out, powers are delegated and defined by the legislature. The definition of powers and duties by the legislative branch is not a real difference between employees and officials because, while all public officials have their duties defined by the legislature, many public employees also have their jobs ultimately defined by the legislature.

The oaths described in paragraph 5 are also taken by officials and employees. The taking of an oath may be a prerequisite for all public officials, but, since World War II, most public employees have also had to take oaths of loyalty to the government as a prerequisite to employment. Although differences may exist in the nature and complexity of the oaths, they are oaths nevertheless. (Chapter 5 will be devoted to an examination of loyalty oaths for public employees and the constitutional problems that have arisen.)

One way in which public officials and public employees do differ is that public officials take their jobs only after being confirmed by the legislative branch of their particular body, be it the United States Congress (Senate) or a branch of the state legislature or city council. Public employees, on the other hand, get their jobs by being hired by their particular employing agency or by a general personnel bureau, such as the Civil Service Commission, without the necessity for confirmation officially by a different branch of government.

The confirmation-nonconfirmation difference can serve to answer the question of who are public employees and who are public officials, but will not answer the question of the real, significant difference between officials and employees in terms of legal status.[7]

The real significance, in legal terms, between public employees and public officials lies in the characteristic found in paragraph 4: "The duties must be performed independently or without control of a supervisory power other than the law." This is the concept that really clarifies the distinctions between those persons who *are* the state and those who *work for* the state.

Public officials are public officials because they owe their ultimate duty to the state as a legal entity, and they may remain in office, theoretically, only as long as they effectively carry out their duties under the law.

7. In United States v. Germaine, 99 U.S. 508 (1879), the United States Supreme Court held that a surgeon appointed by the commissioner of pensions was not an officer since he was not appointed by the president or a department head:

> The Constitution for purposes of appointment very clearly divides all officers into two classes. The primary class requires a nomination by the President and confirmation by the Senate. But forseeing that when officers become numerous, and sudden removals necessary, this mode might be inconvenient, it was provided that, in regard to officers inferior to those specially mentioned, Congress might by law vest their appointment in the President alone, in the courts, or in the heads of the departments. Not all persons who can be said to hold an office under the government about to be established under the Constitution were intended to be included in one or the other of these modes of appointment, there can be little doubt.

Unlike employees, the performance in office of public officials is not judged in terms of simple efficiency, but rather in terms of fulfilling the mission of the particular office held. The standard of judgment is not a personal standard, but rather an official one with the ultimate verdict being whether or not the office has been enhanced by the incumbent, whether the purpose for which the office was established has been advanced.

In many cases, the office was established to assist the chief executive in carrying out the administration of his office, as in the cabinet departments of the federal government. In either situation, while the chief executive is ultimately responsible for the performance in office of subordinate officials, the chief executive is not acting in the role of supervisor or "boss," but rather as the incarnate of the law. In such a situation, his judgments are not personal ones, but have the imprimatur of law. The fact that in actuality a chief executive is making decisions on the performance of other officials in just as personal a manner as a supervisor judging a subordinate employee does not matter. What matters is that legally the judgment is not a personal one, but rather constitutes an exercise of an official judgment on a matter of state, namely the administration of a given branch of government. This difference has significant legal effects.

Public employees are judged in their job not according to standards set by law, but rather by the personal judgments of those with responsibility for their job performance. Not that judgments of supervisors on their subordinates do not constitute governmental action—they do. But unlike judgments on public officials and their performance in office, such judgments do not constitute an official act of government. They are purely personal decisions based on the requirements of good administration in the sense of efficiency of operation, without reference to whether or not the mission of the agency is being fulfilled.

This personal standard of judgment is significant, because cases of efficiency or inefficiency have nothing to do with policy or the wisdom of a given policy. A public employee, unlike an official, is not theoretically involved with the making of policy; his purpose is to effectuate the carrying out of a given policy by performing a given task in a given manner. While in actual practice public employees are beginning to demand and receive a role in the policy-making process, especially in those areas, such as teaching, where policy is often derived from employee performance, the theoretical differentiation that public officials make policy while public employees perform assigned tasks in furtherance of that policy still holds true.

The public official has always been judged at a different and higher standard of accountability than the public employee. As the public employee became a fixture on the scene as government expanded, however, the doctrines developed to protect the country against public officials misusing their power of office were gradually incorporated without a careful scrutiny into the case of the public employee. Indeed, in studying the development of specific cases, this fear of public officials misusing their office is seen to loom large in decisions concerning the treatment of public employees, even though the relationship of the public employee to his job has always been quite different from the relationship of the public official in his office. Yet the reader should also remember that the purpose of having a civil service is to ensure continuity, while the constitutional basis of the political systems is to ensure change. Thus the philosophical underpinning between the two types of governmental personnel demands that, except for the military, the system must find ways to protect employees while subjecting officials to scrutiny.

Tenure of Office

The second line of thinking concerning laws for public employees was based on the fear that the English system would be transplanted into the United States. Before the American Revolution, the concept developed in England that a person had a property right in his office; because of that property right, he could therefore hold a given office for his entire life. Such a doctrine could, of course, develop only because England was a monarchy and the inheritance of positions and titles was based on primogeniture, rather than merit or election; that is, the office was inherited through the firstborn son.[8]

When the Constitutional Convention met in Philadelphia in 1787, delegates opposed the creation of lifetime offices. Congress solved the prob-

---

8. In the case of Harcourt v. Fox, Shower 532, 535, Lord Holt, the Chancellor of England, held:

> I am the more inclined to be of the opinion because I know the temper and disposition of the Parliament at the time when this act was made, their design was that men should have places, not to hold precariously or determinable at will or pleasure, but to have a certain durable estate, that they may act without fearing of losing them.

This case arose in the context of debate over the removal of an officer of the Realm. The decision was to preserve hereditary rights. However, the same language could be a rallying cry for an independent Civil Service with removal for cause only.

lem by setting fixed terms of office for the president and vice-president and members of the Senate and House of Representatives, and it significantly created lifetime tenure in jobs only for members of the federal judiciary, where independence and nonaccountability were a virtue. All officers, whether serving for limited duration or holding life tenure, were subject to removal through the impeachment process or through a form of impeachment for members of Congress.[9]

A related constitutional question arose: if certain offices had a duration and tenure prescribed by law, what constitutional basis was provided for the duration of government offices not specifically mentioned in the Constitution? This problem arose, of course, with respect to whether or not the president, who had the power to appoint certain officials, also had the power to remove these officials. This was especially true in those offices in which the Senate had to confirm the appointment, and was destined to remain an unresolved issue until well into the twentieth century.[10]

The issue of whether the power of removal is incident to power of appointment in the executive first arose before the Supreme Court in the case of *Ex Parte Hennen*.[11] At issue in that case was whether or not a

9. However, in an early Massachusetts case the English tradition was carried over. In Avery v. Tyringham, 3 Mass. Repts. 160 (No. 4), the plaintiff was elected town munster in 1788 (one year before the Constitution was ratified). In 1803 he was fired at a public meeting. No specific grounds were alleged, just that the town wished to be rid of him. He sued for his salary and won. The Court held there is a life contract.

10. In response to a question of the secretary of the Navy in John Tyler's administration as to whether the president could, without court martial, after a favorable finding by a court of inquiry, strike the officer from the rolls. The attorney general held:

> Whatever I might have thought of the power of removal from office, if subject was *res integra*, it is now too late to dispute the Constitution of 1789. It is according to that construction from the very nature of executive power absolute in the President, subject only to his responsibility to the country (his constituents) for a breach of such a vast and solemn trust. It is obvious that if necessity is a sufficient ground for such a concession in regard to officers in the Civil Service, the argument applies *a multo fortiori* to the military and naval department. . . . I have no doubt therefore that the President had the constitutional power to do what he did, and that the officer in question is not in the service of the United States. [4 Opin. 1 (Atty. Gen. opinion), quoted in Blake v. United States, 103 U.S. 230, 232 (1880). See Barry's case, 4 Opin. 612; Lansing's case, 6 Opin. 4; United States v. Perkins, 116 U.S. 483 (1886).]

11. 13 Pet. 259 (1839). See also Kendall v. United States, 2 Pet. 524 (1838).

federal district court judge could dismiss the clerk of the court. While the issue in that case did not concern executive appointment as such, the Court, in attempting to decide the case, discussed the matter in terms of whether there is a power of removal inherent in the power of appointment. The Court found that there was an intrinsic connection between hiring and firing.

In later cases, on the issue of the constitutional power of the executive to remove his appointees, the Court followed doctrine that, in cases of a purely executive appointee, the president does have the power to remove that person. In one case, the Court ruled that the president had the power to remove a U.S. attorney, who held the appointment for a specific four-year term pursuant to a congressional statute.[12] In 1926, in a major case concerning the right of the president to remove a postmaster at will without the advice and consent of Congress, the Court ruled that the president did in fact have that power.[13]

This view of executive power was somewhat modified in several later cases which limited the right of the president to dismiss the persons he appointed to federal agencies on the grounds that these agencies were made independent for the very purpose of keeping them out of the presidential power to remove.[14]

The view that an inherent power of removal accompanies the power of appointment is technically correct when discussing the matters of intergovernmental power structures. A properly managed government would almost be impossible if the Congress or any legislature had to approve every removal of a person to whom it had given its original advice and consent. However, the fact that the president (or any executive), as a matter of constitutional power, may in fact remove without the advice and consent of the legislature those persons whom he had originally appointed with the advice and consent of the legislature, does not mean that the president, or for that matter any other executive of government, be it a federal or state official, has the absolute and unrestrained power to fire or dismiss any person within the executive branch for cause subject only to specific legislative limitation of the power.

12. Parsons v. United States, 167 U.S. 324 (1897). See also Shurtleff v. United States, 189 U.S. 311 (1903).

13. Myers v. United States, 272 U.S. 52 (1926). However, Justices Brandeis, Holmes, and McReynolds in dissent indicated that the Constitution should not be held to give Congress the power to control removal of federal personnel, in order to prevent arbitrary dismissals. This has been expanded to cover judicial protection from dismissals for unconstitutional reasons and is the basis of much of this book.

14. Humphrey's Executor v. United States, 295 U.S. 602 (1935); Wiener v. United States, 357 U.S. 349 (1958).

The Hennen Case

The *Hennen* case, cited as the basis and origin of this doctrine, is unfortunate, in that its ruling on executive power was completely unnecessary to the decision of the case; an examination of the case shows that this holding was in no way a logical conclusion to be derived from the facts. First of all, the Constitution gave life tenure to federal judges to run the administration of their courts in a way in which no federal agency could run the administration of its department with respect to persons working in that department. Second, even leaving aside the differences between the judiciary and the executive as a matter of constitutional development, the relationship between a clerk of court and a judge is a very special type of working relationship which does not usually prevail in a normal employer-employee relationship in the government or, for that matter, in private industry. Because the ability of a judge, any judge, to manage the business of his court is dependent upon the work of the clerk (which in the *Hennen* case meant the chief administrative clerk, not just a deputy clerk), the office of the clerk of court should have been looked upon as being a position with such intimate relationship to the judgeship itself that a judge could use wholly subjective criteria or personal whim for the filling of such a post. If, in fact, the Supreme Court in *Hennen* was influenced by the relationship between a judge and his clerk, then, and this was strong in their thinking, the language of the court which would seem possibly to allow summary dismissal in all cases at the whim of the appointing officer should not have been given such broad interpretation.

The issue should, instead, have been narrowed down to the office of the clerk, rather than serving as a precedent for all governmental officers or employees. While the original *Hennen* court cannot be completely faulted for unsophisticated thinking, since this was a case of first impression, subsequent courts which have cited *Hennen* as a precedent to justify dismissal of public employees should have realized that the relationship between the judge and his clerk of court is a special relationship, not analogous to normal public employer-public employee relationships.

First of all, the clerk of court is more of a public official than an employee, in that the clerk's signature or seal are often required to make various documents official. This is as true today as in the 1830s. Second, the court acts through the office of the clerk in many cases; thus, the public sees the clerk as the judge's alter ego. Thus any friction between a judge and his clerk has a deleterious impact on the court itself, again making the clerk more of a public official than an employee.

Hennen should thus have been limited to its particular facts; whether or not the *Hennen* court would have extended its ruling to employees rather than to officers (and judicial officers at that), no legitimate basis exists for giving this case such precedental value.

The Inherent Rights of the Employee

While Congress or, for that matter, the executive acting alone can alter conditions of employment to meet valid interests, such as the end of a military conflict or a reduction in budget, entirely different issues are raised when the dismissal of an employee is based not on changing general policy affecting all employees in a given class, but on questions of moral character or qualifications of the particular employee or groups of employees.

The fact that the constitutional status of the governmental employers allows them to control the personnel administration, based on the needs of the government and the needs of the policy in a way that a private employer could not do where contractual relationships are involved, does not mean that government employers can treat individual employees or groups of employees with respect to their personal qualifications of employment in the same ways that private employers can treat their employees. The same constitutional basis which allows the government to make general policy which might violate contractual relationships also prevents it from making unlimited, nonrebuttable judgments as to individual personnel qualifications.

Around the turn of the century, courts incorporated private labor management relation law into governmental employment relation law, thus allowing governmental employers absolute free power over their employees. In recent years, when the trend has fortunately been away from this type of law, lawyers and legal commentators, studying the origins of such doctrines, found that they did not inevitably flow from constitutional decisions. In fact, as far back as the 1870s and 1880s eminent jurists had been formulating theories concerning the rights of public employees which not only did *not* allow the government absolute power over the employee, but also provided the legal framework through which the Supreme Court has, in recent years, reversed the old law. The concept of limited power by government employers over their employees has been adopted almost completely in the areas of First Amendment rights of public employees, including association and belief, but accepted only on a limited basis in regard to political activities and rights of procedural due process. This development can now be examined from a conceptual standpoint. First the ways in which public employment differs from private employment must be discussed, since this will explain why public employees seek special legal protection both as to their jobs and their rights as citizens.

Public Versus Private Employment

A vast constitutional difference exists between public employment and private employment, even if the work being done by one is indistinguishable from the other. Private employment is simply a job, and any rights an employee has in his job are due to a contract with his employer, whether it is a personal or a labor union contract. In private employment, any rights not specified in the contract simply do not exist.

Public employment is different, not simply a job, but a public trust. The rights that exist between the governmental agency doing the employing and its employees are not simply questions of "master-servant" relationships. In public employment, theoretically no such thing as employers and employees exists; all public employees are servants of the general public, no matter what position they hold. While in actual practice the institutional arrangements of public agencies and their hiring practices do not differ significantly from private employers, this theoretical difference is absolutely crucial. The problem with the old law was that it treated governmental employment as similar to private employment, and thus applied the rules prevalent in determining private employment rights to the public sphere.

When this problem is understood, the crucial difference becomes evident. While the owners of a private business can be identified, if not by name, at least by class, with real property rights inuring to certain classes of people, the same is not true for public agencies. For example, Mayor Koch does not own New York City, nor is he the agent of any owner of New York City. His actions are judged by the impact they have on the people for whom he is elected to serve, and the legality of his actions are determined according to their impact on the rights of the people he serves. Thus, public employees cannot strike, not because it displeases any other public official, but because of the impact on the general public and because it violates a public trust.

In determining the rights of public employees, the function which the employee is performing is critical. If an employee is carrying out an official function of the agency employing him, the rights and loss of rights inherent in public employment come into play. The only exception would be a person employed as a personal aide to another public official, or whose job is to assist another public official. In that case, a private employment relationship exists, even though in a public context.

In all other cases, the rights of public employees are determined according to public law. This is not to say that a public employee has unlimited freedom to do what he wishes and that he is not subject to discipline. The difference is found in looking at the rights of public employees, starting with the premise that as citizens they are entitled to all of the rights inherent under the Constitution by virtue of their citizenship.

The next question is: What rights have they, as public employees, been required to give up in order to perform their public function? The crucial factor in answering this question is that, unlike private employment, the determination of which rights are to be given up by taking public employment is not measured according to the whim of any person similarly employed. The test is: When the people set up a particular agency and through it a given job, what rights otherwise possessed by the employee have to be given up in order to carry out properly the specific task? In short, an across-the-board rule covering all public employees cannot be drawn. Some public jobs, by their very nature, will quite legitimately require the holder to give up some rights which another public employee still possesses.[15] But, unlike the old law, which stated that a public employee does not have any rights except those given to him by his particular agency, the new theory states that a public employee still has all his rights except those he must give up because of the nature of his job.[16] This is quite a difference. The rights that a public librarian must give up as part of his job will be quite different from the rights that a Central Intelligence Agency (CIA) agent, for instance, will have to lose.[17]

The first espousing of the theory that the power of the executive or the legislature to regulate the business of government is in fact subject to certain constitutional limitations was found in a case having absolutely nothing to do with public employment.[18] In that case, the legislature of Wisconsin enacted a statute stating that if any out-of-state insurance company removed a suit brought against it in a state court to a federal

15. This requirement can be taken to an extreme, as with dress and hair codes. Unfortunately the Supreme Court has upheld it; see Kelley v. Johnson, 425 U.S. 238 (1976).

16. This theory had nearly gained complete acceptance before the ascension of the Burger court. Indeed, much of this book is devoted to examining the conflicting legal theories which are embodied in the approaches of the Warren and Burger courts.

17. See United States v. Marchetti, 466 F.2d 1309 (4th Cir. 1972); cert. denied 409 U.S. 1063 (1972).

18. Doyle v. Continental Insurance Co., 94 U.S. 535 (1976).

court, the state could revoke its license. The Supreme Court upheld the validity of the statute, stating that if the state had the power to exclude altogether, it could not be limited in lesser matters within the ambit of absolute power. In that case, Mr. Justice Bradley, along with two other justices, held in dissent that the fact that a state may have the power to exclude something altogether does not mean that it can subject such a governmental program to any and all conditions. Justice Bradley stated:

> The argument used, that the greater always included the less and therefore, if the state may exclude the appellees without any cause, it may exclude them for a better cause, is not sound. It is first just as unsound as it would be for me to say that, because I may without cause refuse to receive a man as my tenant, therefore I may make it a condition for his tenancy that he shall take the life of my enemy, or rob my neighbor of his property. This concept of the theory of the lesser effect as it is known will come to play an extremely important role in formulating the rights of public employees.[19]

Six years later, Justice Bradley, again in dissent, extended his idea that the fact that the government may have the power to exclude the greater does not mean that it can subject the lesser to any and all conditions to the field of public employment. The case at issue involved the constitutionality of a statute prohibiting any employee of the government from soliciting, receiving monies, or other property from other employees of the government for political purposes.[20] While, ironically, Mr. Justice Bradley was really wrong in opposing the constitutionality of this statute because it would seem to be a perfectly valid one, his theory in opposing would have great benefit for public employees at a later time. He stated:

> . . . thus, in effect, making it a condition of accepting any employment under the government that a man shall not, even voluntarily and of his own free will, contribute in any way through or by the hands of any other employee of the government to the political cause which he desires to aid and promote. I do not believe that Congress has any right to impose such a condition upon any citizen of the United States. The offices of the government do not belong to the Legislative Department to dispose of on any conditions it may choose to impose. The legislature creates most of the offices, it is true, and provides compensation for the discharge of their duties: but that is its duty to do, in order to establish a complete organization of the functions of government. When established, the offices are, or ought to be, open to all. They belong to the United States, and not to Congress; and every citizen having the

19. 94 U.S. at 553.
20. Ex Parte Curtis, 106 U.S. 371 (1883).

proper qualifications has the right to accept office, and to be a candidate therefore. This is a fundamental right of which the legislature cannot deprive the citizen, nor clog its exercise with conditions that are repugnant to his other fundamental rights.[21]

While Bradley was no doubt wrong about the statute in question, because its purpose was not to limit the exercise of political rights of employees but rather to prevent the political coercion of public employees, nonetheless this dissent was critical and will be, at a later date, critical to the development of law because it first raised the concept of unconstitutional conditions in the context of public employment.

The theory of unconstitutional conditions in connection with the theory of the lesser effect provides the best vehicle possible for deciding questions of governmental power in individual rights in the context of the employment policy. The thing to remember about the theory of the lesser effect is that it can only be applied, in terms of governmental power, either in the negative or in total. That is, the government has an absolute power not to engage in a type of governmental program and it likewise has a power to abolish the entire program. When the government chooses to institute a program or policy, it can do so only by implementing it in conformity with constitutional requirements. Thus, no constitutional requirement forces the government to pass a social security program, but it cannot choose to administer such a program on a discriminatory basis.

According to Justice Bradley, and now according to most courts and modern legal commentators, the same theory applies to public employment. While the government had no obligation to engage in public employment and indeed, if it chose, could wipe out all public employment as it could wipe out all social security benefits so long as each and every person is equally affected, it cannot administer its employment relations in a discriminatory way or subject the operation of a government program to the condition that a person, in order to receive the benefits of such a program, must give up his protected constitutional rights. This is especially true in a situation in which the government could not directly through legislation limit the exercise of the constitutional rights; thus it was thought that it could not indirectly do it by the conditioning of the employment relationship.

As Robert O'Neill has aptly pointed out, this distinction between complete inaction and action is not limited to the area of government employment, but has been recognized for a long time in areas completely unrelated to government benefits. In the areas of contract, property, and torts, the law has long recognized that the reliance of a person on the

---

21. 106 U.S. at 376.

unsolicited offer by another may create legal obligations on the part of the volunteer. This is true if a person agrees to store another person's goods; he must store them with a sense of due care. Even if a person voluntarily comes to the aid of another person, unless he is specifically immunized by laws such as the good samaritan act he is obligated to pursue such assistance with good care and could be held liable for any negligence on his behalf.[22]

While Mr. Justice Bradley's view in the *Curtis* case was certainly not a majority view by any means, nonetheless during the 1880s other courts did in fact follow his position, which showed that such a view of the law was not only viable, but was considered to be a very valid approach to the problem. In a Virginia case in 1884, the Virginia Supreme Court ordered the reinstatement of a county officer who was removed for violating a statute prohibiting participation in politics by public employees.[23] In trying to uphold the firing, the state put forward the *Curtis* case as holding that, because the employee is the incumbent of his office, the legislature in the exercise of its general powers may impose upon him such conditions or restrictions as it may seem for the public good. The Virginia court specifically rejected such an interpretation of the *Curtis* case:

> We cannot read that case and regard it as giving countenance to Congress or to any other Legislative body to seal the lips of citizens and exclude them from the assembly of the people unless they will sit down among their fellow man and to forbid their holding communion with their fellow citizens on governmental questions, to directly or indirectly influence the vote of others.
>
> That the Legislature may correct abuses in official conduct; that official malfeasance or misfeance if liable to punishment none will deny; but there is no pretense of such in this case. The act is not entitled an "act to correct official misconduct or the abuse of official station," but is entitled "an act to prohibit the act of participation of politic of certain offices of state government."
>
> If the Legislature has the power to forbid the exercise of one political privilege, why may it not forbid the exercise of another? If one may forbid the officers of government to speak or write according to his sentiments on public affairs, why may it not forbid the officer from voting according to his sentiments, and why may it not impose other restrictions and other disqualifications, until the officer is driven from his office because of the exercise of his constitutional privilege?[24]

22. Robert N. O'Neill, *The Price of Dependency* (New York: Dutton, 1970).
23. Louthan v. The Commonwealth, 79 Va. Rpts. 196 (1881).
24. 79 Va. Rpts. at 204, 205–6.

Keeping in mind this legal background, in which a leading jurist on the Supreme Court spoke of the rights of public employees, and at least one state supreme court during this period recognized and followed his lead, the case from the 1890s which held that the public employee had no rights in his job and could have his constitutional rights conditioned by the fact of employment can now be examined.[25]

Holmes and the Right-Privilege Doctrine

The basis of the denial of public employee rights became known as the right-privilege doctrine, which was a judicial term for the idea that public employment was a privilege granted by the state and not a right of the individual; thus employment could be subjected to any conditions, including the limiting of the employee's constitutional rights.[26] This doctrine, along with the *Hennen* case concept that the power to appoint includes the power to remove, had been the basis of a great deal of hardship for public employees until the 1960s. This doctrine, its development and the long struggle to erode it must be examined to fully understand the present status of public employee rights, especially since the fight to erode this doctrine is the single most important issue in public employee law, and its implications touch every aspect of public employment relations.

If this concept was not completely contrary to existing law, it at least showed a failure on the part of the courts involved to properly take into account a very valid and prominent contemporary legal theory. Ironically, the chief culprit in this judicial mistake was none other than Oliver Wendell Holmes, Jr., considered by many to be the greatest legal mind ever produced in the United States. Indeed, it was the sheer prominence of Oliver Wendell Holmes which transformed a judicial error in an ob-

---

25. Other courts of the period had a more conservative view of the power of government employers over their employees. In People v. Robb, 126 N.Y. 180 (1891), a policeman suffering from an incurable illness was dismissed. He sued to keep on the payroll. He lost.

> It would be a very narrow construction of the statute to hold that the Board does not possess the power to dismiss a policeman for mental or physical incapacity to perform the duties of the place without the delays and formalities of written charges and a public trial or investigation in order to settle the question whether such incapacity in fact exists. [126 N.Y. at 186. See also People v. Higgins 15 Ill. 110 (1853).]

26. See generally Van Alstyne, *The Demise of the Right-Privilege Doctrine in Constitutional Law*, 81 HARVARD L. REV. 1439 (1968).

scure Massachusetts case into a sanctified doctrine of rights versus privileges which had such a deleterious effect on public employees for the next sixty years.[27]

The case in question was an 1892 decision of the Supreme Court of Massachusetts, written by then Chief Judge Holmes, entitled *McAuliffe v. New Bedford.*[28] McAuliffe was a patrolman in the city of New Bedford, who in his off-duty hours became involved in local politics. In the course of his political activities he made some speeches in favor of his particular candidate, and as a result was brought before the mayor and town council of New Bedford and summarily fired for making a speech. He in turn sued the mayor and town council of New Bedford, asking to be reinstated on the grounds that the firing violated his constitutional rights. The case eventually reached the Supreme Court of Massachusetts, where Chief Judge Holmes upheld the validity of the firing in language not only unnecessarily broad for the issues involved in the case, but so broad as to be a millstone around the necks of public employees for many years to come. Holmes stated:

> Petitioner may have a constitutional right to talk politics but he has no constitutional right to be a policeman. There are few employments available to him in which the servant does not agree to suspend his constitutional right of free speech, as well as idleness by the implied terms of his contract. The servant cannot complain as he takes his employment on the terms which are offered him.[29]

The sad part of the *McAuliffe* case is that not only is it wrong in terms of the present-day approach to constitutional rights, but it was questionable in terms of prevailing theory in 1892 concerning governmental power, without even taking into account the constitutional rights of the individual employee. While Holmes's views were probably the prevailing views in the country, as he was the preeminent jurist of his day even before his ascension to the Supreme Court, the tragedy of the opinion is that it not only failed to take into consideration Bradley's dissent, but overlooked a historic precedent in Massachusetts when in 1842 Judge Lemuel Shaw allowed certain forms of trade unionism.[30] While that concerned private labor relations, if Holmes had wanted to use an

27. While Holmes was renowned in the legal world by 1892 for, among other things, his classic book on jurisprudence, *The Common Law* (Mark DeWolfe Howe, ed., Cambridge, Mass.: Harvard Univ. Pr., 1963), he did not become the towering public figure of his present general reputation until his dissents with Brandeis following World War I. See Abrams v. United States, 250 U.S. 616, 624 (1919).
28. 155 Mass. 216, 29 N.E. 517 (1892).
29. 155 Mass. at 220.
30. Commonwealth v. Hunt, 4 Metc. 111 (1842).

analogy to private sources, he should have recognized the major precedent in his state, at least in theoretical absolutist terms. If not, he should not have used the master-servant analogy, since the 1830s was a period of the highest antiunion feeling.

At the heart of Holmes's opinion was the analogy of public employment to private employment: since private employers could offer employment under any and all conditions, so could the government. In some Supreme Court cases, however, the Court held that the government could, as a matter of general policy, enforce a reduction in manpower and a reduction of employee salary where private contractual rights might have prevented that, simply because the government has the power to control without reference to contracts governing property, except that states cannot pass laws revoking or impairing contracts. Likewise in *Curtis*, when the Court upheld the statute limiting political activities of public employees of a certain type, the basis of that holding was not that the Congress or the legislature had the right to subject employees to any and all conditions, but rather that the government was not subject to concepts of private property or contract, in that in its pursuit of legitimate governmental interest it may pass reasonable limitations on the political activities of governmental employees. This holding is certainly a far cry and quite different from the dogmatic holding of the *McAuliffe* case.

Aside from the erroneous analogy of private employment, Holmes could have easily reached the same decision he did without having to issue such a broad and dogmatic statement. Following the lead of the Supreme Court in *Curtis*, Holmes could have easily ruled that a policeman, because of the sensitive nature of his job, should not go around making public partisan political speeches. A holding like that, as noted in the discussion of further developments of the law, would probably have been correct even under modern theory. At the same time, it would have avoided a decision as to the constitutional rights of all employees engaging in all types of protected constitutional expression, based on a case applying to a special type of employee engaging in a very special type of protected expression, one which would quite legitimately have an adverse effect on his ability to properly perform a specific type of job.

While Holmes was not, at this time, a member of the United States Supreme Court, nonetheless, because of his family background and his brilliant written work, he was considered to be one of the most prominent jurists in the United States. His ruling on this matter was taken with much more authority than it would have been if he were lesser known.

To make matters worse, several years after the *McAuliffe* opinion Judge Holmes, in another case concerning a conviction of a minister who had violated a municipal ordinance in Boston by speaking on the Boston Common without a permit, reaffirmed in absolute language the power of a governmental body to subject a public benefit to any and all conditions. This case eventually went to the United States Supreme Court, where it was upheld.[31] Judge Holmes wrote:

> For the Legislature absolutely or conditionally to forbid public speaking in a public park is no more an infringement on the rights of a member of the public than for the owner of a private house to forbid it in his house. When no proprietary right interferes, the Legislature may end the right of the public to enter upon the public place by putting an end to the dedication of public uses. So it may place the lesser step of limiting the public use to certain purposes.[32]

It seems ironic that Oliver Wendell Holmes, who later in his career as a Supreme Court Justice formulated the clear and present danger test and, with Justice Brandeis, espoused in dissent the earliest and most forceful positions of First Amendment rights, would expound such a reactionary view of constitutional rights. While on the Supreme Court, Justice Holmes did change his views as to the rights of citizens to engage in First Amendment activities, although not as much as attributed to him. He consistently maintained his view of the right of government to impose all conditions on public benefits. In a case in which the Supreme Court held that the state of Kansas could not impose a certain tax on foreign businesses doing business within the state, Justice Holmes dissented. The basis of the majority opinion was that the court's decision was a violation of due process of law and was an intrusion upon interstate commerce. Holmes dissented on the grounds that the power of a state to exclude a corporation entirely included the power to subject that corporation to any and all restrictions and taxes.[33]

31. Commonwealth v. Davis, 162 Mass. 510, 39 N.E. 113 (1895); affirmed 167 U.S. 43 (1897).
32. 162 Mass. at 511.
33. Western Union Telegraph Company v. Kansas, 216 U.S. 1 (1910). This reasoning was severely criticized by Thomas Reed Powell:

> Logically a thing which may be absolutely excluded is not the same as a thing which may be subjected to burdens of a different kind, even though such burdens would be regarded all as less onerous than the burden of absolute exclusion. The power of absolute exclusion is a term not identical with the power of relative exclusion or the power to impose any burdens whatever. [*The Right to Work for the State*, 16 COLUMBIA L. REV. 111.]

See also Atkin v. Kansas, 191 U.S. 207 (1903); Heim v. McCall, *supra*, note 3.

Instead, Justice Holmes could have legitimately and probably correctly dissented on the grounds that the Fourteenth Amendment due process clause was designed to protect individuals, especially newly freed slaves, from having their constitutional rights taken away from them by state governments; it was never designed to shield businesses from legitimate regulations and taxes.[34] Nevertheless, Holmes chose to dissent on the same grounds on which he had decided the *McAuliffe* and *Davis* cases. Likewise, in a case involving New York state statutes which prohibited aliens from obtaining government employment or working on government projects, Holmes again held that the Constitution, in that case the equal protection clause, had no application to government employment because the state, like any employer, either public or private, has the absolute right to hire whomever it wishes for the reasons it wishes and to determine every condition of employment.[35]

While Holmes's position was certainly the law at that time, nonetheless it was not universally accepted by legal commentators as the proper position of the law. Thomas Reed Powell, in the same article previously discussed, savagely attacked Holmes and his whole concept of right-privilege distinction. He states:

> What is true of the relation between the power of absolute exclusion and the power of relative exclusion or power to impose any burdens whatsoever, as applied to the relation between a state and foreign corporations, is likewise true of the relation between the power to exclude all and the power to exclude some and not all, as applied to the relation between a state and the selection of its employees. The latter right cannot be deduced logically from the former. The fact that the right of the state to exclude some by excluding all is not denied by the due process clause, has no bearing upon the question whether the right to exclude some but not all is denied by the Equal Protection Clause.
>
> The view of the Supreme Court, therefore, that because no one has any right to work for the state, the state may make such discrimination as it pleases in selecting its employees, seems unsound in logic and opposed to the judicial opinions above cited. It is submitted, therefore, that in so far as Heim v. McCall [the alien exclusion case] stands for the proposition that the equal-protection-of-the-law Clause sets no limits whatever to the power of the state to discriminate by statute in the selection of its employees, the decision is unsound in principle and not warranted by previous decisions.[36]

---

34. This can be traced back to the Slaughter House cases, 16 Wall. 36 (1873), and the Civil Rights cases, 109 U.S. 3 (1883).

35. Heim v. McCall, *supra*, note 3.

36. *The Right to Work for the State*, 16 Columbia L. Rev. 111–12.

The high point of the Holmes doctrine was reached in the appeal to what was probably the most famous trial of the century, the so-called Scopes Monkey Trial. While most readers are familiar with the dramatic confrontation between Clarence Darrow and William Jennings Bryan at the trial itself, very few realize that after Scopes was found guilty and fined, he appealed his case to the Tennessee Supreme Court. While many of the issues he raised concerned the effect of the statute on the freedom of religion, he also claimed that the statute made it impossible for him to teach his subject of biology according to his best professional ability. The result of the appeal was a disaster.[37]

At the heart of the decision was the theory that the Fourteenth Amendment had absolutely no relevance to rights of public employees in their jobs and that, since Scopes's employment was a privilege, the state could subject teacher employment to any restriction, including what may or may not be taught in the classroom.

While the Tennessee Supreme Court was reiterating in this most celebrated case the hard line doctrine of Holmes in the *McAuliffe* case, the United States Supreme Court in two cases unrelated to public employment had made a major change in constitutional doctrine, a change which was to have great beneficial effects at a later time for public employees.

The Rise of Due Process

In 1925 in *Gitlow* v. *New York*, the Supreme Court upheld the conviction of Benjamin Gitlow, a leading Communist, for violation of the criminal anarchy law.[38] However, in rendering its decision the Supreme Court mentioned almost in passing that it assumed that the Fourteenth Amendment was made applicable to the states by the First Amendment. Mr. Justice Holmes, while disagreeing on the upholding of the conviction, nonetheless was firmly in support of this view in his dissent.

37. Scopes v. State, 154 Tenn. 105, 289 S.W. 363 (1925). Then the Court held:

> [Scopes] had no right or privilege to serve the state except upon such terms as the state prescribed.
>
> The statute before us . . . is an act of the state as a corporation, a proprietor, an employer. It is a declaration of a master as to the character of work the master's servant shall, or rather shall not perform. In dealing with its own employees engaged upon its own work, the state is not hampered by the limitation of the Fourteenth Amendment to the Constitution of the United States.

38. 268 U.S. 652 (1925). See also Whitney v. California, 274 U.S. 357 (1927).

This change of law was extremely critical, because a doctrine of law existed holding that the original Bill of Rights was only applicable to the actions of the federal government and not to state governments. This doctrine was originally espoused by John Marshall in an 1833 case, *Barron* v. *Baltimore*, involving the power of a state to take property without just compensation.[39] The post-Civil War amendments, especially the Fourteenth, were supposed to remedy this problem so that, in conjunction with the Civil Rights Acts of 1866 and 1870, federal courts would be able to hear cases involving deprivation of constitutional rights of its citizens.[40]

However, these amendments were not effective because the Supreme Court, in the so-called Slaughter House Cases of 1873, in effect emasculated the Fourteenth Amendment by holding that the only new substantive provision was equal protection of the laws and it then only applied to Negroes, since it must be read with the Thirteenth and Fifteenth Amendments which only applied to Negroes. In effect the Supreme Court read the due process clause out of the Fourteenth Amendment. The exclusion of equal protection had a serious impact on public employees especially at the state and local levels, in that discussions of their rights could only take place within a legal framework not involving basic constitutional rights. Such weakening contributed to the development of the right-privilege doctrine, since the limitation on the employee could only be judged within the theory of the powers of government employers and not the constitutional rights of the employees. Thus a two-pronged limitation was imposed on employees. First, the right-privilege doctrine gave public employers absolute control, as a matter of public administration law over their employees. Second, a constitutional remedy outside the employment relationship was lacking.

Gitlow initiated the constitutional remedy for persons subjected to government action, including public employees. *Gitlow* was not concerned with public employees and indeed was substantively restrictive, but it did remove a fifty-year-old legal barrier and provided to the public employee, at least where First Amendment rights were concerned, a legal basis for challenging arbitrary action; indeed, it would have been applicable to the *McAuliffe* case if it had come after *Gitlow*.

The other barrier to public employees was, of course, the right-privilege doctrine. This became somewhat weakened in the rather obscure

39. Barron v. Baltimore, 7 Pet. 243 (1833).
40. For a background on the post-Civil War amendments, see Jacobus TenBroek, *Equal under the Law* (New York: Macmillan, 1965).

case *Frost Trucking Company* v. *The Railroad Commission.*[41] In this case the issue was simply whether a state could impose certain types of regulation on state-owned highways. In deciding that case, the Court assumed that no one had the constitutional right to force a state to build public roads, and if the trucking company could not haul goods because of lack of public roads, it would have no recourse. But the Court then went one step further and considered whether this situation meant that the state could arbitrarily attach any condition it wished on the use of the roads, claiming that they were a "privilege that the state was free to withhold entirely." In very significant language, the Court stated that the right to withhold entirely the building of public roads does not give the state the power to subject the use of the roads to any and all conditions.[42]

While the Supreme Court in the mid-1920s in effect did away with the underlying theory on which the original *McAuliffe* case was based, it nonetheless took another twenty-five years before the public employee reaped the benefits of this new change in theory, and then only because of the catastrophic impact of the loyalty-security programs, following World War II, on the situation of public employees.

The year 1933 saw the advent of the New Deal, and in 1941 the United States entered World War II. The nature of these emergencies was such that the public employment sector was literally mobilized in a crusade. With the public sector playing such an important national role, morale among public employees was so high that the conditions of underlying bitterness, found in any group, which traditionally leads to great movements in the law, simply did not exist. Since the Supreme Court historically selects cases to hear not so much on their individual merit but

---

41. 271 U.S. 583 (1926). See also Linde, *Constitutional Rights of Public Employees: A Comment on the Inappropriate Uses of an Old Analogy,* 16 UCLA L. REV. 75 (1969).

42. The Court's language was:

> It would be a palpable incongruity to strike down an act of State legislation which, by words of expressed devestment, strip the citizens of rights guaranteed by the Federal Constitution, but to uphold an act by which the same result is accomplished under the guise of a surrender of a right in exchange for a valuable privilege which the State threatens with withdrawal.
>
> If the state may compel surrender of one constitutional right as a condition of its favor, it may, in a like manner compel the surrender of all. It is inconceivable that guarantees embedded in the Constitution of the United States may thus be manipulated out of existence. [271 U.S. at 586.]

See Van Alstyne, *The Constitutional Rights of Teachers and Professors,* 1970 DUKE L. J. 841.

rather as representative of some broad (legal) movements, the lack of continuous pressure from public employees clamoring to have their rights vindicated meant that the Supreme Court simply was not compelled to rule on questions involving the conditions of public employee rights.

At the same time, the Supreme Court was responding to events in the turbulent 1930s; questions of free speech were especially of utmost public interest. As early as the mid-1930s, even before Roosevelt's famous Court Packing Scheme which, while a failure, resulted in a liberalized Supreme Court, the Supreme Court began to greatly expand the scope of the First Amendment to the point where it became known as a "preferred right."[43] This development would be of incalculable value to public employees when they became a target of post-war loyalty hysteria.

While public employees suffered some very severe legal setbacks early in the post-war era in such cases as *Bailey* v. *Richardson*,[44] where the Supreme Court upheld the firing of a federal employee after a hearing in which anonymous charges of unexplained grounds of disloyalty were the basis of evidence against the employee, and *Adler* v. *Board of Education*,[45] where a loyalty program which made membership in a listed organization the sole basis of discharge (this whole area will be explored in a later chapter), it was the development of theory in the area of First Amendment rights which made possible a counterattack by public employees. This counterattack also had a great impact on the rights of persons not public employees, although this has not been without resistance, with the fight far from won.

In 1952, in *Wieman* v. *Updegraff*,[46] the Supreme Court for the first time in its history found that the action of a state government (or for that matter, any government) had the effect of destroying or limiting a constitutional right held by the public employee, and was thus unconstitutional. That case featured a certain type of loyalty oath which had the effect of punishing any membership in an organization on the attorney general's list, even if such membership was innocent. The Court found that this oath had the effect of violating the employee's right of free association. However, this decision was hardly a full-blown grant of rights for public employees to engage in First Amendment activities. Because this was a "loyalty case" and because as Justice Clark, writing for the

43. This statement was found in a footnote by Justice Stone in the case of United States v. Carolene Products Co., 304 U.S. 144 (1938).

44. 182 F.2d 46 (D.C. Cir. 1950); affirmed by equally divided court 341 U.S. 918 (1951).

45. 342 U.S. 485 (1951), discussed in chapter 5 along with the preferred rights doctrine and other cases of the 1930s.

46. 344 U.S. 183 (1952), discussed in chapter 5.

majority, stated that a finding of disloyalty becomes in the community a "badge of infamy," the Court, rather than granting full rights of public employees, in effect carved out an exception to the normal Holmes doctrine when the situation involved a finding of disloyalty.

The *Wieman* case could not, however, be underestimated because, as in all areas of law, a doctrine granting a measure of rights for individuals in one particular fact situation will always be attempted to be applied for entirely different situations. Thus, while the Supreme Court may have been thinking only in terms of loyalty-security cases, once it found that an area could exist in which the state unconstitutionality impinged upon the protected First Amendment rights of its employees, it became impossible for this Court or for any court to limit such a theory and finding exclusively to the area of loyalty-security cases.

For the next fifteen years almost all the favorable decisions, indeed all the favorable decisions for public employees, came up in cases involving a loyalty-security program. However, the civil rights movement in the late 1950s and early 1960s generated cases which, while ostensibly of the loyalty-security type, in reality had nothing to do with loyalty investigations, but were in fact an attempt to destroy civil rights organizations such as the National Association for the Advancement of Colored People (NAACP). In the most famous of these cases, *Shelton* v. *Tucker*,[47] the state of Arkansas passed a statute requiring all teachers to disclose all organizations to which they had belonged in the last five years. While this decision will be discussed in much greater detail in a later chapter, in striking down this statute the Supreme Court based its decision both on the right of association and on limitations on the right of public employers to condition employment upon disclosure of that right. Thus the right-privilege doctrine suffered a major blow—one which provided the conceptual framework which has resulted in its abolishment as a viable doctrine of law, although its vestiges remain in the guise, sometimes justified, of administrative necessity. Indeed, the doctrine became so eroded that in a 1967 case the Supreme Court could state as a doctrine of the Court: "The theory that public employment which may be denied altogether may be subject to any condition, regardless of how unreasonable, has been uniformly rejected."[48]

Through 1967, however, all cases holding for public employees came in an area involving loyalty-security programs or programs falsely claiming a loyalty-security purpose; not until 1968 did the Supreme Court in two important decisions find for public employees in regard to the assertion of a constitutional right in cases having nothing to do with loyalty

47. 364 U.S. 479 (1960), discussed in chapter 5.
48. Keyishian v. Board of Regents, 385 U.S. 589 (1967).

or security investigations, but rather to assertion by an individual public employee of a basic constitutional right solely in an individual capacity.

In *Pickering* v. *Board of Education*,[49] the Supreme Court held that a school board could not dismiss a teacher because he wrote a letter to a local newspaper unfavorable to the school board. The *Pickering* case leaves open many subtle and difficult questions concerning how far and what type of speech a public employee may engage in without being subject to discipline; nonetheless, it states in no uncertain terms that public employment may not be offered on the condition that the employee give up his rights of First Amendment freedom of expression and that any expression so limited can only be limited by the supreme court of a state and must be of valid compelling state interest with respect to the employment. The Court put the particular problem this way:

> To the extent that the Illinois Supreme Court's opinion may be read to suggest that teachers may constitutionally be compelled to relinquish First Amendment rights they would otherwise enjoy as citizens to comment on matters of public interest in connection with the operation of the public schools in which they work, it proceeds on the premise that has been unequivocally rejected in numerous prior decisions of this court [cite omitted].
>
> At the same time it cannot be gainsaid that the State has interests as an employer in regulating the speech of its employees that differ significantly from those it possesses in connection with the regulation of the speech of the citizenry in general. The problem in any case is to arrive at a balance between the interest of the teacher, as a citizen, in commenting upon matters of public concern and the interest of the state, as an employer, in promoting the efficiency of the public services it performs through its employees.[50]

The language in *Pickering* has pushed forward the law concerning the rights of public employees to engage in constitutionally protected activities into an entirely new sphere. The Holmes doctrine is dead, although the *Pickering* case is by no means an absolute grant of full First Amendment rights to public employees. Implicit in this decision is the idea that the state may still place some limits on the First Amendment rights of its employees because of the special demands inherent in public employment. However, the essential changes in the concept can be seen in the shift of emphasis, from the idea that a public employee must take his employment as he finds it, even if the conditions of that employment included the giving up of his constitutional rights, to that of the statement

49. 391 U.S. 563 (1968).
50. 391 U.S. at 568.

in *Pickering*, that the otherwise inviolate First Amendment rights of public employees might, under certain circumstances and because of certain compelling government needs, be limited in these special cases. The difference is more than language; it is in real substance.

The second major decision for public employees brought the problem of public employees' rights full circle. This 1968 case was the curious one of *Epperson* v. *Arkansas*,[51] which concerned an Arkansas statute against the teaching of evolution, one almost identical to the statute found in the *Scopes* case. While the *Epperson* decision leaves many questions unanswered, especially in the area of academic freedom, it took the *Pickering* case one step further and held again, in an entirely different context, that the state cannot impose any and all conditions on public employees, or specifically teachers, as a condition of their employment.

While much of the decision focused on how the prescribing of a particular dogma, in this case one based on the required teaching of religious tenants in the public schools, violated the establishment of religion clause of the First Amendment, the Court also looked at the effect this law had on teachers. The Court held that the "First Amendment does not permit the state to require that teaching and learning must be tailored to the principles or prohibitions of any religious sect or dogma." Relating this rule directly to teachers, the Court stated:

> The State's undoubted right to prescribe the curriculum for its public schools does not carry with it the right to prohibit, on pain of criminal penalty, the teaching of a scientific theory or doctrine where that prohibition is based upon reasons that violate the First Amendment. It is much too late to argue that the State may impose upon the teachers in its schools any conditions that it chooses, however restrictive they may be of constitutional guarantees.[52]

Thus the Court, in a case ironically similar to the *Scopes* case, a high point of the absolutist right-privilege doctrine, laid this outdated rule of law permanently to rest.

The Current State

The years since the *Epperson* case have been somewhat disappointing. An awaited breakthrough, one wiping out legal restraints for public employees, has not happened; indeed the cause of the public employee is in

51. 393 U.S. 97 (1968).
52. 393 U.S. at 100.

somewhat of a retreat which, at the time of this writing, seems to be worsening instead of improving.

The primary cause for this change is the composition of the present Supreme Court has changed from a liberal majority under Chief Justice Warren to a conservative one under Chief Justice Burger. This change occurred just as public employees began to take advantage of break-throughs, primarily those in First Amendment areas, to press claims in many other areas. Thus, as the composition of the Court has changed, so has the pressure on it to hear cases involving limitations on public employees in areas not purely under the scope of the First Amendment. Over the last six years the Supreme Court (and, of course, lower federal and state courts) have had to decide many important cases just as the law was changing from the absolutism stance of the right-privilege doc-trine to a stance featuring the balancing of administrative interests of an agency as weighed against the right of the employee. Obviously, in such a state of flux, the law is subject to many inconsistencies.

The Supreme Court has not extended full rights of procedural due process to public employees; it has refused to overrule the *Mitchell* case,[53] upholding the validity of the Hatch Act;[54] and recently it has declared constitutional a hair and dress code imposed on policemen.[55]

On the other hand, the refusal to extend certain doctrines of law to public employees in the fullest extent that they might wish does not mean that the old days of the right-privilege doctrine has returned. The Su-preme Court in the *Roth* and *Perry*[56] cases has specifically guaranteed to public employees First Amendment rights, while at the same time limit-ing rights of procedural due process. Likewise, while upholding some loyalty oaths, the Supreme Court has not returned to the days of the early 1950s when public employees were at the mercy of the witch-hunter.

Indeed, the problems that public employees are facing now are similar to problems facing many other groups and persons in this country con-cerning the reforms of the Warren years; should they be continued, kept at the same level, or in fact reversed? The new Supreme Court majority is extremely unpredictable, finding certain things constitutional which

53. United Public Workers v. Mitchell, 330 U.S. 75 (1948), discussed extensively in chapter 4.

54. In a series of cases entitled United States Civil Service Commission v. Na-tional Association of Letter Carriers, 413 U.S. 548 (1973), the Supreme Court up-held the validity of the Hatch Act and voted to overrule Mitchell. This is discussed in chapter 4.

55. Kelley v. Johnson, 425 U.S. 238 (1976).

56. Board of Regents v. Roth, 408 U.S. 564 (1972); Perry v. Sindermann, 408 U.S. 593 (1972). These cases are discussed exhaustively in chapters 3 and 6.

most observers believed to be unconstitutional, especially in actions related to freedom of the press and criminal law. At the same time, this new Court has thrown out antiabortion statutes, declared capital punishment at present unconstitutional in certain cases, and limited many other attacks on the First Amendment. Thus, although the law concerning public employees is uncertain, this same uncertainty also affects other segments of society.

This situation is further complicated by the fact that a new president will appoint new Supreme Court judges and new lower federal judges as well, and those judges will, for the most part, doubtless have a different judicial philosophy than those appointed during the last eight years. This combination of inconsistency in the Supreme Court and a new president sets up an interesting situation in terms of the willingness of lower federal courts to make decisions affecting public employees rights.

The relationship between the Supreme Court and lower federal courts is a very complex one. Federal courts are, of course, obligated to follow the Supreme Court where the Supreme Court has clearly ruled. However, when rulings are unclear or nonexistent, lower courts either rule on their own interpretation of the law or attempt to anticipate Supreme Court ruling. Since cases take several years from inception to a hearing before the Supreme Court, public employees might find that lower courts are more favorable to them in anticipation of the possibility that, if and when that case or a similar one comes before the Supreme Court, the composition of the Court will have changed enough so that the trends of the Warren court will again become law.[57]

Likewise, the Supreme Court might react to the changing conditions in the country and, while not necessarily becoming more liberal, it might defer taking cases which would be strongly criticized by the political majority, thus allowing a further development of the law to take place in lower federal courts or state courts. In short, the premium will be placed on cases factually sound, in which a ruling could be justified in terms of general equity rather than broad ideology.

For that reason public employees should begin to understand the concepts of balancing interests so as not to lose cases which, although theoretically strong, are factually weak or contain issues which alone could justify government action. The rest of this book is designed to explore various trends and to show the legal traps which might befall public employees seeking to assert their rights.

57. The most ominous cases are Bishop v. Wood, 426 U.S. 341 (1976) and Aldinger v. Howard, 427 U.S. 1 (1976) which have been an indication of a possible return to the right-privilege doctrine. These cases are discussed in chapters 2 and 6 in their proper contexts.

Exclusion and Dismissal from Public Service

In the vital area of exclusion and dismissal of persons from the public service, two basic approaches to the problem exist. In general, the exclusion or dismissal is challenged on the grounds that governmental action violates a constitutional right held by the applicant or employee as a citizen. Pervasive questions of the legitimacy of employee behavior and any recourses open to them when in danger must be defined in terms stated in the Constitution. This chapter is instead concerned with an examination and definition of the grounds by which governments can exclude persons from public employment where the issues do not rise to the level of constitutional challenge in a classic First Amendment sense.

The particular issues discussed in this chapter are those acts of the employee which cannot be easily fitted into the category of an obvious assertion of a constitutional right, such as a letter to the editor, or of an obvious administrative justification, such as gross incompetence. These problems can best be described as quasi-constitutional.

Two particular types of problems should be considered. The first involves an action based on the elements of a personal life style which, while not necessarily constitutionally prohibited, are arguably so irrelevant to the legitimate needs of the government employer as to subject any job action based on those reasons to scrutiny as a possible violation of the due process clause of the Fifth or Fourteenth Amendments (the

Fifth Amendment applies to the federal government; the Fourteenth to state and local governments).

The second area concerns limits on otherwise justifiable administrative actions of the employer by virtue of standards against which the basis of dismissal can be measured. This would concern the concept of cause. This problem arises because in many cases, especially those involving federal agencies, cause is a legalized standard for dismissal.[1] Likewise, many state and federal courts, in interpreting state action, have imposed a standard on the government for those matters where the basis of the job action has so little relationship to the real needs of the agency that it in effect becomes arbitrary action tantamount to deprivation of due process of law.[2] The reader should note that a court will not interpose itself into subjective decisions of a purely administrative nature such as qualification or ability, barring special circumstance such as racial or sexual discrimination. The same is true for such issues as promotion, barring discrimination or provable relation to an assertion of a constitutional right, which will be discussed separately.[3]

When the basis of an action is not concerned with the ability to perform a job or similar generalized personnel matters, but is also not an assertion of a constitutional right, however, legal problems may arise; this is the basis of this chapter. Because these matters are generally fact questions based on special circumstances, the best that can be done is to explain areas in which such problems have arisen and show how courts or legislatures have approached them, as guidance for employees who might find themselves caught in this legal twilight zone.

Not to discuss this issue would distort this examination of the law, because an area exists between the assertion of constitutional rights and purely administrative action in which the employee can either be caught or, conversely, seek a remedy outside the agency. For an employee seeking to prevent or reverse an action against him, taken for reasons to be discussed, this is as much an assertion of his rights as if he was being punished for making a speech or writing a letter to a paper.

1. See 5 U.S.C. §7501(a) and 5 Code of Federal Regulations (CFR) §752.104 (1964) for federal regulations as the providers of procedural due process to federal employees. This act is the old Lloyd-La Follette Act of 1912, and the accompanying Civil Service Commission regulations permit removal "only for such cause as will promote the efficiency of the service." The procedure will be discussed in chapter 6, on procedural due process. The only concern here is the concept of just cause.

2. This will be discussed later in the chapter. See Scott v. Macy, 349 F.2d 182 (D.C. Cir. 1965); reheard 402 F.2d 644 (1968). Norton v. Macy, 417 F.2d 1161 (D.C. Cir. 1969).

3. Bishop v. Wood 426 U.S. 341 (1976), discussed extensively in chapter 6.

Procedural Safeguards

Even when no direct constitutional issue exists, applicants and employees are still not bereft of any relief from government actions. To protect against injustice, courts have been evolving rules which determine: (1) whether a given ground of exclusion or dismissal is relevant to the needs of the agency; and (2) whether in a given case, even if the grounds are sufficient, the evidence presented against the employee is sufficient to sustain such a charge.

As a general rule, courts have held that governments have wide latitude in establishing criteria for the hiring and dismissal of employees.[4] This power has been recognized as inherent in the power of the executive branch (at all levels) to administer the government.[5] For many years it was felt that the main purpose of an agency or department was the accomplishment of the mission for which it was established. In this context, personnel were just another factor of administration to be equated with other factors such as physical facilities, budgetary allotments, and so on. The employee took his employment as he got it. Unless legislation or rules of the agency gave the employee certain rights, he had none since there was no property right in the job. If the agency could hire without limitation, it could then fire without limitation. As one early case put it: "Where the power of appointment is conferred in general terms and without restriction, the power of removal in the discretion and at the will of the appointing power is implied and always exists unless restrained and limited by some provision of law."[6]

This, of course, is the old right-privilege doctrine transposed into the area of administrative necessity. But, as in the issue of the right-privilege doctrine, the absolutist position breaks down or has recently met legal challenges when the administrative decision is not made because of a change in general policy but from a judgment involving the moral character or qualifications of a particular employee or group of employees. The same is true, of course, when the employee is challenging the legality of an administrative action and is punished for it—a kind of "administrative Nuremberg Trial," in which a special responsibility may devolve on the employee. Since these issues have a quasi-constitutional basis and

4. See Hilton v. Sullivan, 334 U.S. 323 (1948), in which this rule was delineated in the context of a congressional act giving hiring preference to honorably discharged veterans.

5. Ex Parte Hennen, 13 Pet. 230 (1839); Myers v. United States, 272 U.S. 52 (1926).

6. 13 Pet. at 231.

may touch on protected constitutional rights, they must be discussed to fully understand the relationship between employee rights and administrative necessity.

Just as the courts have begun to evolve rules which delineate the limits of governmental interference with the constitutional rights of public employees and applicants for public employment, so too have courts begun to develop rules which limit the powers of government bodies to exclude and dismiss persons from public employment based on decisions as to personal qualifications not based on the actual ability to perform a given job.

This judicial function is important at the federal as well as the state level, even though federal employees by law cannot be dismissed except "for such cause as will promote the efficiency of the service." Since the statutory law does not define "just cause," judicial interpretation is essential to insure some degree of justice to the employee.

The Concept of "Cause"

The actual subject of this area is the concept of "cause." It is almost a shibboleth that a person can be excluded or dismissed from government employment for cause or just cause. Thus the real issue to be faced is: What kinds of behavior or personality traits constitute cause for dismissal or exclusion of a person from public employment?

The best way to clearly understand what is meant by cause as a legal concept is to examine two cases in which the main issue was the presence of sufficient cause to dismiss the public employee.[7]

Tom Carter was hired by the Federal Bureau of Investigation as a clerk in the Identification division. After working for a year, he enlisted in the U.S. Air Force. After discharge he returned to his old job. Because he was unmarried and Washington is an expensive place to live, especially for someone earning a government clerk's salary, Carter shared an apartment with three other FBI employees. One day the FBI received an anonymous letter complaining about Carter which read as follows:

> Dear Sirs: Would like to make a complaint about a fellow working for the FBI, his name is Tom H. Carter who lives at Kennebeck House or Apts; sleeping with young girls & carrying on; it annoys me terrible; I wish you can do something about it. Thank you.

7. Carter v. United States, 407 F.2d 1238 (D.C. Cir. 1968); Lefcourt v. Legal Aid Society 312 F. Supp. 1105 (S.D. N.Y. 1970).

The letter was never identified; but since the letter was sent directly to the particular division where Carter worked, the writer must have had some knowledge of both Carter and the FBI.

Carter was called in by his supervisor and asked about the matter. He said that a girl he had been seeing for years had stayed over at his apartment and, while they had slept together, they had not undressed nor had they had sexual relations. The supervisor questioned his roommates separately, all of whom confirmed his story. Nevertheless, the FBI dismissed Carter for "conduct unbecoming an employee of this bureau." When the FBI refused to allow him to resign he brought suit for reinstatement.

Because the FBI is exempt from Civil Service requirements of dismissal for cause, its action would have stood up except that Carter, as a veteran, was protected by a provision of the Universal Military Training and Service Act, which shielded returning veterans from firing from any job to which they returned for a period of one year "except for cause." Thus the question in the *Carter* case was simply whether his acts could constitute "cause for dismissal."[8]

The United States District Court dismissed Carter's claim, but on appeal the Circuit Court for the District of Columbia reversed and ordered a trial on the facts. In discussing the concept of cause the court made it clear that it applies only to those governmental bodies not specifically exempted, in addition to all employers, governmental and private, covered by special statute. It made clear that the government as employer is under greater restrictions than private employers who, unless specifically restricted, can fire employees for purely personal reasons.

In discussing the criteria for cause the court held that the ultimate criteria is the reasonableness of the act—the showing of objective conduct on the part of the employee that satisfies some objective standard of cause. Because it is not possible to set out all possible grounds for discharge, the test that the court uses is that a government employee must "conform to the ordinarily expected standards of personal conduct." The court uses a good analogy when it compares this to the "common law of the shop" standard used to determine the validity of employer action in labor-management grievance procedures.[9]

---

8. A special facet of this case, like Hilton v. Sullivan, was the veteran's preference. While Carter had no statutory rights to employment by virtue of being a veteran, Section 96 of the Universal Military Training and Service Act, 50 U.S.C. App. §459 (c)(1964) imposed a cause standard similar to the Civil Service laws, which is the burden of proof as to causes.

9. See Textile Workers Union of America v. Lincoln Mills of Alabama, 353 U.S. 448 (1957), establishing a common law concept to govern substantive decisions in

The ordinarily expected standards test is a very good one because actions are not judged by the particular rules of the agency, but by widely held standards of what constitutes proper conduct in a work environment. These rules need not be written out, but are clearly understood by most people as the proper way to conduct oneself on the job. This is not to say that an agency may not have specific rules and standards of behavior for its employees; but the very specificity of the rules makes it possible to judge them by other standards, such as whether they contravene a right of an employee, whether they can be easily followed, and whether they can be easily understood—as opposed to being too vague.

In this particular case, the court posed the question of whether the employee understood that this type of behavior was known to be prohibited. An employee can be held to have knowledge that a certain practice is prohibited, even though not expressly stated, if it is "the kind of job-related misbehavior that is inconsistent with proper attention to work or proper loyalty to the employment relationship."[10]

The court held that, as a matter of law, an employee of the FBI could not be held to have knowledge that this kind of behavior was behavior "unbecoming an employee of this bureau." The FBI tried to justify its act by saying that the standard of behavior for all employees of the bureau was, to give credit to Harold Ross, the standard of "the little old lady from Dubuque," as expressed in the FBI handbook. However, the court pointedly noted that the FBI handbook also specifically allows FBI employees to engage in legal gambling and the use of intoxicants during off-duty hours. Thus the court ordered Carter to be given a trial where the facts of the case, including a definition of community and FBI standards, could be aired.

The *Carter* approach is extremely useful, especially in cases where the employee's conduct is neither clearly protected by the Constitution or statute nor clearly in violation of a valid, well-known rule of behavior. By applying a common sense standard the court has avoided becoming entangled in problems of absolute powers of government or absolute rights of employees in situations where no constitutional questions are present. I submit that this is the approach that all courts should use in cases of dismissal for behavior not quite constitutionally protected, but not clearly violative of a valid rule.

labor law cases. The statute which gives federal court jurisdiction in certain types of cases gives these courts the power to fashion rules of decision without reference to specific statutory language or state law. I believe that the same process has developed in cases brought under the Civil Rights Act, 42 U.S.C. 1983.

10. 407 F.2d at 1244.

Disloyalty and Insubordination

To see how this rule works in practice, the case of *Lefcourt* v. *The Legal Aid Society* can be examined.[11] Gerald Lefcourt was graduated from law school in June, 1967. He had been extremely active in civil rights and civil liberties activities. In his last year he was a student volunteer with the Legal Aid Society. After graduation he joined the Legal Aid Society as a full-time staff attorney. Six months later he was discharged for behavior that was "not in harmony with the welfare of the organization." He went into district court and lost. Unlike Carter, he did not appeal the decision and the decision sticks.

Just as the *Carter* case cannot be understood only in the context of the unique standard of behavior applied by the FBI to its employees (this could not have served as grounds for dismissal in many other agencies), so the *Lefcourt* case has to be understood in the context of what was happening to the legal profession in 1968. The Legal Aid Society of New York was founded to provide legal assistance to indigent criminal defendants. It long predated the Legal Aid Agencies formed under the Office of Economic Opportunity (OEO), and was not connected with the federal program. (While a question arises as to whether the Legal Aid Society was a state agency, the court assumed it was for purposes of argument—I agree that it clearly should be treated as such.) The tradition of the Legal Aid Society was conservative. Their tradition was to defend persons accused of crime according to the rules of the system, not to change the system.

However in June of 1968, a new breed of lawyer was emerging. The experiences of the Mississippi summer, Selma, and the Vietnam War had convinced these young lawyers that to protect the individual the system itself must be changed. But even among these new young lawyers, Gerald Lefcourt would be considered an activist. It was inevitable that Lefcourt and his supervisors would clash. He was openly critical of the way in which the Legal Aid Society was operating and was instrumental in forming the Association of Legal Aid Attorneys of the City of New York. Indeed, Lefcourt claims he was fired solely for his speeches and his activities in regard to the association.

The society, on the other hand, claimed they fired Lefcourt not because of his speeches or organizational activity, but because of his behavior on the job and his attitude toward his superiors. The society claimed that he continually nagged his supervisors about changes in duty hours; he

11. See note 7, *supra*. Contrast with Crocker v. United States, 127 F. Supp. 568 (Ct. Cl. 1955).

refused to accept a transfer to a different office; he requested time off to attend to personal matters; and he was generally disrespectful.

Whether or not these charges were sufficient to justify a dismissal as a matter of law is difficult to judge. However, the trial judge thought they were sufficient, and attempted to differentiate this conduct from conduct protected by the Constitution.

Judge Lasker characterized the reasons for the dismissal as being "a frictional relationship developing during the course of his employment between Lefcourt and some of his superiors which, capped by his strongly critical statements, caused those who were managing the Society [as I have stated above], to conclude in good faith that Lefcourt's service was not in harmony with the welfare of the organization."[12]

He compared Lefcourt's situation with that found in *Pickering* v. *Board of Education*, where a public schoolteacher was dismissed for writing a letter critical of his school board.[13] Judge Lasker found that Lefcourt's case differed from *Pickering* in several important respects. Lasker held that in *Pickering* the statements of the teacher were directed to the public at large, while in this case they were directed at persons with whom Lefcourt had daily contact, raising questions of discipline and harmony. Second, Pickering's statements did not interfere with his daily performance in class, while Lefcourt's had a definite impact on the workings of the Legal Aid Society. Finally, Pickering's statements must be considered public debate and thus protected, while Lefcourt's statements formed no part of public debate.

While Judge Lasker showed his awareness of some of the hidden issues in the case, the decision represents the traditional law on the responsibilities of public employees and the grounds for which they can be fired. In the usual case involving First Amendment rights of public employees, the issue is generally public statements made by the employee, which may or may not concern a matter relevant to the job. While public utterances were present in *Lefcourt*, the main issue was purely internal statements and actions. In the court's view the issue was not whether Lefcourt's statements and actions fell within the range of permissible speech. Rather, the court looked at the entirety of the situation and characterized Lefcourt's behavior as being disruptive activities, which often took the form of statements critical of the policies of his superiors.

If the facts as presented by the Society are accepted as true, then Judge Lasker's characterization of Lefcourt's behavior is essentially correct. Likewise, under traditionally accepted notions of the law, activities

12. 312 F. Supp. at 1112.
13. 391 U.S. 563 (1968). This critical case is discussed in detail in chapter 3.

which lead to the promotion of disharmony in an organization would be valid grounds for dismissal of the employee.[14] Yet a different factor should also be considered in judging what is disruptive behavior. The Legal Aid Society and the newer Legal Aid Societies chartered under the aegis of OEO can be characterized as being in the service sector of the government. As previously noted, the legal profession is undergoing a great change brought on by the emergence of young lawyers burning with a desire to make the legal system work for all. This is not unlike the attitude of many teachers and social work professionals for their professions. As with teachers and social workers, these lawyers consider themselves as having a stake in changing the legal system, rather than simply serving their clients. Nowhere is this feeling more widespread than in the various legal aid offices.

Perhaps Lefcourt's behavior and attitude would be considered disruptive even in the most socially aware legal aid office, but his criticisms of the New York Legal Aid Society are not without merit, and could have been afforded more weight. However, the judge was correct in not wanting to pass on an internal dispute of the Legal Aid Society. When Lefcourt went public, he obviously made his tenure on the faculty untenable.

Internal criticism of the basic policies of one's employer which reach the point of insubordination are usually considered to be a valid ground for dismissal. Yet public employees in many different sectors are now raising questions of the basic policies of their employers, especially in areas where they are as well-trained as their supervisors. A new approach should be taken to define improper criticism; in fact, is criticism of policy, in the service sectors, not an inherent part of a job? How far can it extend?

Some guidance can be gleaned from a California case, *Parrish* v. *Civil Service Commission of Alameda County*.[15] Benny Max Parrish was a social worker in the Oakland, California, Welfare Department. In 1963, welfare departments all over the country, but especially those in California, conducted "midnight raids" on the homes of welfare recipients to see if any woman receiving aid to dependent children was violating the so-called man in the house rule, which barred aid to any woman living with an able-bodied man who could support her and her children. At the time

14. See McAuliffe v. New Bedford, 155 Mass. 219, 19 N.E. 519 (1892); however see Roberts v. Lake Central School Corporation, 317 F. Supp. 63 (N.D. Ind. 1970), in which a teacher who was also a union leader was fired for statements made at a union meeting where he accused the school board of trying to buy off the union. The court held that this constituted protected speech and could not be classified as insubordination.

15. 57 Cal. Rptr. 623 (1967).

of the incident in question neither the midnight raids nor the man in the house rule had yet been declared unconstitutional by any court.

However, when the Alameda County Welfare Department decided to conduct such a raid, Parrish refused to take part on the grounds that such an activity was unconstitutional. The raids took place without Parrish and he was fired for insubordination. He sued for reinstatement and eventually won in the California Supreme Court. The court ruled that Parrish, a public employee, had a right to refuse to participate in a governmental activity which he truly believed unconstitutional or illegal. In the same decision the California court agreed with Parrish and held such raids to be illegal searches and violative of the recipient's right of privacy.

The importance of this case is that, at the time that Parrish acted, such practice was not illegal or unconstitutional. This should be differentiated from a situation in which a certain practice has been declared unconstitutional, but a given governmental agency continues to engage in such practice and the public employee refuses to engage in the clearly illegal practice. In such a case the legal question will be easy, as no public employee can be forced to engage in an illegal act and be fired for not doing so.[16]

Parrish goes much further, because Parrish was acting on his own sense of values as to what is proper behavior by a public employee, not on legal precedent. In effect, he made a legal challenge to a practice of his employer and won.

The *Parrish* rule is a good one, though it is limited to situations where the public employer is engaging in an illegal or unconstitutional practice. I do not think that it can be stretched to cover an individual who refuses to participate in an activity of his employer because he considers such activity is unwise or foolish. The law clearly states that public officials can legally engage in foolish and unwise activities; such activities are subject to change in the normal political ways, but refusal to follow such policy while it is still policy is clearly insubordination. However, this does not mean that public employees cannot act to change unwise policy. One of the prime goals of employee organizations, especially teachers' unions, is to effect a change in administrative policies in their given agencies. However, this is a continuing activity done while still working under existing rules. When large groups of public employees strike, especially over nonwage issues, the action remains illegal, but special counter-

16. The cases of Ernest Fitzgerald and Gordon Rule, budget analysts with the Air Force and Navy respectively, were subject to job action for "blowing the whistle" on improper budget practices with cost overrides in weapons projects. They were both reinstated after protracted fights. Fitzgerald's case is discussed in chapters 3 and 6.

vailing factors are present in the situation of a mass strike rather than individual refusal to work under a given policy.

One question that was not answered in *Parrish* was whether he could have been reinstated if he was wrong. That is, even though he deeply believed that the midnight raids were unconstitutional, if the court had found them to be legal, could he still have been reinstated, since he believed them to be unconstitutional? Probably not. Because a public body is often subjected to varying pressures on the proper way to conduct policy, an activity which is proper at one time or in one context might be all wrong in another context. However, constitutional questions present more difficulty, especially when the question is not the power of the agency but the right of the citizens against whom the action was taken. Thus, fairly good guesses can be made as to what is legal and what is not. The decision not to participate in an activity of one's employer because such activity is illegal or unconstitutional is a very serious decision, one that should not be made in a casual fashion. To fashion a rule allowing a public employee the right to refuse to participate in unconstitutional activity, even before it is held unconstitutional, and to hold him strictly accountable for his legal judgment, would thus be proper. Allowing public employees continually to sue their employers in behalf of public clients is not good policy; legal problems aside, the presumption that governmental agencies usually act illegally is not valid. This does not mean that public employees must be silent or that they cannot try to change policy. However, this recognizes that a public employee does owe a certain level of loyalty to his employer, even as he is attempting to change the policy of the public employer.

Yet situations like *Parrish* do arise in which the government engages in clearly unconstitutional acts which shock the conscience of a public employee to the point where he cannot participate in such activity. A public employee should not be punished if he is correct about such illegality. Loyalty to one's organization can go far but there are limits, and this clearly constitutes the limits of employee loyalty. If the employee is wrong, then in effect his act should be treated as a resignation, as he has said, in effect, that he cannot continue to work in this agency if the agency engages in such practices.

An important recent case concerning the concept of cause, though unfortunately not terribly favorable to the employee, was the case of *Arnett* v. *Kennedy*.[17] In this case Kennedy, a field representative of the Office

17. 416 U.S. 134 (1974). See also Krennrich v. United States 340 F.2d 653 (D.C. Cir. 1965), cert. denied 382 U.S. 870 (1965), where the employee anonymously sent defamatory letters to a supervisor and a fellow employee's wife. The court held that the mere sending of the letter was sufficient grounds for dismissal irrespective of whether or not the charges were true.

of Economic Opportunity, was charged with having made intentionally false public statements that a regional director and an assistant in OEO had offered a bribe to a potential grantee in return for a statement against Kennedy and another employee violating some kind of policy directive. Charges were brought against him by his own supervisors and he was dismissed after a short hearing.

Once his local agency had found against him, Arnett was faced with two types of remedy. The first was to follow administrative provisions given to federal civil service employees by the Lloyd-La Follette Act of 1912, which permitted removal of public civil service employees only for such cause as would promote the efficiency of the service, or to file in federal court claiming that this just cause standard was too vague. The Supreme Court by a six to three vote reversed a lower court decision and held that the standards of dismissal were not impermissably vague or overbroad; in other words, were not so sweeping in terms as to render both legal and illegal activities equally wrong, thus rendering the whole provision unconstitutional.

While much of the opinion concerned the constitutionality of the procedural due process provisions of the statute, which will be discussed later, nevertheless the upholding of the just cause standard has the effect of shifting the burden from the agency to the employee to prove that the agency's actions were not correct. Also, this rule differs from the law of freedom of expression in which a great differentiation is established between constitutional consequences of speech made as part of and relating to one's job and speech made about matters not directly concerned with one's job, in determining whether or not certain nonconstitutional grounds can be the basis for a public employee's dismissal, especially from federal employment. The use of the just cause and promotion of the efficiency of the service standard means that no differentiation, as a matter of law, is made between matters of policy and matters of personal behavior which might have a relationship to function. Thus the line of lower court cases such as *Carter*, which feature the disapproval of life styles, may be seriously weakened. Since the facts in the *Arnett* case concern an action which immediately affects the working relationship in the most direct way possible, the case should be read as narrowly as possible, with the understanding that unfounded allegations of misconduct made by an employee against his employer is just cause. Factually this case is closer to *Lefcourt* than *Carter*.

In the recent case *Kelley* v. *Johnson*, however, the Supreme Court upheld the validity of the Suffolk County (New York) hair length regulations for policemen.[18] The Policemen's Benevolent Association sued,

18. 425 U.S. 238 (1976).

claiming that such regulations had no valid relationship to public health and safety, and violated the individual policeman's personal liberty, as protected by the Fourteenth Amendment.

The Supreme Court held that this regulation need not be viewed in terms of the general public but rather in terms of how the county wished to establish its police force. Thus the county need not establish a public need for such a regulation; since it deals with a uniformed service, the regulation is to be deemed valid unless shown to be completely arbitrary. Whether the basis of the regulation is the need for similarity of appearance or for a desire for esprit de corps, either choice would validate the regulation.

A dissenting opinion, filed by Justice Marshall and joined by Justice Brennan, stated that the right of a citizen to choose his own personal appearance was beyond question, and in terms of the stated justification for the regulation this right was not overcome, since it is the uniform, not the hair, which makes the policeman. Likewise, since a vast majority of the officers affected were plaintiffs in the suit, this regulation could not help the esprit de corps.

This case is probably less significant in terms of its ruling than in the attitude expressed. Since the fact of uniform was the basis of the ruling it probably could not be extended to most other employees. However, this Court showed a strong tendency to find in favor of administrative justification over individual rights, and this bodes ill for public employees, especially in cases where the conduct in question is not protected speech and bears directly on the employment relationship.

Arnett and *Kelley* should not be read as meaning that the right-privilege doctrine has returned. Both cases had unique fact situations, in that *Arnett* was clearly job-related, and *Kelley* concerned a uniformed service where at least universal regulation could be traditionally justified, though *Kelley* is much harder to justify factually than is *Arnett*.

What public employees should do in the future is avoid confronting their employers where confrontation is avoidable, since disruptive action is now considered just cause. If confrontation is to occur, it is obviously best for the employee if the agency causes the confrontation, and even better if the employee can relate his situation either to actions unrelated to the job or to more traditionally protected First Amendment activity. However, as previously stated the possibility of new, less conservative judges being appointed at all levels may mean that the 1975–76 terms of the Supreme Court were the low point for public employees. Indeed, that point may have been reached in two very recent Supreme Court cases.

In *Aldinger* v. *Howard*,[19] a schoolteacher was dismissed from her job

19. 427 U.S. 1 (1976).

without a hearing because she was allegedly living with her boyfriend, though her work was considered excellent.

She sued the county treasurer in federal court under the provision of the Civil Rights Act, which only allows suits for damages against officials, not state agencies. As part of her suit she tried to include a state law claim against the county by virtue of a time-honored procedure called ancillary jurisdiction, under which a federal court may also hear purely state law issues growing out of a case if there is proper federal jurisdiction. The Supreme Court refused to allow this procedure, although the Warren court, lower courts, and numerous commentators had been prescribing this method as a way to avoid dual litigation.

The second and most important case, the one with the most ominous meaning for public employees, was *Bishop* v. *Wood*.[20] In that case a policeman in the town of Marion, North Carolina, was dismissed without a hearing by the city manager, who charged that the policeman failed to follow orders, had a poor attendance record in classes, caused low morale in the department, and generally engaged in conduct unsuitable to an officer. The city ordinance under which he was hired provided that he would be classified as a permanent employee, and the United States Supreme Court, in previous cases discussed in greater detail in other parts of this book, held that a person classified as a permanent employee, such as a teacher on tenure, is guaranteed rights of procedural due process as part of any job action taken against him.

The case was further complicated by the fact that the charges against the policeman were based on false or mistaken information. Thus the city manager's action against the policeman was clearly not based on just cause, but at the same time was not based on a provable interference with an otherwise protected constitutional right, such as the right to freedom of speech. Thus the question before the Supreme Court was whether, in a situation involving an arbitrary dismissal of a state public employee for grounds not involving an attempt to proscribe otherwise protected constitutional rights, a federal court could assert jurisdiction over the matter and order either reinstatement based on arbitrariness of action or, at the very least, order that the employee be reinstated and that dismissal proceedings be instituted following so-called procedural rights of due process.

The Court held that neither of these were required. On the first grounds the Court held that in situations where there is no claim that a public employer was motivated by a desire to curtail or penalize the exercise of an employee's constitutionally protected rights, the federal court was not an appropriate forum to review the "multitude of personnel

20. 426 U.S. 341 (1976).

decisions that are made daily by public agencies." What this means is that an arbitrarily dismissed public employee who claims that he was dismissed on false or misleading information concerning job performance and who is not given a chance to prove the falsehood of the information prior to dismissal, can only sue in a state court, rather than federal court.

While at face value this is not in itself totally fatal to the public employees' right to challenge arbitrary, nonconstitutionally motivated job actions, nevertheless it can have serious curtailing effects on them. Many state courts are quite competent and able to try such matters; however, from a strictly administrative point of view, many such state courts also have overcrowded dockets, due to the enormous criminal case load plus the multitude of other civil litigations not found in federal court. Thus the employee may have his claim delayed to the point where it is meaningless. In addition, the substantive basis for relief in various state courts is not at all uniform. While many state courts have recognized infringements on constitutional rights or arbitrary action on government employees as being violative of state law in the same way an action could be maintained under federal law, this is by no means true in all states. Federal courts, while having some variation from court to court, tend to have more uniform decisions on cases involving constitutional rights. However, the real problem lies in the procedural rather than the substantive areas. This is not an insignificant matter, because while federal courts have obvious problems of overcrowding of the docket, they are much less crowded than most state courts.

Federal criminal law tends to center on white collar crime, with some notable exceptions, but the normal range of criminal matters, assaults, burglary, and so on, are never seen in federal courts. Since crime statistics show that these crimes are the most frequent, the federal courts are much less burdened than state courts in criminal matters. The same is true in civil cases. Because of more limited federal jurisdiction due to jurisdictional amounts far higher than in state courts and the need for a federal issue, except in suits between citizens of different states, the vast run-of-the-mill civil matters are never seen in federal court.

Thus, as a rule a hearing in a federal court will come much sooner than in a state court. Indeed, my experience in federal court has been that cases are often set too quickly, in a matter of months, while state cases may take years to be litigated, and this in an average-sized state. Thus the public employee attempting to get a claim heard not only is competing against criminal cases, but even in areas where different judges are assigned to criminal and civil cases, the public employee has to fight for court time against the multitude of automobile accidents, property disputes, domestic relation cases, and other matters not found in federal court. In addition, many state judges are former officials of the locality in which the employee is suing, not necessarily the case in federal court, which of course will present problems. Again, this is not an across-the-board, hopeless situation; the courts also have competent state judges and incompetent federal judges, and in many areas state courts would probably be better than federal courts.

In the area of the rights of public employees, however, many suits have already been tried in state courts. This means that federal courts, traditionally more receptive to claims by state employees of arbitrary dismissal not necessarily based upon interference to protect constitutional rights, no longer have this jurisdiction, and the public employee is now required to go into state courts. Many state courts were secretly pleased to be relieved of cases such as these, which often involve lengthy trials; thus public employees suddenly forced into state courts are doubtless going to receive an icy reception from court administration.

Another serious ramification to the lack of access to federal courts bears on the substantive claim. While rights to procedural due process, discussed in detail later in this book, do not seek to answer the question of right or wrong of evidenciary facts, nevertheless, in the context of federal court jurisdiction prior to *Bishop* v. *Wood*, the right to be given procedural due process for those public employees held to be permanent employees, or given that right by contract, in effect constitutes a substantive doctrine of federal law. Thus, the denial of procedural due process becomes the denial of a remedy—an important remedy to public employment. If the court finds that procedural due process is denied, the dismissal is held to be illegal. In short, even if no damages are assessed and the employee can be subsequently dismissed after a fair hearing, the employee is at least reinstated as of the date of the earlier dismissal and is entitled to his salary going back to that particular date. This, of course, is a major impediment to arbitrary dismissal.

However, in this case the Supreme Court held that, contrary to its previous decision in the *Arnett* case, the methods of procedure for a dismissed employee may be determined by the employer along with the grounds for the dismissal, provided that the grounds do not constitute a punishment for exercising a protected constitutional right. Thus, the right to be fired only for just cause is in effect contingent upon the procedures that the government has set up to handle grievances of punished employees. Cause accordingly becomes inseparable from existence to evaluate cause. Four justices of the Supreme Court, dissenting in this case, specifically made mention of this contradiction and how it in effect wiped out what they had thought was a proper balancing of interests in *Arnett*:

The majority thus implicitly concedes that the ordinance supplies the grounds for discharge and that the city manager must determine them to be "adequate" grounds before he may fire an employee. The majority is holding that the petitioner had no property interest in his job in spite of the unequivocal language in the city ordinance that he may be dismissed only for certain kinds of cause rests then on the fact that state law provides no *procedures* for assuring that the city manager may dismiss him only for cause. The right to do his job is thus redefined according to majority by the procedures provided for in the third sentence and is redefined as infringed only if the procedures are not followed.[21]

This is precisely the reasoning embraced by only three, and expressly rejected by six, members of the Court in *Arnett*. The argument of concern was whether or not rights of procedural due process for those employees held to be covered by procedural due process as a matter of nonconstitutional statutory law or regulation (Arnett was held not to be covered) would be protected from dismissal, except for just cause. That the procedures for determining whether or not just cause was present would occur "not by legislative grace but by constitutional guarantee" was understood. What this all means for a state employee is that the employee's right to challenge an arbitrary dismissal is based strictly on state law, both procedurally and substantively. If a state does not have a state law equivalent to procedural due process made applicable to its employees, the public employee cannot complain against the methods by which he was dismissed. Likewise, if the state law does not have a basis for determining what is or is not just cause, no other complaints can be made.[22] This situation is really unfortunate, because even if the United States Supreme Court felt that matters such as this could be best handled

21. 421 U.S. at 350.
22. That is, federal court actions can no longer be based on denial of procedural due process unless the state violates its own law. Likewise state employees can no longer complain in federal court that the state did not have just cause, in a nonconstitutional sense, to dismiss the employee. Of course the state employee may sue in state court, if the state provides a remedy, or in federal court if there is a substantive court constitutional issue involved. However, Bishop v. Wood would seem to stand for the position that if no constitutional issue is present and no state remedy exists the employee is out of luck. In most states public employees can assert some form of equitable procedure to get a court hearing at least as to reinstatement. However, actual damages may not be available in the absence of specific legislative authority. The Civil Rights Act permits both equitable relief (injunction of reinstatement) and actual and punitive charges. In many states an aggrieved person can sue either for equitable relief or damages, but not both. Thus, on very practical grounds, public employees are in a much poorer position unless the claim has as its basis the violation of a substantive right. Bishop v. Wood, 426 U.S. at 349, 350.

in state court as a matter of administration, nevertheless the constitutional guarantees of procedural due process would still be applicable to state court proceedings except for the second part of the decision, and the state court would have been required to determine whether procedural due process was present. As of now the protections of the state public employee are in limbo, and his rights to challenge arbitrary dismissal are based not on constitutional rights but depend instead entirely upon the particular laws of his state. While this decision will doubtless be modified or changed as the Supreme Court changes, nevertheless it is the law now.

However, this does not mean that arbitrary decisions are the law in all jurisdictions. Both the federal government and many states do provide some mechanisms to determine whether or not dismissal was proper. Thus, those situations in which a proper forum can be found and in which an employee is able to make a claim based upon the improper proof of facts must now be considered. The facts that can and cannot be the basis of just cause in areas other than job-related matters must be considered, because these would seem to present most of the legal difficulties.

"Immoral" or Criminal Conduct

The area of greatest legal difficulty with regard to the exclusion or dismissal of public employees for cause where no constitutional issues are involved is the area of "immoral" or criminal activities. The reason this is so difficult is that the conduct involved invariably takes place outside of the employment situation, and the question is whether such conduct has relevance to the employment situation. Two issues flow from this larger issue: (1) whether such conduct itself should even be considered relevant to employment; and (2) if so, what is the degree of behavior necessary to be considered relevant to one's employment?

As in all these areas, First Amendment questions are present, since many people claim that certain conduct considered immoral may indeed be constitutionally protected. However, those issues will be discussed with the First Amendment rights of public employees. For the purpose of this discussion, assume that all such activity can legally be classified as immoral or criminal or both; the only issue is under what circumstances commission of such acts can serve as a disqualification for public employment.

Before attempting the difficult questions of definition and application of terminology, the easier problems should be considered. No matter how immoral or criminal acts are defined, clearly some types of acts are immoral or criminal under anybody's definition of the term. These are crimes involving what is called moral turpitude. All acts involving the afflicting of violence upon another, except in self-defense, would be one type. Fraud or illegal appropriation of another's property would be another. So would sexual aggression on unwilling persons, or the sale of narcotics and other drugs, in effect crimes with victims. Because they may easily be classified as untrustworthy, persons can clearly be disqualified from public employment for the commission of such offenses, unless the offense is so far back in time as not to have any present relevance, or if special extenuating circumstances are present. Even if such circumstances are present, the general rule of disqualification would prevail, with burden on the individual to prove the rule should not apply to him.

However, once this class of activity has been considered, the waters indeed become murky. Here are found the so-called crimes without victims—prostitution, gambling (perhaps), "pandering" and the like, possession of marijuana, and so on.[23] No definitive rule as to what conduct is absolutely disqualifying and what is not is possible; each case has to be taken alone, and the mere commission of a certain class of conduct cannot be the sole grounds of disqualification.

The place of commission of the conduct is a relevant factor; clearly, if any of the previously described actions were performed on the job, or if the job site was used to set the groundwork for the commission of such an act, such a factor could provide a basis for dismissal, especially if the job site was a relevant factor in the act. By job-related activity I do not mean that such an activity was done with either a fellow employee or a person the employee got to know through his work. This would not necessarily indicate that such activity was job related, provided no other factors were present. If the job was merely incidental to the activity, then the activity might not lead to job action; save that the employee engaged in such activity with a fellow employee, it should not be considered job related. What really is relevant is first, the seriousness of the act; second, whether other employees were affected or work impaired; and, finally, whether the job site was, in effect, used as a cover. Thus, forming an office football pool may not be of any importance, but if an employee

---

23. Most cases which I have discovered have involved homosexuality. It may be that for those public employees who have gotten into trouble for gambling, drinking, etc., the social implications are so much less serious that it is not much of a disability in finding different employment. Also, governments seem intent on persecuting employees who are homosexual. One case which involves a different type of "moral offense" is Pelicone v. Hodges, 320 F.2d (D.C. Cir. 1963). In that case Pelicone was discharged from a federal job for taking a prostitute to a hotel room. He was fired for involvement in a criminal act, but this was not criminal. Thus he was ordered reinstated.

acts as a bookie or an intermediary with a bookie it might. Since the facts will be unique in this type of situation, no hard-and-fast rule can be developed to cover all situations.

Of course, the facts must be examined to see whether any inducement or seduction was present. If a public employee can be shown to have induced another employee to enter into acts he would not have done but for the inducement, this situation could clearly be the grounds for job action, even if the fellow employee enjoyed such activity. Aggressive behavior to those not connected with one's public employment could be grounds for dismissal if it justifiably raises the fear that the employee would engage in aggressive conduct against other employees.

Alcohol

An example of conduct which could be permissible or impermissible, depending on the circumstances, is the consumption of alcoholic beverages. This example is vital because "drinking" is usually legal except in certain circumstances, in contrast to gambling, which is usually illegal except in certain circumstances. In either case, the person can engage in such activity alone; only those who furnish the means of engaging in such conduct are acting in a manner not easily duplicated by the individual.

Drinking, while usually legal, is considered by many to be immoral. No matter how drinking is characterized, the consumption of alcoholic beverages can have a detrimental effect on one's work.

In looking at the possible consequences drinking might have on the job, extremes should be examined first. No one would doubt that chronic alcoholism or repeated instances of intoxication while at work can be grounds for dismissal or exclusion from public employment. Degrees may be involved, but the ultimate question of whether such activity can lead to dismissal must be answered affirmatively. Likewise, no one can claim that drinking in one's home, without any ill effects, or even the offering of alcohol to fellow employees, no matter how distasteful this might be to them, should, except in exceptional circumstances, be grounds for dismissal. Exceptions always can be found to both rules, but usual behavior is the major concern here.

However, a great many types of conduct involving alcohol are not subject to easy answers. An example would be public drunkenness. Can an arrest for that crime be the grounds of dismissal of a public employee, even if the employee never drinks on the job or has his job performance impaired by the use of alcohol? It depends.

The nature of the job is certainly a factor. Some jobs require the employee to maintain a spotless public image, and even a single arrest for public drunkenness could be a disqualification. With some other jobs it might not be a relevant factor, though repeated instances could lead to a valid decision that one is incapable of controlling his vices, with the strong possibility of job-related activity occurring.

A more difficult case is a conviction for drunken driving. This is an extremely serious offense, which involves endangering the lives of others. Yet such a condition should not bring automatic disqualification. An employee who has two drinks may be just as guilty of drunken driving as a thoroughly intoxicated person, and may indeed be subject to equally severe criminal penalties. Yet, in judging if this is a disqualification for public employment, other factors come into play. While the criminal law is designed to cover those persons who may not think they are affected by alcohol, but are still a driving menace, such a strict liability standard would be inappropriate for determining disqualifications for public employment. The relevance of criminal convictions to public employment is that the evidence of the conviction or commission of certain behavior often provides good evidence of what a person will do on the job. Aside from the fear of a person committing certain crimes while employed, the existence of criminal behavior will often mean that a person has very poor attitudes toward authority or the lack of a sense of responsibility. This is not necessarily the case; thus factors other than the mere existence of criminal activity should be accounted for in determining whether the activity justifies a disqualification.

Gambling

The same analysis should be used for other activities which, though possibly criminal, do not involve other persons except in a passive sense. Gambling, as previously mentioned, is another example. A compulsive gambler, like a chronic alcoholic, can be excluded or dismissed from the public service because sooner or later the gambling will affect job performance. Likewise, occasional betting, whether legally at a racetrack or illegally through a bookie (on something like a major sports event, where the primary motive is interest in the event rather than the gambling itself) should not be cause for expulsion.[24]

Without getting into too much detail, large grey areas of activity that could be grounds for disqualification exist, depending on individual circumstances; these can only be handled case by case.

---

24. An ironic aspect of this issue concerns the late J. Edgar Hoover. As director of the FBI he imposed a code of conduct on his agents and employees which was puritannical in the extreme; see Carter v. United States, note 7, *supra*. Yet he was a habitué of the racetracks and saw nothing wrong with placing bets.

Drugs

The one area which will present the courts with the most difficulty in the years ahead is the area of private use of drugs. Unlike gambling and the use of alcoholic beverages, which have both legal and illegal aspects, the mere possession of many popular drugs is a criminal act—in some cases with very severe penalties.

One would be rather naive to think that the current general use of drugs has not reached the ranks of public employees. Indeed, one reason for the dearth of reported cases of public employees dismissed for using certain classes of drugs is that the use is so widespread that public officials do not want to set precedents which might be used against them in the future.

Another difficulty connected to the drug problem is that the use of certain types of drugs is engaged in by large numbers of persons with full knowledge that such activity is illegal—indeed, the very illegality may perhaps account for the popularity of the use. Thus, the legal situation involves whether conscious criminal conduct of a certain type should always be grounds for dismissal.

No easy answer presents itself. Obviously use of a prohibited drug on the job or coming to the job under the effect of a prohibited drug should be grounds for dismissal. Likewise, a conviction for the sale of a prohibited drug would also be grounds for dismissal, because a person who has engaged in the selling of an illegal commodity could be a threat to the harmony of the working environment; if he sold it in one place he could sell it on the job site or to fellow employees. The key is to establish a nexus between the nature of the criminal activity and the possible adverse effect on the employment situation.

The real problem involves the person convicted for the possession or use of a drug when the offense took place in private, with no work relationship whatsoever. The Alaska Supreme Court is the only court that has ever found a right of privacy in the possession or use of prohibited drugs if used in private and without affecting any other person. Thus the act of possessing or using drugs is a criminal act in every other jurisdiction in the United States, and for that matter in the entire world.[25]

However, the multiplicity of laws on drugs contain many varying kinds of penalties for possession or use of the different types of drugs. In all jurisdictions the possession or use (though use can usually only be proven through possession) of opium derivatives is a serious felony. Clearly any

25. Though many areas have now decriminalized, if not legalized, marijuana possession.

conviction from possession of an opium derivative should be a ground for dismissal.

However, penalties vary greatly as to other drugs. Penalties as to the most controversial drug, marijuana, vary from noncriminal treatment, to a misdemeanor with small fines or a jail sentence in states like New Jersey, to treatment as a felony, although most jurisdictions have now eliminated the felony aspects of marijuana possession.

With the widespread use of marijuana in all sectors of society inevitably cases will arise of public employees found guilty of possession or use of marijuana, cases in which the employers have decided to dismiss the employee based on the crime of possession of marijuana. When this occurs some public employees will inevitably go to court to attempt reinstatement. The problem facing courts is whether they should impose special tests to protect a public employee convicted of a crime which, though minor in nature, was based upon an activity the employee knew at all times was illegal and which could have been easily avoided.

Courts will probably begin to apply a test to determine whether, under the facts of the conviction, a determination could be made that would render the employee unfit to perform his particular job. While visualizing the many possible fact situations which might arise is impossible, the fitness-to-perform test could bring in a number of factors, such as prior performance on the job. Was the conviction merely another example of the employee's willingness to disregard existing rules? Was the employee acting in a discreet manner when arrested or was he in a situation where detection was very likely? What is the nature of his job? If the employee is expected to keep up a respectable front, within a reasonable level, an understanding could have existed that any public employee would be found unfit to continue his job based on a single conviction for possession and use of a drug like marijuana.

Homosexuality

An area presenting questions similar to those of drug use, one involving a great deal of litigation, is the area of homosexual acts and the homosexuality of public employees; so much so that this has become the leading edge of the law, with precedent value far beyond the issue itself.[26]

Like the use of prohibited drugs, homosexuality, or at least a type of sexual activity such as sodomy, which is part and parcel of male homosexual activity, is illegal in most jurisdictions in the United States and

26. Dew v. Halaby, 317 F.2d 582 (D.C. Cir. 1963) cert. dismissed 379 U.S. 951 (1964); Morrison v. State Board of Education, 1 Cal. 3d 214, 461 P.2d 375 (1968);

in most places in the world as well. If the activity is not considered to be criminal in all its aspects, it is still considered to be immoral conduct by all governmental bodies. While certain legal limitations are naturally in effect on this approach, especially as to racial or sexual discrimination, experience with the Nixon administration shows that, when the basis of discrimination is a category not declared by law to be "suspect," and where the factor is not easily discernible, real across-the-board exclusion can occur. Thus a legal standard is needed for persons who have certain personal characteristics not otherwise protected by law, so that they are not excluded or dismissed from public service.

Among individuals with personal traits that could legitimately put them in a discernible category or subject them to special treatment, often unfavorable, homosexuals form by far the most prominent group, and as such generate legal issues which have much broader implications. For that reason the law concerning public employment disabilities of public employees or generalized employment prejudice against persons having unique personal traits (not gender or race) must be discussed.

Administrative Attitudes. The federal government has been especially notorious in excluding homosexuals. While no explicit written policy of the Civil Service Commission bars the employment of homosexuals, an open secret in Washington indicates that homosexuals just do not get hired if the applicant is known to be a homosexual, and the disclosure need not simply come through criminal records but could also be discovered through medical reports, admission, notoriety, or any other way, including anonymous reports.[27] The federal policy against hiring or retaining known or accused homosexuals is an across-the-board policy applying to homosexuals as a class.

The basis of the decision to exclude homosexuals from federal service is based on a broad interpretation of the power given the Civil Service Commission to "prescribe such regulations for the admission of individuals into the civil service as will best promote the efficiency of that service." The concept of promotion of efficiency is the basis for the decision not to allow known homosexuals in the federal service.

Yet the real reason for excluding homosexuals is not lack of efficiency, but because of prejudice against them. Kimbell Johnson, director of the

Scott v. Macy, 349 F.2d 182 (D.C. Cir. 1965); 402 F.2d 644 (1968); Norton v. Macy, 417 F.2d 1161 (D.C. Cir. 1969). See generally note, Government Created Employment Disabilities of the Homosexual, 82 HARVARD L. REV. 1738 (1968).

27. The Civil Service Commission has based its decision to exclude homosexuals from public employment on its interpretation of the power given it under 5 U.S.C. §3301, to "ascertain the fitness of applicants as to age, health, character, knowledge and ability for the employment sought."

Bureau of Personnel Investigations of the U.S. Civil Service Commission, in an interview reported in a student note in the *Harvard Law Review, Government-Created Employment Disabilities of the Homosexual*,[28] admitted the reason for excluding homosexuals is the desire to preserve public confidence in the Civil Service. This is an outgrowth of the Mc-Carthy era, when homosexuals in the government were considered as bad as communists in the government, and possibly synonymous.

This does not mean that homosexuality could not be the basis of exclusion or limitation of employment. Unlike the use of drugs or alcohol, substances which actually affect the ability of a person to perform his job, homosexuals are no less efficient because of their homosexuality, no matter how promiscuous. Homosexual activity could, of course, have an effect on fellow workers or persons met during the course of employment; homosexuality is considered repugnant by many people and the feelings of these people cannot be brushed aside. Yet homosexuals should not be punished for the prejudices of the general public. A policy of employment for homosexuals which strikes a balance between avoiding prejudice against homosexuals while still preventing an undermining of public confidence in the Civil Service should be achieved.

One criterion for hiring could be the degree of homosexual activity. Homosexuals who restrict themselves to private acts are less offensive than those indulging in open solicitation. Clandestine homosexuals are less likely to arouse public hostility than those who openly profess their homosexuality. And professed homosexuals are, in turn, less offensive than those whose conduct is notorious.

While no hard-and-fast rule should be drawn to bar all of a certain kind of homosexual, certain types of homosexual behavior lend themselves more readily to serve as the basis of dismissal or exclusion. A person who makes a homosexual advance on fellow workers could easily be barred from employment. Yet a person who makes repeated heterosexual advances could be just as easily dismissed. Likewise, a person who has engaged in homosexual solicitation, even if off the job, might be barred because of the fear that he will engage in such activity while on the job. Each case should be decided on the basis of the particular facts of that case and not on general rules of exclusion.[29]

In addition, a person never involved in known homosexual conduct but who nevertheless uses stereotyped homosexual actions should not

28. 82 HARVARD L. REV. 1738 (1968).

29. The California Supreme Court in the case of Morrison v. State Board of Education rejected the argument that homosexuality per se was a disqualifying trait. On the basis of a casual homosexual relationship with another teacher, Morrison had his

be barred from public employment. Since these stereotyped mannerisms, rather than actual homosexual behavior, often are offensive, however, a valid personnel policy might be to employ persons with such mannerisms and traits, whether or not homosexual, only in jobs having the least contact with the general public. To deny employment because fellow employees might not like these character traits would not be valid, especially if evidence of homosexual solicitation of fellow employees is absent.[30]

Other factors should also be considered. One is frequency of homosexual acts. Is the person exclusively homosexual, or are his homosexual activities infrequent? Another factor is length of service. A person who has held a job for many years without any known homosexual behavior who suddenly is either publicly exposed as a long-time homosexual, or who is caught while engaging in an infrequent homosexual act, should not be treated the same as a person without an ascertainable work record in the same position. The determining factor should not be service in a given job, but past work performance.

According to a note in the *Harvard Law Review* (cited previously in note 26), the Civil Service Commission has already taken tentative steps toward liberalizing its almost blanket prohibition on the employment of homosexuals. The present policy of the commission is not to expel employees with many years service; minor criminal convictions two or more

license to teach revoked for "immoral and unprofessional conduct and an act involving moral turpitude."

The court held that there must be shown that the conduct in question indicated an ineptness to teach. The court focused on the fact that no attempts were ever shown as to improper relationships with students nor any lack of qualification as to teaching duties.

> Before the Board can conclude that a teacher's continued retention in the profession presents a significant danger of harm to students or fellow teachers, essential factual premises in its reasoning should be supported by evidence or official notice. In this case despite the quantity and quality of information available about human sexual behavior, the record contains no such evidence as to the significance and implications of the incident. Neither this court nor the superior court is authorized to rectify the failure of uniformed speculations or conjectures as to a petitioner's conduct. [461 F.2d at 392–93.]

30. A particularly fascinating case developed recently in New Jersey, when a teacher underwent a sex change operation and sought to be reinstated in the school she previously taught in as a male. The school board refused, holding that her presence would be so disruptive and controversial that normal school operations would be disrupted. Likewise, her notoriety was such that employment in other schools would be impossible.

years before application are also no longer grounds for exclusion. The policy now excludes only those whose homosexuality is a matter of public knowledge or record.

The federal government's standards for exclusion from service for reasons of homosexuality were set out in a letter to the Mattachine Society dated February 25, 1966.[31] This letter was introduced by the government in the case of *Scott* v. *Macy* to define the government's standards as to homosexuality.[32] According to the letter, the persons "about whom there is evidence that they have engaged in or solicited others to engage in homosexual or sexually perverted acts with them, without evidence of rehabilitation are not suitable for federal employment." The letter qualifies this to the extent it is concerned only with conduct, not tendencies, with many considerations involved including the "total impact of the applicant upon the job."

The letter stresses the fact that homosexuality is illegal in almost all jurisdictions of the country, but tries to deny that the government does or can inquire into private sexual conduct. It states, "as long as it remains truly private, that is, remains undisclosed, it is not the subject of an inquiry."[33]

This definition is broad and would include most persons who are homosexuals; indeed, compared to many state and local governments, the exceptions are actually liberal. Thus, for most purposes, the known homosexual is still barred at all levels of government, with the exceptions to this policy very limited in nature. Accordingly, the homosexual who wishes to be employed by the government or who wishes to retain his government job has recourse only to the courts.

---

31. The Mattachine Society of Washington is a civil rights organization for homosexuals with emphasis on securing employment rights for homosexuals in government and preventing discrimination against them in the granting of government benefits, etc. In the famous cases of Leonard Matlovitch and Vernon Berg, the Air Force sergeant and Naval officer discharged for admitted homosexuality, the society was outspoken in its support.

32. 349 F.2d 182 (D.C. Cir. 1965); reheard 402 F.2d 644 (1968).

33. The authority the Civil Service Commission cites for its position is based on 5 U.S.C. §631 (1964) as amended; 5 U.S.C. §3301 (Supp. II 1967) and Civil Service rules promulgated thereto; 5 CFR §731.201 (1968).

> The Commission may deny an applicant examination, deny an eligible appointment and instruct an agency to remove an appointee for any of the following reasons. . . .
>
> (b) criminal, infamous, dishonest, immoral or notoriously disgraceful conduct.

Fortunately, as a result of such cases as *Scott* v. *Macy*, *Norton* v. *Macy*, and other cases which will be discussed later, the Civil Service Commission has revised its rules concerning employment of homosexuals. The new regulation which covers the area states:

> Individuals' sexual conduct will be considered under the guides discussed above. Court decisions require that persons not be disqualified from federal employment solely on the basis of homosexual conduct. The Commission and all agencies have been informed not to find a person unsuitable for federal employment solely because that person is homosexual or has engaged in homosexual acts. Based on these court decisions, an outstanding injunction, while a person may not be found unsuitable based on unsubstantiated conclusions concerning possible embarrassment to the federal service, a person may be dismissed or found unsuitable for federal employment where the evidence establishes that such a person's sexual conduct affects job fitness.[34]

Thus, while no absolute ban now exists under Civil Service regulations or from court decisions, obviously a great area of latitude is present both for the employee and the government to determine whether or not sexual predilection can be the basis of disqualification from government employment. Just as in the area of free speech, government employees will see that a form of balancing test has been introduced, weighing the interests of government efficiency and noninterference with the agency's mission as opposed to the personal right of the individual to maintain a nonobtrusive sexual predilection. Because of this balancing test, the importance of factual analysis becomes absolutely critical. Accordingly, as the question of judicial attitudes toward the use of homosexuality as a basis of exclusion dismissal are discussed, the factual nuances which developed in these cases must be kept in mind; the establishment of a broad rule in the form of a dogma should not be attempted.

Judicial Attitudes. A public employee or applicant for public employment who finds himself excluded or dismissed because of homosexual behavior will find that courts, just as the rest of society, have an ambivalent attitude toward the power of the government to exclude or dismiss persons from the public service because of homosexual behavior. In some cases courts refuse to look behind the stated reasons of dismissal or exclusion and simply accept the agency's findings of fact as determinative, while others seek a relationship between the conduct and the person's fitness to perform the job. Fortunately, courts are beginning to make

34. 5 CFR §731.202(b).

factual examinations to determine whether alleged homosexual behavior could be the basis of the action taken.

This trend in judicial attitudes can be clearly seen if the change in judicial thinking that has taken place in one court is examined. This court is the important United States Circuit Court for the District of Columbia, which handles all appeals from determinations of federal agencies in Washington, including, of course, the Civil Service Commission.

William Dew had been working as an air traffic controller for the Federal Aviation Agency for twenty months and had earned a satisfactory rating. In a routine check of Dew's personnel file, the personnel officer discovered that, prior to coming to the FAA, Dew had applied for a position in the Central Intelligence Agency. As part of the application, he was required to undergo a lie detector test. During that test he admitted to having participated in several homosexual acts when he was eighteen years old. On the basis of this evidence Dew was dismissed from service. The reason given by the agency was that a person of Dew's background might adversely affect the efficiency of the service, even though his performance on the job had given no indication that his work could be subject to unusual influences. Dew even introduced psychiatric evidence that he was now a stable married parent with no tendency to repeat the acts committed while an adolescent.

Despite the evidence, indicating that Dew no longer had any homosexual tendencies, the district and circuit courts affirmed his dismissal. The basis of the decision was simply that, even though no evidence existed to indicate that Dew's prior immoral acts had exerted any impact on his actual job performance, the court refused to challenge the hearing examiner's determination that employment of a person with such a background might nevertheless adversely affect the "efficiency of the service."[35]

This decision was unsophisticated in the extreme, because the court deliberately closed its eyes to evidence showing that the homosexual acts had absolutely no bearing upon Dew's performance in his job. Indeed, if the personnel check had not been performed, the acts would never have been uncovered and Dew would have continued in his job with his superiors completely unaware of his past and without any reason to doubt his ability to do his job.

This case, while bad law, did have a happy ending. After losing in the court of appeals, Dew appealed the case to the United States Supreme Court which, to the surprise of many, agreed to hear it. The Court never

35. Dew v. Halaby, 317 F.2d 582 (D.C. Cir. 1963). Cert. granted 376 U.S. 904; cert. dismissed by agreements of the parties, 379 U.S. 951 (1964).

did hear the case, however, as the FAA quickly reversed itself and agreed to reinstate Dew to his former position with back pay.

This FAA decision did not mean that the government had changed its position on homosexuals in government service. Instead, it meant that the government preferred to give Dew his job back rather than to have the Supreme Court reverse the court of appeals and, in the process, issue broad guidelines which would have required government agencies to show that dismissals for homosexuality, or for any other ground, were based on a factual showing that the behavior of the dismissed or excluded person had or would have an adverse effect on his ability to perform his job. The government knew that the court of appeals' decision could not stand; that it was weak.[36] Yet, the lesson of the granting of the writ of certiorari was not lost on the Court of Appeals for the District of Columbia; the next time it was faced with a case involving homosexual activity of a public employee which could not be resolved on procedural issues, it took an entirely different tack, strongly hinting that the change in the law should come from it, rather than from the Supreme Court reversing one of its decisions.[37] This case was *Norton* v. *Macy*,[38] which involved facts much less favorable to the employee than those in *Dew* v. *Halaby*.

Norton was a high-level budget analyst in the National Aeronautics and Space Administration (NASA). One night in October of 1963 he was observed by two officers of the Washington, D.C., Morals Squad. He drove up to a man in Lafayette Square, picked him up, drove around the square and dropped him off at the starting point. The two men drove off in separate cars, followed by the officers. Both men were eventually arrested; the second man stated that Norton made a homosexual advance and invited him up to his apartment. The ostensible reason for the arrest was a traffic violation incurred during the chase; nevertheless, the police interviewed Norton and the other man for several hours concerning their sexual history. When Norton stated that he worked for NASA, the police notified the chief of security for NASA, who came to the police station.

---

36. From a tactical viewpoint the decision of the government to concede Dew v. Halaby was sound. In 1963, the Warren court was first beginning to hit its stride and, based upon this fact, some of its most far-reaching decisions in affirmation of personal liberty came during this period. There is no doubt that the Supreme Court would have reversed in very sweeping language.

37. The Scott v. Macy cases were decided between Dew v. Halaby and Norton v. Macy. However, their significance was less in the question of what kind of "immoral activity" must be shown to justify dismissal than in the question of how the government must act in moving against employees on these grounds.

38. 417 F.2d 1161 (D.C. Cir. 1969).

He was allowed to see the confidential arrest record and to monitor a special interrogation, conducted for his benefit. During the interrogation, Norton denied having made any homosexual advance. After Norton was finally given his summons, the security officer identified himself and asked Norton to come down to the NASA office for a talk. During the discussion, Norton allegedly conceded that he had engaged in some minor homosexual activity while in high school and college, and admitted that while drinking he occasionally experienced some homosexual desires. He further admitted that on several occasions he had blacked out while drinking and may have engaged in some homosexual conduct. He admitted having had some kind of blackout on this particular evening, but stated that he only invited the man to his apartment for a drink.

On the basis of this evidence, later formally confirmed by Norton, the agency decided that he had indeed made a homosexual advance on the night in question and that this act "amounted to immoral, indecent, and disgraceful conduct." It further concluded that, on the basis of these admissions, Norton possessed "traits of character and personality which render [him] . . . unsuitable for further Government employment."[39] Norton lost all Civil Service appeals and the district court dismissed his case on motion of the government. He appealed to the court of appeals, which reversed its position from the *Dew* case and ordered him to be reinstated.

This decision bears some close scrutiny, because although the particular factual issue was homosexuality, the method of analysis used by the court is of great benefit in deciding many other types of cases where an employee has engaged in conduct which may or may not indicate a lack of fitness to perform a government job.

At the outset, the court rejected the idea that once the Civil Service Commission or any other agency has labeled conduct as immoral, the court is precluded from inquiring any further into the basis for dismissal. It rejected any presumption of special expertise on behalf of the Civil Service Commission or any other agency as to what is or is not immoral behavior:

> However, the Civil Service Commission has neither the expertise nor the requisite anointment to make and enforce absolute moral judgments, and we do not understand that it purports to do so. Its jurisdiction is at least confined to the things which are Caesar's and its avowed standard of "immorality" is no more than the prevailing mores of our society.[40]

39. 417 F.2d at 1163.
40. 417 F.2d at 1165.

Having disposed of any claim by an agency of unique qualifications to decide questions of the moral behavior of its employees, the court then ruled on the vital question of the circumstances under which homosexual behavior could properly be the basis of agency action. It concluded that a government agency was not in the business of enforcing community standards of morality as a matter of general principle. An agency, in order to dismiss an employee for immoral conduct, must find something in that conduct which could have an ascertainable deleterious effect on the efficiency of the service:

> We are not prepared to say that the Commission could not reasonably find appellant's homosexual advance to be "immoral," "indecent," or "notoriously disgraceful" under dominant conventional norms. But the notion that it could be an appropriate function of the federal bureaucracy to enforce the majority's conventional code of conduct in the private lives of its employees is at war with elementary concepts of liberty, privacy, and diversity. And whatever we may think of the Government's qualifications to act *in loco parentis* in this way, the statute precludes it from discharging protected employees except for a reason related to the efficiency of the service. Accordingly, a finding that an employee has done something immoral or indecent could support a dismissal without further inquiry only if all immoral or indecent acts of an employee have some ascertainable deleterious effect of the efficiency of the service. The range of conduct which might be said to affront prevailing mores is so broad and varied that we can hardly arrive at any such conclusion without reference to specific conduct. Thus, we think the sufficiency of the charges against appellant must be evaluated in terms of the effects on the service of what in particular he has done or has been shown to be likely to do.[41]

The key to this part of the decision is the use of the term "ascertainable deleterious effect." This shifts the burden onto the agency to justify its action in terms of definable and provable interests. The court then spells out what some of these interests might be. In some cases, the possibility of blackmail, which would jeopardize real security interests, would justify the government in not risking the employment of homosexuals in security related jobs. However, even this might be taken too far; in one case an admitted homosexual was denied a security clearance to work at a private research laboratory, despite the argument of the employee that his public admission of homosexuality insulated him from susceptibility to blackmail.[42]

41. Ibid.
42. This is the case of Benning Wentworth. It has its recent counterparts in the Matlovitch and Berg cases mentioned in n. 31 *supra*. As for the latter case, unless the

The court stated that overtures on the job or truly notorious conduct, which could have adverse reactions on fellow employees or the public, could be taken into account. The court said of these types of acts "whether or not such potential consequences would justify removal, they are at least broadly relevant to the 'efficiency of the service.' "

In Norton's case, the court cited the testimony of his superior that he did a very good job and that he was not worried about any possible effect on his performance. Norton's duties did not bring him in contact with the public, and his fellow employees were completely unaware of his immorality. However, he was still dismissed because, as his superior stated, dismissal for any homosexual conduct was a "custom within the agency," and he decided to follow the custom because continued employment of the appellant might "turn out to be embarrassing to the agency," in that "if an incident like this occurred again, it could become a public scandal on the agency."

The court rejected the use of potential embarrassment as a cause for discharge because, as it aptly put it:

> A claim of possible embarrassment might, of course, be a vague way of referring to some specific potential interference with an agency's performance; but it might also be a smokescreen hiding personal antipathies or moral judgments which are excluded by statute as grounds for dismissal.[43]

In other words, some specific, reasonable, forseeable connection must be present between potential embarrassment and the efficiency of the service. Without it the dismissal is illegal.

In this case the court found no such specific connection. It characterized Norton as "at most an extremely infrequent offender, who neither openly flaunts, nor carelessly displays his unorthodox sexual conduct in public." This lack of frequent activity minimized the potential for embarrassment to the point where the court could call the dismissal, on these grounds, as being arbitrary.[44]

---

composition of the present Supreme Court changes rapidly, there is absolutely no chance they could ultimately prevail.

43. Norton v. Macy, 417 F.2d at 1167.

44. At this time this is the very best ruling that could be expected. In view of the Supreme Court's action in Doe v. Commonwealth's Attorney, 425 U.S. 985 (1976), no constitutional attack on sodomy laws applying to consenting adults can be successfully made in federal court. While some states, such as Illinois and Oregon, have repealed these laws, this is not yet the prevailing trend in the country. However, I would guess that within five years "sexual preference" discrimination will be mostly ended.

The importance of the *Norton* case cannot be overstated. In the area of the law involving the powers of government, the District of Columbia Court of Appeals is the real pacesetter, since it has the most expertise and has tried the most cases. Traditionally, the United States Supreme Court has followed the lead set by the D.C. Court of Appeals in this type of case. Sometimes the lead has not been good, as in *Bailey* v. *Richardson*, in which an equally divided court upheld the dismissal of a public employee on security grounds, despite the fact that the action was based on secret testimony. The Supreme Court can also be expected to follow the lead of the D.C. Court of Appeals with regard to questions of the basis of dismissal of a federal employee. If the Supreme Court does not accept any cases in this area, the *Norton* case is that much more important, since it is really the most authoritative law to date in any jurisdiction in the country.

Several cases have followed *Norton* in this area, though none tried before the Supreme Court. In all these cases Norton was used as the standard; this fact is vital when reading the most recent cases. The Norton rule has in no way been abrogated or overruled. Quite the contrary; the Norton rule remains the standard, and the only issue is how far it can stretch, and the kinds of conduct it will or will not permit the government to use as a basis of dismissal or exclusion.

The District of Columbia Circuit Court followed up *Norton* in 1973 with a case called *Gayer* v. *Schlesinger*.[45] This case involved an attempt to deny a homosexual a job in a Defense Department agency, and established the principle that in order to deny someone employment, the government must establish factually a rational connection between the employee's homosexuality and the efficiency of the service. Emphasized was the concept that facts are all important, though in determining whether or not a rational connection existed, some deference must be accorded to the decision of the agency that "the degree of deference must be the result of a nice but not easily defineable weighing of ingredients of which the particular case is comprised."[46]

This case in effect reaffirmed the balancing test set out in *Norton*, and raised the paramount need for a good factual record. In order to see how this balancing test works, two cases from the West Coast will be discussed, both of which became subsequent to *Norton* and *Gayer*, and both of which cited *Norton* and *Gayer* as the controlling legal authority.

45. 490 F.2d 740 (D.C. Cir. 1973).
46. 490 F.2d at 750–51.

In *Society for Individual Rights, Incorporated* v. *Hampton*,[47] an organization of homosexuals and a discharged employee brought suit challenging the Civil Service Commission's policy as heretofore stated and as it existed during *Scott* v. *Macy*. In that case the district court held that the employee had to be reinstated, since homosexual activity alone could not be the basis of discharge, but the judge further warned that homosexuals do not form a "suspect category," that is, a group which, by the mere existence of the classification, would indicate the possibility of discrimination. This is, of course, usually used when talking about blacks, women, or Spanish-speaking people. In the present case the district court issued a blanket injunction against the Civil Service Commission, the same injunction referred to in the revised rules which caused the change in the Civil Service Commission's regulations, previously discussed.[48]

However, the judge's warning in *Hampton*, that homosexuals are not immune from job action based upon their homosexuality, was borne out in a subsequent case in Seattle, Washington, *Singer* v. *United States Civil Service Commission*.[49] This case had an ironical factual situation, in that the employee was dismissed from a job with the Seattle District Office of the Equal Employment Opportunities Commission. Singer was employed for many years with the EEOC. He was discharged after a hearing on the basis of the following allegations: (1) he was publicly engaged in kissing incidents with his boyfriend in front of the elevator of the Federal Building in Seattle; (2) he wrote a strong article for the local paper attacking so-called closet queens; (3) he purposely wore clothes and engaged in personal mannerisms which accented the homosexual stereotype; (4) he became organizer and president of the Seattle Gay Alliance, and in that capacity obtained a great deal of publicity, all of which identified him as an employee of the federal government; (5) he wrote voluminous articles and letters to different sources in which he virtually flouted his homosexuality; and (6) he applied for a marriage license to marry his boyfriend under circumstances which guaranteed maximum media coverage.[50]

The Court of Appeals for the Ninth Circuit ruled that under these circumstances the dismissal was proper, distinguishing this case from *Norton* in that here the defendant was not being dismissed because of his homosexuality, but rather because the public activities he engaged in were of such a nature that it affected the efficiency of the service. The court further held that Singer's homosexuality or the fact that he made

47. 528 F.2d 905 (9th Cir. 1975).
48. 5 CFR §731.202(b).
49. 530 F.2d 247 (9th Cir. 1976).
50. 530 F.2d at 250–51.

public statements were not the sole basis for affirming his dismissal. His flaunting of homosexuality, making it a public issue, were held to be the type of notorious conduct covered in the new regulations of the Civil Service Commission.

One caveat to *Singer*; reading *Singer* after *Norton* may produce the impression that those who try to hide their homosexuality are better protected than those who admit to their sexual predilection. However, *Singer* actually indicates that those who flaunt their unorthodox behavior, whether sexual or otherwise, can be subject to disciplinary action; the nature and degree of this flaunting, as opposed to admission of behavior, has to be weighed under the circumstances of the case.

One test seems to be whether or not the person "goes public," that is, identifies himself as an employee of the federal government. If, for instance, a federal employee wrote a letter to the editor complaining about the treatment of Singer and identified himself as being gay without identifying himself as a federal employee, or at least without identifying his agency, then of course he should be protected; this is not the flaunting of notorious behavior found in *Singer*. On the other hand, a person who wishes to protect his predilection should also not be punished, though some recent cases indicate that, while a person cannot be dismissed for his homosexuality, the refusal to give such information on an application form can be the basis of dismissal. This is somewhat unfortunate, since it puts the employee in an impossible spot; either he admits he is a homosexual and finds his application rejected, or denies homosexuality and finds he is subsequently dismissed for failure to disclose the information on an application form. This matter is hard to resolve; the best advice this author can provide to a prospective employee who happens to be gay is that he is better off admitting the information if legitimately requested, especially when the request pertains to any organization the individual may have belonged to and if one of these organizations was the Gay Student Alliance at his given college or university. Of course personal predilections cannot be the basis of a legitimate question, but the organization question is not so easily resolved, and the employee should be aware of the possible problems that might arise.[51]

51. The recent trend of Supreme Court decisions has become so alarming to civil libertarians that at the 1976 American Civil Liberties Union Biennial Convention, long discussions were devoted to encouraging ACLU attorneys not to bring cases they cannot expect to win on the facts, since the Supreme Court seems to be looking for cases which it can use to limit rights of public employees. Even a victory at the lower court can be appealed by the government (unless there is an acquittal at the trial level in a criminal case) to the Supreme Court and has often been done so to the detriment of the employee. See Board of Regents v. Roth, discussed in chapters 3 and 6.

Since factual questions are so paramount, the next question that must be discussed is whether any special legal requirements exist which apply in the actual weighing of the interest, irrespective of the particular substantive grounds being weighed.

Judicial Limits on "Cause"

If the *Norton* case is instructive on the question of substantive requirements necessary to justify a dismissal for cause, then the next question which must be dealt with is the levels of proof the government must offer to substantiate the connection between the actions of the defendant and the ascertainable deleterious effect on the efficiency of the service.

Remember that in the *Arnett* case the United States Supreme Court upheld the concept of "just cause" as constitutionally satisfactory, neither overbroad nor vague. That, however, does not define "just cause." Since these problems generally arise when the individual is being punished for his own personal behavior rather than as an administrative attempt to intimidate a broader group (though that is always present in the case of homosexuals), these cases will lack a broad public issue. That the United States Supreme Court will take any of these cases and issue a broad mandate, favorable or unfavorable, is unlikely. Thus these cases will be decided at lower court levels, with variations among different courts, both federal and state, as to their attitude toward the public employees involved.

This is not to say that legal standards applicable to other, similar cases cannot be established. Quite the contrary; these rules of law will, however, be heavily dependent upon the factual matters developed, and courts will often rule based on feelings of general fairness, even if the particular court may tend to favor the agency or the employee.

In short, these cases are actually going to turn on the standard of proof necessary to justify a particular action. This is a legal, not a factual matter, because many decisions have been made in the area of administrative law in which a standard of level of proof must be reached before the agency can justify its acts, at least where the basis of the charge against the employee is not purely job-related and has no outside factors, such as those previously discussed.[52]

52. This issue was raised squarely in Charlton v. United States 412 F.2d 390 (3rd Cir. 1969). In that case, Charlton was dismissed for allegedly failing to report a bribe. There was a factual challenge to the finding of the Civil Service Commission. The district court held that a federal court has a limited right of review as to the *factual* issues in a dismissal case. The Court of Appeals for the Third Circuit revised,

In the area of "immoral or criminal behavior" of the employee, when the charges against the employee could be the basis of job action (or exclusion for nonemployees), the issue becomes the level of proof of the relationship between the act done and the needs of the agency necessary to justify the job action. Subsidiary problems involve who has the burden of proof and the nature of the administrative hearing in which such proof is provided.

The problem of burden of proof is especially critical, because even if a court has rules similar to *Norton* which requires that a connection be made between the act and the agency's need, this type of rule can easily be circumvented if the agency is allowed to meet its requirements by merely showing that an act has been committed. This act could serve as the basis of dismissal, leaving it up to the employee to prove that his act would not come within this standard.

What is needed are rules which set minimal standards of proof, standards that an agency must meet in showing this relationship. While these rules are often expressed in such terms as "beyond a reasonable doubt" or "clear and convincing," they have no real meaning unless they are related to actual fact patterns. Thus a premium is placed on real litigatory skills at the administrative level, if for no other reason than to make a record which could be of benefit in court.

As a brief aside, the reader will obviously discern that this emphasis on purely litigative skills and problems is not misplaced. In every chapter of this book, no matter the particular substantive issue or the rule of law applicable, no areas of absolutism exist any longer, either for or against the employee. Whether courts balance the administrative interests against the employee or require a higher substantive justification, especially where protected constitutional rights may be involved, all parties in the public employment relationship have become very conscious of litigation; for better or worse, as in professional sports, much daily personnel administration is conducted with an awareness on all sides that what is said or written may someday be of value in court. This is neither good nor bad; it is a fact of life.

holding that a court must go beyond merely determining whether procedural requirements have been met. Instead, a court by virtue of the authority of 5 U.S.C. §706 must review the entire record and can determine if the factual decision was arbitrary, capricious or an abuse of discretion or was unsupported by substantial evidence. This case discussed the theoretical limits of the standard of evidence, but did not explore what kinds of evidence would or would not suffice to meet the test. Thus we will look at the D.C. Circuit Court cases for guidance. For a general look at the problem, see note, Dismissal of Federal Employees: The Emerging Individual Role, 66 COLUMBIA L. REV. 719 (1966).

Therefore, the issue of standard of proof for administrative job action becomes very important. As usual, the leading court in terms of judicial discussion is the district and circuit courts of the District of Columbia. Thus an examination of how these courts have handled the problem of standard of proof, especially in the area of immoral or criminal conduct, will be of great value to other courts, since these problems are now, so to speak, "coming out of the closet."

The first judicial breakthrough in this area came in 1963 in a most unusual case, *Pelicone* v. *Hodges*.[53] Pelicone was a pressman with the Commerce Department with many years of satisfactory service. He was dismissed on the basis of admission on a personal history statement that he was arrested for "Disorderly Conduct—Prostitution" (he took a prostitute to a hotel room). Especially interesting was the fact that no such crime existed, either in name or in fact.

The actual grounds for dismissal were "conduct unbecoming to a government employee" and "criminal, infamous, dishonest, immoral or notoriously disgraceful conduct." However, clearly the basis for the charges was the arrest, not the actual nature of the conduct.

The court of appeals reversed the dismissal, holding that, since the acts charged were not criminal in nature, but the basis of dismissal was criminal conduct, the dismissal could not be upheld. The court refused to discuss whether such conduct could be the basis of a charge of immoral conduct, but it strongly indicated that so little relationship was shown between the conduct—patronizing a prostitute—and the so-called efficiency of the service that, had the criminal conduct issue not have been present, the dismissal would probably still have been reversed.

Pelicone v. *Hodges*, while important, was still a case involving a rare set of facts as the basis for discharge. The key case would be one in which a person was being discharged or excluded from government service on the basis of vague charges of homosexual conduct supported by flimsy evidence, where the person denied culpability: in short, a new *Bailey* v. *Richardson*, without the presence of the loyalty-security issues.

Such a case appeared in 1965 and the opinion (really opinions, as two separate decisions arose from the same facts) of the Court of Appeals for the District of Columbia was one of the most important, yet least known cases in the area. The case, or more precisely cases, are known as *Scott* v. *Macy*.[54]

Bruce Scott had passed his Civil Service examinations and was eligible for employment with the federal government. However, an investigation

---

53. See note 23 *supra* for discussion of this case in a somewhat different context.
54. 349 F.2d 182 (D.C. Cir. 1965).

prior to his being put on the lists uncovered an arrest in 1947 for "loitering" and an arrest in 1951, plus some derogatory information supplied by various sources which stated that Scott was a homosexual. Scott was called before an investigator; he attempted to explain the circumstances of the arrests, but refused to answer any questions about the alleged homosexuality because he did not believe the question was pertinent to matters of job performance.

He was disqualified for employment because of immoral conduct. He then requested a specification of how, when and where he had allegedly conducted himself immorally so that he could adequately answer the board's indefinite allegation of immoral conduct. In answer to this request, the Civil Service Board of Appeals and Review responded only that the record gave convincing evidence that he had engaged in homosexual conduct.

Denied any administrative relief, Scott brought suit in federal court to have himself reinstated on the list and made eligible for employment without any disabilities.

He lost at the district court level but, on appeal to the circuit court, the decision was reversed, with Warren Burger dissenting. The two-judge majority split as to the proper grounds for reversal. Judge Bazelon was very concerned with the stigma that would attach to Scott as a result of the disqualification, which he said, "not only disqualified him from the vast field of all employment dominated by the government but also jeopardized his ability to find employment elsewhere."

Since this "stigmatizing conclusion" was based only on statements that Scott was a homosexual or had engaged in homosexual conduct, such statements required clarification. In view of this, Bazelon would require that:

> The Commission must at least specify the conduct it finds "immoral" and state why that conduct is related to "occupational competency or fitness," especially since the Commission's action involved the gravest consequences. Appellant's rights to be free from governmental defamation requires that the Government justify the necessity for imposing the stigma of disqualification for "immoral conduct."[55]

Viewing the facts in this case and the weak evidence presented in support of the charges, Bazelon concluded:

> The Commission may not rely on determination of "immoral conduct" based only on such vague labels as "homosexual" and "homosexual

---

55. Contrast this with Board of Regents v. Roth 408 U.S. 564 (1972), in which the Supreme Court refused to recognize the possible stigmatizing effect of dismissal from government service.

conduct," as a ground for disqualifying appellant for government employment.[56]

Judge McGowan, concurring in the decision to reverse, took a somewhat different tack. He was not concerned, as was Judge Bazelon, about the "stigmatizing effect" of the disqualification, nor even of what proof the government must offer to justify a finding of immoral conduct. What bothered McGowan were the inadequacies, in terms of procedural fairness, of the notice given to appellant of the specific elements constituting the "immoral conduct" relied upon as disqualifying him for all federal employment. He was most disturbed that when Scott asked for specifications, he was only told that he had engaged in "homosexual conduct."[57]

The two opinions are really complementary to each other, because they represent solutions to different stages in the process of disqualification or dismissal. McGowan's view, though somewhat more limited than Bazelon's, is important in its own right. The problem of evidence and proof is usually dependent upon the question of what elements of a charge must be proven. By requiring the government to give factual specifications in regard to a broad charge, the proof question is resolved, at least to the extent of eliminating irrelevant material on events not the basis of the charge.

This is important but it is not enough. What Bazelon is saying is that, even though the government may specify exactly what behavior or acts are being used to justify a conclusion of immoral conduct, the evidence used by the government must in fact show that the acts of the employee or prospective employee did constitute an actionable charge, with such charge serving as the legal basis of dismissal. Recall the *Carter* case and that of the teacher fired for sleeping with her boyfriend; in short, instances may arise where the charge, even if proven, may not be a valid basis of dismissal. The question is one of standard of proof since, if the agency can merely make assertions such as "immoral conduct," without specifying the underlying factual basis, the employee will be under a great disadvantage. (This problem is also tied in with problems of procedural due process, discussed in a later chapter, where the issue is whether an agency can be required to give its reason and provide a hearing.)

This chapter presupposes a requirement that reasons be given and some hearing be held. The issue, thus, is how detailed must the reasons be and to what degree must the agency substantiate the basis of those

56. Unfortunately, Arnett v. Kennedy may have approved the use of such broad labels as not being unconstitutionally vague, though admittedly in a somewhat different context.
57. 402 F.2d at 645, 646.

reasons. This leads to a separate but directly related problem of proof, that of confidential statements made by anonymous informants which provide part or all of the basis of dismissal. While this will be explored in great detail when loyalty and security programs are discussed, this has great relevance in the area of immoral or criminal conduct. Indeed, it was part of *Scott* v. *Macy*, and can be explored in the context of that case.

Informants and Anonymous Statements

Judge Bazelon was also concerned about the use of the confidential statements of informants relating to alleged homosexual conduct on the part of Scott (or informants in any other situation). In this case the government not only did not give the names of the informants, but also did not give specifications of the conduct allegedly committed.[58]

The two problems can be separated. Even if a rule protecting the identity of informants could be justified, a rule prohibiting the person from knowing what specific charges of misconduct are being used to justify disqualification or dismissal cannot. In most cases, revealing the conduct could be done without revealing the precise source of the information. For instance, if the person was accused of making a homosexual advance to a fellow employee, revealing that this information was being used to justify dismissal would not reveal the source of the information. However, it would be of great use to the employee to know that this charge was being made so that he might refute it.

Yet in most cases, the real reason for not revealing the information or the source is that the information really consists of conclusory statements that the person is a "homosexual" (or a communist or any other label), and these conclusions are merely based on general impressions or even prejudices, rather than facts. If this is the real basis of evidence, then such evidence should not be used, and no justification can be offered for a rule protecting not only the source, but the information itself.

The protection of the source can be a more difficult problem. Circumstances may include the necessity of protecting a source, especially when the allegations might lead to criminal prosecution. Here, not only might protection of the source be correct, but the information itself might also be withheld. However, this is a really limited situation, and should be handled like situations involving police informants. Under Supreme Court

58. This is the Bailey v. Richardson situation, in which a public employee was dismissed for being a security risk upon the basis of anonymous statements in which the author was not identified. This is discussed in great detail in chapters 1 and 5.

decision, evidence obtained on the basis of search warrants based on informant tips can be valid if the prosecution can prove the reliability of the informant.[59] A variant of that rule could be used in cases of informant information concerning alleged misconduct of government employees. However, since the need of an informant system is necessary to the functioning of a police department and the danger of physical harm coming to police informants is very real, the basis of the determination of reliability need not be too intensive.

These problems do not occur, except in rare instances, in the area of government employment, however, and a much stricter test of reliability could be introduced. One possible way of handling the problem is that if a federal court (or a state court in certain states such as California) gets a case of a dismissal or the exclusion of a person from government service based on charges such as immoral conduct, and the basis of the evidence is confidential statements from informants, then the following procedure (or one similar to it) might be instituted. If the employee makes a request for the name of the informant, for the information given, or both, the government should be required to go before the trial judge and, in an ex parte proceeding,[60] justify the protection of the name of the informant, the evidence given, or both. The judge would then make a determination, subject to interlocutory appeal if the decision goes against the government, as to what may be protected. The court might require the government to produce the informant under conditions of security, and make the informant testify under oath as to the validity of the information so given. The only difference is that the employee or his counsel will not be present or apprised of the proceedings. While the employee could end up having the information justified without his being given what he requested, with all things considered, this would be a good system. If the individual relies on the decision of the court, he should rely as well on the judgment of the court as to the need to protect the informer or his information. If the government loses and still prefers not to reveal the information, they can reinstate the employee.[61]

Judge Bazelon alluded to the problem of security investigations, specifically citing *Bailey* v. *Richardson.* However, he declined to make a

59. Aguilar v. Texas, 378 U.S. 108 (1964); Chimel v. California, 395 U.S. 752 (1969); Adams v. Williams, 407 U.S. 143 (1972).

60. In which only one side is present. Used mostly in obtaining temporary relief such as stays or temporary restraining orders, in situations where the moving party would be subject to unfavorable injury without immediate ruling but the other party would suffer little or anything pending a full hearing.

61. A similar procedure was used to test the admissability of certain portions of the Watergate tapes.

judgment on that case, holding that such matters were not applicable in a nonsecurity case. This discussion of dismissals on security grounds will also be deferred at this time. However, the reader is asked to remember this case when security dismissals are discussed, since the reasoning applicable here is also applicable to such cases.

The decision in this case did not end Bruce Scott's difficulties with the Civil Service Commission. Soon after the decision, Scott was given a report of the commission which set forth the following information: (1) the 1947 arrest; (2) the 1951 arrest; (3) statements alleged to have been made by appellant to a former supervisor when he was in state employment that he was a homosexual, that he had been "perverted" since youth, and that he lived with a "lover"; and (4) that appellant had stood mute when a neighbor had characterized him as a homosexual.[62]

After specifying these four allegations, the commission again asked him whether or not he was a homosexual. Scott again gave a detailed explanation of the 1947 and 1951 arrests. He denied ever making such a statement to the supervisor, and stated that he felt no obligation to reply to his neighbor's allegation. He again refused to answer the question of whether or not he was a homosexual because of constitutional reasons.

Scott was again disqualified from government service. The basis of the disqualification was a letter from the chief of adjudication of the Civil Service Commission, which stated that he was being dismissed for violation of civil service regulations which permit dismissal for many reasons, including "criminal, infamous, dishonest, immoral or notoriously disgraceful conduct," in addition to failure to give information. The letter mentioned failure to answer the question of whether or not he was a homosexual, plus his failure to deny the allegation made by his neighbor. However, the letter was very vague and never specified exactly the reasons for the dismissal.

When the case eventually reached the court of appeals again, the government lost. The court characterized the first decision as holding that Scott's exclusion "could not be sustained upon the record before us, and we directed that a judgment be entered which would have the effect of restoring appellant to the status of one eligible to be considered for federal employment, absent any further valid action by the Commission to accomplish his absolute disqualification."[63]

The issue was, then, whether or not the second disqualification was based on the grounds not approved in the first case or on entirely new grounds. The government contended that the real reason for the exclu-

62. 402 F.2d at 645.
63. 402 F.2d at 644–45.

sion was not immoral conduct but refusal to give testimony, namely to answer the questions about whether or not he was a homosexual. The court agreed that failure to give information could be a basis of dismissal or exclusion, but in this particular case it was impossible to determine what the real grounds for the dismissal were.

The confusion lay in the fact that, while the letter mentioned that refusal to testify could be the basis for exclusion as well as immoral conduct, the letter only specifically cites (2), which relates to immoral conduct as a grounds for exclusion of Scott, but it omitted (4), referring to refusal to give testimony.

The court then decided that, where an exclusion could have rested on two distinct grounds, one valid and one invalid, and it could not be determined which was the basis of decision, then the decision must fail.

> We are unable to conclude, however, that the Commission's decision did not in fact rest upon a finding of "immoral conduct." Therefore, the current disqualification cannot stand. Where individual rights of substance turn upon whether the Commission acted for one reason rather than another, we think it not too much to expect that the Commission will not leave its motivations clouded by inexactitude of expression. Civil Service investigators are doubtless not unlike the rest of us in being slow to relinquish a conviction of the correctness of an action once taken for the reason it was taken. If a wholly new and different reason is to become the mainspring of this action, that should be made clearly to appear and the resources of language are fully up to this task.[64]

As in *Dew*, the Civil Service Commission chose to reinstate Scott rather than take the risk of appealing the case to the United States Supreme Court. This was actually unfortunate; this area needs a Supreme Court ruling setting out some of the ground rules for permissible agency action with regard to dismissal or exclusion where no issue of infringement of protected constitutional rights is present.

However, given the present Supreme Court, it is best that the issues of both whether homosexual behavior can be cause for dismissal, and if so what level of proof must be presented before a dismissal, is not presently before the Court for a decision. With the authority of *Scott* v. *May* and some of the older Supreme Court cases in force, a standard of evidence applies at least to proceedings involving federal employees, which can be applied in the Circuit Court for the District of Columbia and used, as prudent, by other courts. What *Bishop* v. *Wood* means to the issue of standard of evidence is open to dispute. That case denied the

64. 402 F.2d at 648.

constitutional basis of procedural due process and denied federal jurisdiction to employment cases in which no substantive constitutional issues
were present. However, in that case the dismissal was based on false or
misleading statements. Whether they could prevail as to a federal employee is doubtful. But the Court may have given state courts carte
blanche to fashion any rules they please with regard to levels of evidence
in state and local dismissals. Only time will tell, though with the new
administration possibly getting a chance to appoint Supreme Court justices, the dangers of *Bishop* v. *Wood* may be prevented from intensifying.

Chapter 3

Freedom of Expression

This chapter explores the question of whether or not a public employee loses any of the rights of freedom of expression guaranteed by the First and Fourteenth Amendments to the Constitution, and held by all citizens of the United States, simply by virtue of being a public employee. For the purposes of this chapter the discussion is limited to those rights practically known as freedom of speech. Likewise, the discussion is concerned only with those expressions of the public employee neither criminal nor illegal. The only issue discussed in this chapter is whether or not something inherent in the nature of public employment, or in the nature of a specific kind of public employee, allows a government employer to proscribe certain types of First Amendment rights of expression, which in the context of a private citizen or private citizens would be completely inviolate.

Several types of First Amendment activities are intimately involved with the activities of public employees, but will not be discussed until a later chapter. One, of course, is the political rights of a public employee. Although considered to be a basic, if not the basic, First Amendment right, nevertheless, within the context of public employment, this right has been subject to very special and restrictive rules.[1] Likewise, the area

1. The entire area of political rights of public employees, especially as to the constitutionality of statutes such as the Hatch Act, 5 U.S.C. §7324, which severely limit these rights, as discussed in the next chapter. See United Public Workers v. Mitchell,

of loyalty and security programs affecting public employees also concerns their First Amendment rights; because of clerical reasons as much as anything else, however, this area has to be specially treated and not discussed as part of the general topic of freedom of expression of the public employee.[2]

Historically, laws have changed from a doctrine which held that public employees lost all their First Amendment rights simply by virtue of their public employment, to the more modern doctrine which holds that there cannot be an absolute ban on public employees engaging in otherwise protected First Amendment activities. However, this evolution of the law does not mean that the public employee has the right to engage in all types of First Amendment activities on the job or off, work connected or not.

Ironically one of the most famous champions of First Amendment rights, Mr. Justice Oliver Wendell Holmes, was the architect of the law restricting the First Amendment rights of public employees. As Chief Judge of the Massachusetts Supreme Court he coined the famous epigram which stated, "Petitioner [a public employee] may have a constitutional right to talk politics, but he has no constitutional right to be a policeman." This became the bedrock of the law concerning public employees which the Supreme Court made in a subsequent Massachusetts case, adopting the position that if the government could absolutely prohibit all public use of a public facility, it could also prohibit certain individual uses of the facility. In other words, the power to exclude the greater also included the power to exclude the lesser. This became known as the right-privilege doctrine. Eventually a counterargument developed which stated that even though the government had a right to prohibit something absolutely or not to do something absolutely, no requirement

330 U.S. 75 (1947); Democratic State Central Committee v. Andolsek, 249 F. Supp. 1009 (D.C. Md. 1966); Fort v. Civil Service Commission, 61 Cal. 2d 331, 38 Cal. Rptr. 625, 392 P.2d 385 (1964); Bagley v. Washington Township Hospital District 65 Cal. 2d 499, 55 Cal. Rptr. 401, 421 P.2d 409 (1966).

2. The entire area of loyalty-security programs also cuts across the First Amendment rights of public employees, but in a criminal or quasi-criminal context. Thus, even though many important principles of First Amendment law have been developed in cases involving some aspects of the loyalty-security program, the very special impact, or as Mr. Justice Clark put it, the "badge of infamy" which faces a public employee in his relationship to the loyalty-security programs, requires that such programs be considered separately from the issues discussed in this article. See Wieman v. Updegraff, 344 U.S. 183 (1952); Keyishian v. Board of Regents, 385 U.S. 589 (1967); Elfbrandt v. Russell 384 U.S. 11 (1966); Baggett v. Bullitt, 377 U.S. 360 (1964); Cramp v. Board of Public Instruction, 368 U.S. 278 (1961); United States v. Robel, 389 U.S. 258 (1967); Schneider v. Smith, 390 U.S. 17 (1968).

obligated the government to adopt social security or have a draft for the service, or engage in any type of governmental activity. Accordingly, once the government does, in fact, engage in certain activities, its power is limited when making distinctions and discriminations in the context of its programs. Thus, if the government does in fact decide to hire employees, the mere fact that it did not have to hire them in the beginning does not mean that it can control all aspects of their lives once hired.[3]

Since this has been discussed previously in greater detail, suffice it to say for the purpose of this chapter that in many different contexts concerning public employees, including the context of freedom of speech, these two contradictory philosophies swirled and jousted for supremacy in the courts. Finally, in 1967, the United States Supreme Court decided a case which, while not totally eliminating the right-privilege doctrine, nevertheless, in the context of First Amendment rights of public employees, took a position at least halfway between, if not somewhat shaded in favor of, the public employee.

This case, called *Pickering* v. *Board of Education*,[4] involved a teacher in a small Illinois town who was fired for writing a letter to the editor complaining about certain practices of the school board. After the letter was published, the teacher, Pickering, was dismissed from his position on the grounds that the letter contained some false information in its statements (which in fact it did), and that the letter "unjustifiably impuned motives, honesty, integrity, truthfulness, responsibility and competence of the school administration."

The Supreme Court, in ordering Pickering reinstated to his position, took a position midway between the abolition of the right-privilege doctrine and its retention:

> To the extent that the Illinois Supreme Court opinion may be read to suggest that teachers may constitutionally be impelled to relinquish their First Amendment rights that they would otherwise enjoy as citizens, to comment on matters of public interest in connection with the operation of the public school in which they work, received on a premise which has been unequivocally rejected in numerous decisions of this court. . . .
>
> The theory of public employment which can be denied altogether, may be subjected to any conditions regardless of how unreasonable, has been uniformly rejected. At the same time it cannot be gainsaid that the state has interests as an employer in connection with the regulation of the speech of employees that significantly from those that possess it in connection with the regulations of speech of the citizenry in general.[5]

3. Chapter 1 discusses this in detail.
4. 391 U.S. 563 (1968).
5. 391 U.S. at 568.

The court later held that the problem, in any case, was to arrive at a balance between the interests of the teacher as a citizen commenting on matters of public concern and the interests of the state as an employer.

Since the time of the *Pickering* decision, the Supreme Court has been attempting to apply this balancing test to reach a happy medium between the rights of employees and the rights of the state with respect to limiting or not limiting employee free speech. However, this attempt has not been successful, simply because this is an area that resists application of such a test. Traditionally, a balancing test attempts to find a happy medium between positions, with the result that both positions are intentionally limited. While this may be a valuable tool in resolving most disputes, when dealing with protected constitutional rights, it is not necessarily the proper method. After all, the basic philosophical underpinning of the Constitution, as expressed in the Declaration of Independence, is that there are certain inalienable rights; life, liberty, and the pursuit of happiness. While the words of the Declaration of Independence naturally are not law in the sense of the Constitution or succeeding statutes, nevertheless, in any determination of the relative position of the individual with regard to protected constitutional rights, it is "self-evident" that the rights of the individual, while not absolute, certainly are paramount; and balancing the rights actually causes the forfeiting of certain rights.

Subsequent to the *Pickering* decision, but prior to the advent of the Burger court, the Supreme Court developed a new test to determine the rights of public employees, or for that matter citizens as against the government, when dealing with governmental programs. This test has been technically called "the compelling state interest test." It holds that, even when dealing with government benefits, government programs, and governmental administrative requirements, the constitutional rights of citizens can only be lessened in the name of governmental administration if the government shows a "compelling state interest" as to a particular aspect of the public administration.[6]

The Supreme Court found this test easy to apply and used it to hold unconstitutional such governmental administrative programs as an unnecessarily long residence requirement for welfare or voter registration, or the right to be afforded due process before having certain government benefits cut off. The *Pickering* decision certainly was one area in which

6. Carroll v. President and Commissioner of Princess Anne, 393 U.S. 175 (1968), prior restraint on public speech; New York Times v. United States, 403 U.S. 713 (1971), prior restraint on newspapers; Shapiro v. Thompson, 394 U.S. 618 (1969), right to travel and vote; Stanley v. Georgia, 394 U.S. 557 (1969), right to read pornographic material in one's home; Kramer v. Union Free School District No. 15, 395 U.S. 818 (1969), residence to vote.

the Supreme Court should have followed its then natural bent and refrained from the use of the unfortunate phrase "balancing test."[7] Since that time, a much more conservative Court has used the balancing test concept in such a way as to severely limit the gains made by public employees with regard to the assertion of their constitutional rights. As of this writing this trend seems to be accelerating, especially in light of a recent Supreme Court decision, discussed later in this chapter, in which an official of the Office of Economic Opportunity was fired for publicly criticizing his agency superiors and several employees; the Supreme Court upheld the dismissal.[8]

To properly understand and examine the present law concerning the right of public employees to engage in otherwise protected speech, the various elements which must be incorporated into the balancing test must be examined to see the types of expression or categories of public employee subject to limitation and, conversely, the areas open to employees, areas in which they may make any statements or engage in any type of protected First Amendment right without any fear of job action, such as dismissal or lack of promotion. Indeed, to a certain extent, much of the material under discussion will have to be speculative, simply because the *Pickering* case, while eliminating any absolute ban on freedom of speech, has not been followed up by other cases which would define the concept of the balancing test without *Pickering*. Unfortunately, Supreme Court decisions since *Pickering* have served to narrow, rather than expand, the rights of employees within the concept of balancing, while still preserving the proposition that a public employee cannot be disciplined for asserting a protected First Amendment right.

7. Emerson states that the weakness in the balancing test as it affects public employees is that:

> . . . a government employee cannot conceivably know in advance how much weight should be given to the circumstance that he may have a specially "informed and definite opinion" about the issue, or that the agency could "easily have rebutted" his errors. Moreover, the open-ended balancing takes the Court into dangerous and irrelevant territory. Thus the Court finds it necessary to "presume," probably contrary to fact, that Pickering's letter had not "in any way . . . interfered with the regular operation of the schools generally." Here the Court is in the position of suggesting that only innocuous expression is entitled to protection, a view inconsistent with the whole theory of the First Amendment and its own prior emphasis on the need for teachers to be "able to speak out freely." Once again the balancing test proves an ineffectual tool. [*The System of Freedom of Expression* (New York: Random House, 1970), p. 581.]

8. Arnett v. Kennedy, 416 U.S. 134 (1974).

The following examination of the problem will attempt to break down the areas involved in balancing rights of government employers and government employees into two broad categories. The first concerns the nature of the interest asserted by the employer; the second concerns the particular nature of the speech in question. In analyzing such areas both historical developments and court cases will be examined, not only those of the U.S. Supreme Court, but other federal and state courts as well, where applicable. This examination will provide some guidance to the public employee faced with the problem of whether or not a given type of expression could cost him his job. While a great deal might well be speculative, the public employee will at least be able to hazard an informed guess as to whether or not a given type of expression could put him in jeopardy.

The elements used by courts to examine these matters usually fall into two broad categories. The first concerns the nature of the interest asserted —especially by the employer. The second concerns the particular nature of the speech in question. While these broad categories often interlace and overlap, they can nevertheless be distinguished as each has individual peculiarities with special rules. In examining the cases, the presence or absence of a given element in one area is often determinative of a question arising in the other, although the particular order in which the competing interests are examined is unimportant, since the test is a balancing test. In some cases the employer or employee asserts one particular element of one area as the basis of *his* case, while the other is asserting one particular element of the other area as the basis of *his* case. Thus the overlapping subtleties which contribute to the determination of the balance are a matter requiring a great deal of scrutiny. These areas will now be discussed individually.

Nature of the Interest

In determining the constitutionality of questions involving a public employee's assertion of rights of free speech, the outcome of the issue can often be determined without ever making reference to the nature of the speech by simply balancing the various interests that either side brings to bear when asserting the right to prohibit expression. Such an analysis presumes that the expression could not be prohibited but for the fact that the person engaging in such speech is a public employee. Neither an absolute ban of public employee expression can be tolerated, nor can public employees be considered to have as broad a right to free expression as general citizens. An examination of the law in this area indicates that courts have generally recognized five particular interests asserted in dealing with the problem of balancing rights of expression against rights to prohibit expression. These interests are: (1) the nature of the job; (2) administrative perogatives; (3) morale of the organization; (4) interference with employee performance on the job; and (5) special legal status of the employee.

The last interest is of particular importance, since the Supreme Court has recently ruled that the legal standing of the employee is determinative of whether or not the employee is entitled to procedural due process before termination, which in turn has an effect on protected rights of free speech.

The Nature of the Job

One of the prime elements used to determine whether or not a given act of expression can be prohibited is the basic nature of the job held by the public employee seeking to assert his right to speak. Some types of public employment are of such a specialized nature that any kind of extramural expression would be wholly improper for an individual holding such a position, lest his particular position be compromised. Likewise, in some jobs extramural speech would not only be proper, but also warranted in light of public interest.

Situations in which the nature of the public employee's job prohibits his engaging in expression arise in two different contexts. The first is found when the job is of such a nature that expression of any kind would be considered inappropriate; the second is found when only certain kinds of expression would be considered appropriate.

Those cases involving an absolute prohibition of speech concern more of a theoretical than a practical problem. Especially involved are those cases of employment categorized as relating to national security, in which the employee must give up all his rights of expression because the nature of his job requires him to operate in secrecy, or at least anonymity. Any public employee in such a situation would indeed find himself hard pressed to initiate legal action seeking the full measure of constitutional rights for other employees.

Until recently this situation was, in many ways, theoretical; an important case on this very point has now been brought forward, however, but the Supreme Court has refused to review it. The case involves the attempts to publish without deletion the book *The CIA and the Cult of Intelligence*, by John Marks and Victor Marchetti. Marks and Marchetti were former agents of the Central Intelligence Agency; as part of their employment they signed statements, under oath, to the effect that upon leaving employment they would not discuss any matter within the scope of their employment which had not been officially declassified.

After writing the book but before publication the publisher, as a matter of courtesy, sent the CIA a copy of the proposed manuscript. Upon receipt, the CIA proposed some 300 deletions. When the publisher decided to publish it without the requested deletions, the CIA went to federal court in northern Virginia to get an injunction against publication of the book. While the CIA did not get a prohibition against the publication of the book, Judge Bryant nevertheless accepted some 160 deletions. In final form, the book features large spaces, left blank to indicate deletions by the CIA.

The Court of Appeals for the Fourth Circuit, in an appeal taken by the authors and publisher to have all restrictions removed from the book, refused to withdraw the deletions, and indeed strongly indicated that, if the book was not already in print, it would have allowed the entire 300 deletions, rather than the 160 allowed by the district court judge. Since the Supreme Court did not hear the appeal, this decision stands.[9]

Such bans should, however, be limited to very specific situations. An absolute ban doctrine should not apply, for instance, to situations in which the employee is engaged in work of a confidential nature, even though the fact that he is so engaged is not considered confidential. In such cases only those types of expression which might interfere with or compromise his position should be banned. This applies in particular to members of law enforcement agencies, especially the FBI, which has rather strict rules concerning expression of its agents. Nothing in the nature of the employment of an FBI agent (unless he is an undercover operative) should lead to a complete ban of expression in all cases.[10]

In many instances agents are encouraged to become a part of the community where they work and are often posted in a given community for long periods of time. If an agent makes statements on a matter not concerning any kind of federal issue, his position as an FBI agent should not be compromised. Likewise, if the agent engages in some aspect of

9. See also Heine v. Raus, 399 F.2d 785 (4th Cir. 1968); affirmed 432 F.2d 1007, cert. denied 402 U.S. 914 (1971), where executive privilege was invoked by a defendant on the grounds that his statements were made in his capacity as a CIA agent.

10. A well-publicized case concerned the trials of a FBI agent who criticized the late J. Edgar Hoover in a paper submitted as part of a seminar at Columbia University on criminal administration, which he was attending under FBI auspices. When the criticism became public, the agent was banished to the hinterlands and eventually resigned from the FBI. At the same time, the FBI prohibited agents from attending this seminar, even though the professor, Abraham Blumberg, is considered to be one of the leading experts in criminal administration in the country.

expression concerning law enforcement, such speech should not necessarily be the cause of disciplinary action. In such cases a factual determination would have to be made. For example, if an agent made a statement critical of local law enforcement agencies, such a statement should or should not be prohibited, based on such a factual determination. If the statement was simply critical of the capabilities of a given law enforcement official with whom the agent works, the speech should be considered beyond bounds. On the other hand, if the agent made a statement critical of local law enforcement agencies on the grounds that they were not following federal criteria or that they were impeding the federal agency from doing its job, the speech itself should not be banned per se, especially when the agent had attempted to rectify such problems through internal channels but was unsuccessful. In such a situation, as Van Alstyne has so correctly pointed out, "the public importance of the disclosure itself—whether it truthfully brought to light a matter of serious institutional impropriety which would have gone unattended but for the breech of confidence involved in the employee's comment. . . ."[11]—presents the predominant interest which must be asserted. Vindication of the employee's freedom to speak out under these circumstances may outweigh whatever marginal tendency the result has to inhibit other frankness in the normal operation of the agency.

Such a theory may be correctly interpreted from the language of *Pickering* itself. Discussing whether the employee (in *Pickering*, a teacher) had a right to speak out on matters concerning the activities of the board of education, the Court seemed to indicate that, even if a teacher might make a somewhat erroneous statement, nevertheless the importance of having teachers, with their special expertise, speaking out on such matters as the use of funds in school systems, is of such paramount importance that the public need for the expression outweighs any other interests. The Court stated:

> More importantly, the question of whether a school system requires additional funds is a matter of legitimate public concern on which the judgment of the school administration, including the school board, cannot, in a society which leaves such questions to popular vote, be taken as conclusive. On such a question, free and open debate is vital to inform the decision-making by the electorate. Teachers are, as a class, members of a community most likely to have informed and definite opinions as to how funds allotted to the operation of the schools should be spent. Accordingly, it is essential that they be able to speak out freely on such question without fear of retaliatory dismissal.[12]

11. *The Constitutional Rights of Teachers and Professors*, 1970 DUKE L. J. 851.
12. Pickering v. Board of Education, 391 U.S. at 571–72.

Thus, the concept that a public employee, precisely because the nature of his job gives him special expertise, has the obligation to speak up at certain times for the public interest, overcomes any countervailing powers of the government to limit expression. This is apparently an idea on the verge of becoming a matter of major public importance and may lead to major developments in the law, though probably not until the Supreme Court changes. The language in *Pickering*, while referring to a fact situation only mildly controversial, would nonetheless seem to have great validity in matters arising now and in the future on issues of much greater importance to the public and concerning jobs of greater sensitivity.[13]

Anonymous Information

The case of Daniel Ellsberg took the *Pickering* issue to a level of national importance and, but for the stupidity of the governmental agency investigating and prosecuting this case, would have made major law in the area by virtue of the jury verdict.[14] While many factual differences are evident between *Ellsberg* and *Pickering*, in that Ellsberg was not a public employee when he acted and was charged with criminal activity rather than being subjected to discipline on the basis of violating a policy of government, nonetheless the issue in *Ellsberg* is similar in many respects to the issue raised in *Pickering*.[15] Daniel Ellsberg asserted that a former public employee with access to a document of great national importance and immense public interest had an obligation (he was unable to have the information disseminated to the public through a more legitimate source, such as the Senate Foreign Relations Committee) to "go public" with it.

If the theory of *Pickering* states that it is a matter of public importance that certain public employees, such as teachers, should speak out on

13. Emerson is of the opinion that "on the facts of the case Pickering was not a very difficult decision. More troublesome factual situations, which are bound to arise may produce a sharper analysis. . ." (*The System of Freedom of Expression*, p. 581).

14. This refers to criminal charges against Ellsberg for his action in obtaining and releasing the so-called Pentagon Papers. The issues involved in the attempt of the Justice Department to enjoin the publication of the "papers" involve entirely different issues, though they are not unrelated.

15. It should be noted that the principles applicable to public employees are equally applicable to persons not technically government employees, but whose employment is dependent upon government approval. See Greene v. McElroy, 360 U.S. 474 (1959), engineer for defense contractor who needed a security clearance; Spevack v. Klein, 385 U.S. 511 (1967), disbarment proceedings against attorney; Law Students Civil Rights Research Council Inc. v. Wadmond, 401 U.S. 154 (1971), admission to the bar; United States v. Robel, 389 U.S. 254 (1967), security clearance.

matters of public concern because of their expertise and special knowledge of the facts, this doctrine can obviously be expanded to state that, under certain circumstances, a public employee is not only *not* subject to reprisals, but has an obligation to bring to the public information of such importance that only he, as an expert, or others in his position, could release. Again, in such situations, the determination would have to be made on a case-by-case basis after the fact. When dealing with matters involving classified information and policies allegedly affecting national security, such a doctrine places an extremely heavy burden on the employee to be correct, in that if he is incorrect, the very nature of his assertion would not only subject him to disciplinary action but, as the *Ellsberg* case has shown, to criminal prosecution. However, since information concerning covert or secret government activities is most vital for the public to know about, and in this situation, when the initial legal presumptions were in favor of the government as opposed to the employee, the balancing test, weighing the rights of the government to secrecy as opposed to making public the information, would be proper. As opposed to *Pickering* situations, the effect of a balancing test in this case would be to increase, rather than decrease, public information. Since the Republic has not been dissolved by virtue of the revelations of the Church committee, courts will perhaps be more objective in weighing the balances in cases where the government has invoked national security to either suppress dissemination of information or to punish the employee making such information public.[16]

Such a doctrine will have to be part and parcel of other changes in the law; for instance, to what degree should certain types of information be considered "governmental property," in the sense that the releasing of such information or the physical removal of documents containing it constitute a common theft?[17] In the *Ellsberg* case, the first legal step

16. At this time the law on the subject of unauthorized use of government documents would not favor Daniel Ellsberg. See Tribune Review Publishing Co. v. Thomas, 254 F.2d 883 (3d Cir. 1958); United Press Association v. Valenti, 308 N.Y. 71, 123 N.E. 2d 777 (1954); Trimble v. Johnson 173 F. Supp. 651 (D. D.C. 1959); Liberty Lobby v. Pearson, 390 F.2d 489 (D. D.C. 1968); Dodd v. Pearson, 279 F. Supp. 101 (D. D.C. 1968), 410 F.2d 701. See also note, The Supreme Court 1970 Term, 85 HARVARD L. REV. 211, 212 (1971), which suggests that the dilemma might be resolved if the courts breathe new life into the Freedom of Information Act, 5 U.S.C. §552 (1969) by instituting stricter judicial review of the invocation of the national security exception.

17. A distinction might have to be made between the physical property of the papers and the information they contain. In the *Ellsberg* case the release of the information contained in the papers might be protected by the First Amendment while the unauthorized taking of the "papers" might still be a criminal act. Judge Byrne, presiding judge in the Ellsberg trial, posed that very point when, in response to a

would have been to decide whether or not the information contained in the Pentagon Papers, as opposed to the documents themselves, was in fact government property, and whether or not the government could have control over the ideas so contained. If the court had ruled that information was not property in the general sense, it would eventually have had to consider a more general question: Should Ellsberg, or any other employee, be protected when he has information which the public has a need to know, and only he can release?

In a situation such as that found in *Ellsberg* or any similar case, two levels of problems arise. First, can the recipient of the information be subject to sanction for printing or otherwise making public that information? And, second, can the public employee be subject to sanction for serving as the conduit to the ultimate media source?

I think, regarding the first part, that an almost absolute immunity should apply to the ultimate publisher of the information, even when the information could be considered a legitimate government secret. Indeed, the only kind of publication that could conceivably be subject to sanction is one in which the publication might seriously affect the constitutional rights of another under circumstances where publication of the specific information would be unnecessary for legitimate public information. The only area where such repression might have some validity (outside of war, when lives might be placed directly in danger) is the controversial area of publishing information as to pending criminal trials, which could have a disastrous effect on the defendants' rights at trial. Mere allegations of wrongdoing would not be sufficient, no matter how damaging; this is journalism at its best. Involved here are the publication of details of a confession which had been suppressed and which would be relevant in an ongoing criminal trial; this may be contempt of court.[18]

The second problem, involving the possibility of sanctions on employees, is different from *Pickering*. In an *Ellsberg* case, the public employee is not speaking for the record but rather acting surreptitiously in funneling the information to the media with the hope that his anonymity will be preserved. This is a much harder case, since the act done is so obviously damaging to the administrative needs of the agency as to make the employee's situation untenable, greater public need notwithstanding. Yet

government motion which would allow them to question and strike jurors if they were readers of certain publications such as the *Washington Post*, and the *New York Times*, stated that he perceived that there were First Amendment questions as to whether the Pentagon Papers were properly classified at the time Ellsberg had them copied.

18. The Supreme Court recently overruled the use of a gag order issued in a notorious murder case in Nebraska.

a legal rule allowing automatic disciplinary action would also be invalid, since the result would be to prevent employees from disclosing, publicly or otherwise, information concerning the misdeeds of their employers.

In fashioning a legal rule for this type of situation a different kind of test must be developed, since no agency has a legitimate interest in not disclosing its misdeeds, yet the public employer subjected to charges should have some protection from untrue or misleading charges of corruption or inefficiency which could destroy its reputation as easily as the opposite when done to the employee. Such a rule should be based on the idea that source identification is to be encouraged where possible, and any sanction against the employee limited to those situations where the information or charge is knowingly false, such as in *Arnett*, where the employee accused his supervisor of a criminal act knowing the same to be false (assume for this discussion that it is false).

Anonymous sources should be discouraged, except where real harm could come to the employee by disclosure or premature disclosure of the source. This situation would most likely occur when the information concerns criminal or quasi-criminal activity, as per the Watergate revelation. This is, of course, a very difficult problem, especially for lower level employees. Indeed, the formula should take into account the relative position of the employee. The secretary who gives a newspaper a copy of incriminating documents should obviously get more protection, since the information is in such a raw state that further investigation would be necessary before publication. The same need not be true when a relatively high level employee makes a charge in which the very position of the employee gives the information its authenticity. Again anonymity might be necessary; under such circumstances, however, sanctions against the employee might be valid if the employee would have been protected if his name was revealed but greater harm came to the agency by the fact of nondisclosure.

The Ernest Fitzgerald case, discussed later, is a perfect example of how this rule would work in its optimum state.[19] In this case, a high level investigator for the Air Force made statements before a congressional committee concerning cost overruns on a certain air base. He was punished, but a court ordered him reinstated with back pay. If the information he gave publicly was given anonymously to Jack Anderson and his name never disclosed, and if he had properly been identified as the source, his case doubtless would have and should have come out differently. The informant was of a high enough level that much administrative action could not have justified sanctions (they were tried), and the

19. Fitzgerald v. Hampton, 467 F.2d 755 (D.C. Cir. 1973).

only reason for punishment was the information itself. Since the legal issue was narrowed to validity of the speech, the need for anonymity was gone. This is the proper approach to this problem. Since *Ellsberg* was dismissed on unrelated issues, this most vital question will have to await a new case for final resolution.

Administrative Prerogative

While certain types of jobs allow prohibitions on all or certain kinds of speech by employees holding them, jobs also exist where the proper administration of a government function allows the government employer to limit the expression of its employees for the purpose of preserving its policy and its mission. This is somewhat different from the preceding discussion because, in the discussion of the nature of the job, the focus was on the employment situation itself, where requirements of a given job included a limitation or ban on the employees' rights of speech. Here limitations of speech will focus not on the expression per se, but rather on the impact of the expression on the agency in terms of the agency's requirements. This point may best be illustrated by looking in some detail at the case of *Murray v. Vaughn*,[20] which is significant because it is the one case which has brought into clear focus all the issues in the area of limitations on an employee's rights of free speech due to administrative prerogatives.

In the *Murray* case the plaintiff, Steven Murray, was a Peace Corps volunteer in Chile. In May of 1967, a group of Peace Corps volunteers in Chile drew up a petition opposing the war in Vietnam; Murray was one of the signers. When Peace Corps officials suppressed the distribution of the petition, Murray wrote a letter to the editor of the *New York Times* and to a paper in Chile which gave a summary of the signers' views and also complained about the actions of the Peace Corps in suppressing the distribution and dissemination of the petition. As a result of writing the letter, Murray was dismissed from the Peace Corps and later classified 1-A by his local draft board. Murray then brought suit in the federal courts, charging that the dismissal violated his First Amendment rights and asking for reinstatement in the Peace Corps.

The government's defense stated that the dismissal did not interfere with the plaintiff's First Amendment rights because its only effect was to render the plaintiff unemployed, not to prohibit him from speaking. The government also argued in the alternative that even if such a ban affected

20. 300 F. Supp. 688 (D. R.I. 1969); reaffirmed Murray v. Blatchford, 307 F. Supp. 1038 (D. R.I. 1968).

Murray's rights of free speech, it was a reasonable action exercized by the Peace Corps to protect an important interest, namely the apolitical role of the Peace Corps in foreign policy. The court dismissed the government's first premise rather quickly, holding that the action of the government had a "chilling effect" on the First Amendment rights of the employee.[21]

The court then discussed the remaining issue in the context of the balancing test found in *Pickering*. Concluding that a public employee cannot be fired arbitrarily for asserting First Amendment rights, but also that the government does have an interest in preserving the efficiency of the public service and its mission, the court treated the big question, namely whether the action of Murray in the letter violated the government's interest in maintaining an apolitical Peace Corps. The court held for Murray.

Conceding that the government did have a legitimate interest in keeping the Peace Corps apolitical, the court said that the thrust of Peace Corps interest in remaining apolitical was to keep Peace Corps volunteers out of the internal politics of the host country. The court used as an example a volunteer's writing a letter accusing the host country's government of corruption and calling for its overthrow. The government, in this example, would have a legitimate interest in suppressing speech and taking action against the writer. However, the court found that this type of situation was not present in the *Murray* case.

Having made the crucial determination about the real governmental issue in respect to letters such as that written by Murray, the court was now ready to decide the other vital question: What was Murray's interest vis-à-vis the government, and why must Murray's interests prevail? The court stated:

> The more reasonable view of this case is that Murray spoke about matters of vital interest to him as a human being, a United States citizen, and a Peace Corps volunteer. Any inhibition on speech so far removed from the government interest alleged to support it must fall. It is no different than the use of termination from a teaching position in the public schools as a restraining on expressions about school politics differing from those of the school "establishment." *Pickering* v. *Board of Education, supra.* Nor is it substantially different than the use of a loyalty oath or of internal legislative disciplinary procedures

21. 300 F. Supp. at 689. "Chilling effect" doctrine means that a governmental action is unconstitutional if it causes a person to refrain from First Amendment rights for fear that the expression would be punished. See Bigelow v. Virginia 421 U.S. 809 (1975); Dombrowski v. Pfister 380 U.S. 479 (1965).

to expel a duly elected state legislator for expressions of opinion concerning public issues vital to and deeply felt by him. *Bond* v. *Floyd, supra.*[22] To permit a termination such as this would be to value bureaucratic paranoia over the central commitment of the First Amendment to "uninhibited, robust, and wideopen" debate on public issues. *New York Times* v. *Sullivan* [cite omitted].[23] If such a valuation were accepted, then no person in any branch of the government service which touches upon the foreign policy of the United States could make public statements critical of any facet of foreign policy without fear of compelled severance from service. The First Amendment prohibits such a broad infringement. The defendants' motion to dismiss is therefore in this respect also denied.[24]

In the *Murray* case, the court focused with great precision on defining the exact mission or administrative interest of the particular employing agency. It then singled out these particular agency interests and held that no one working for the agency could make statements which would contradict the official point of view, even if the statements had validity and even if these statements would be protected in other circumstances if made by public employees.

This approach could, naturally, lead to the use of the administrative necessity of termination to ostensibly prohibit otherwise protected expression by public employees. However, this problem can be handled by the courts if they define the mission or the administrative needs of the agency (for purposes of proscribing speech) as narrowly as possible.[25] A method available to courts useful for the exertion of judicial scrutiny over government agencies invoking the administrative necessity doctrine against expression of its employees is the test applied to determine whether statutes which proscribe First Amendment activities are overbroad. Courts have often held statutes to be unconstitutional because a

22. Bond v. Floyd, 385 U.S. 116 (1966) referred to the attempt by the Georgia legislature to refuse to allow Julian Bond to have his elected seat because of his anti-war statements.

23. 376 U.S. 254 (1964) held public officials could not sue for libel unless statements made against them were intentionally false with malicious intent. But see Time, Inc. v. Firestone 424 U.S. 448 (1976).

24. 300 F. Supp. at 704.

25. That public employees engaging in speech ordinarily completely protected could nevertheless be proscribed because of administrative necessity arose with respect to two public petitions released by large groups of public employees. The first concerned a group of Justice Department lawyers who complained that the Justice Department was not doing enough to enforce the civil rights laws. The second concerned a group of State Department employees who issued a petition concerning Vietnam policy.

less drastic means of accomplishing the aim of the legislation, without impinging upon First Amendment rights, was available.[26]

Thus at no time would protection of information concerning misconduct on the part of the agency be considered a prime function of the agency, and in view of the revelations coming out of Watergate and related scandals, this whole question of administrative agencies covering up misconduct is a matter of rather prime importance, certainly not to simply be considered on a theoretical level.[27]

Likewise, unless the agency in question is one of peculiar sensitivity, expression of the employee not concerned with the mission and activities of the agency should not be proscribed in any way. In short, an agency can invoke its administrative necessities to prohibit the speech of its employees in those circumstances where it can operate only by not having its employees criticize the persons with whom the agency must deal, or in such situations where, after a discussion of legitimate policy interests, the agency has decided on one policy and employees criticizing such policy could seriously affect the ability of the agency to carry out that policy.

Morale of the Organization

On a somewhat lesser scale than that of possible interference with grand policy of administration is the idea that instances may arise in which certain styles of speech of public employees may be curtailed or prohibited because of their effect on the morale and working efficiency of the organization with respect to other personnel. This situation could develop in instances where a subordinate employee criticized his superior when the two shared an intimate relationship, or where morale of other employees might be affected by certain types of expression. The possibility of the first type of action was raised in *Pickering* in a footnote, which stated:

> Likewise, positions in public employment in which the relationship between superior and subordinate is of such a personal and intimate nature that certain forms of public criticism of this superior by the subordinate would seriously undermine the effectiveness of the work-

26. Shelton v. Tucker, 364 U.S. 479 (1960); United States v. Robel, 389 U.S. 258 (1967); Aptheker v. Secretary of State, 378 U.S. 500 (1964); Keyishian v. Board of Regents, 385 U.S. 589 (1967); Dombrowski v. Pfister, 380 U.S. 479 (1965).

27. See 5 U.S.C. §552(a)(3) (Supp. V, 1970), the so-called Freedom of Information Act.

ing relationship between them can also be imagined. We intimate no views as to how we would resolve any specific instances of such situations, but merely note that significantly different considerations would be involved in such cases.[28]

Morale is such a nebulous term that when conflicts occur between employee and employer over an employee's public expression, the issue of a decline in agency morale is difficult to assess and is usually discussed in different terms. Because the morale so lessened may belong to the administrator alone, he will often try to couch such a disagreement in terms such as "interference with the administration," as previously mentioned. Rather than considering questions of interference with morale as a complete category in itself, they should be considered as elements of other types of interests asserted in determining whether or not the expression of a public employee is protected.

Interference with Job Performance

Of all the grounds which the employing agency can use to limit the freedom of expression of its employees, possibly the strongest grounds (besides those few incidences where the job itself limits expression) is that a given public utterance by a given public employee in a given situation might interfere with the employee's performance of his job.[29] In *Pickering* this was a very important element and the Court held that one of the reasons for its overturning of Pickering's dismissal was that his statements could not be shown to have in any way impeded the proper performance of his teaching job. The Court thus clearly stated

---

28. 391 U.S. at 570; see discussion in chapter 1.

29. One major aspect of the morale question would be the ability to get along with one's fellow employees or the maintenance of discipline in general. In *Pickering*, the Supreme Court thought this was very important and the failure to show that Pickering's statements interfered with such interests was a major consideration in the decision.

> The statements are in no way directed towards any person with whom the appellant would normally be in contact in the course of his daily work as a teacher. Thus, no question of maintaining either discipline by immediate superiors or harmony among co-workers is present here. Appellant's employment relationships with the Board and, to somewhat lesser extent, with the Superintendent are not the kind of close working relationships for which it can persuasively be claimed that personal loyalty and confidence are necessary to their proper functioning. [391 U.S. at 569–70. But see the most recent Supreme Court case—discussed later in the chapter.]

that interference with an employee's job performance would be grounds for dismissal.

In attempting to decide whether or not a given assertion of First Amendment rights by the employee actually impedes his job, several factors must be taken into consideration. One factor involves the speech itself—was it made on job time or after job time, as an extramural activity? In *Pickering*, the fact that the speech was made or the letter written outside the context of the employment relationship certainly was a factor in the Court's decision.

Another factor involves those employees who, while not banned altogether from making public statements because of their job, may, because of certain expectations with respect to that job, be limited from engaging in certain types of speech. Thus, an employee who engaged in such prohibited speech would in fact be undercutting his ability to perform his job. The case of *Lefcourt* v. *Legal Aid Society*[30] is an example of that precise point. In it, a lawyer employed by the Legal Aid Society engaged in such strong criticism of the way his agency was handling its clients that he put himself in a position in which his effectiveness, in terms of his ability to represent his clients, was severely undermined, and his dismissal was affirmed.

Possibly the best example of a situation in which a public employee engaged in speech which would have been protected except for the unusual circumstances under which it was accomplished, is the case of *Goldwasser* v. *Brown*.[31] Goldwasser was a civilian teacher employed by the Air Force. His job was to teach basic English to foreign military officers who were in the country as guests of the United States government on a military officers exchange program. Goldwasser had an unquestioned ability to teach English, but was discharged by the Air Force because, during his classroom sessions, he used his classroom as a forum to express his views regarding the war in Viet Nam and antisemitism in America. Goldwasser sued for reinstatement, but the Circuit Court for the District of Columbia eventually upheld his firing on the grounds that, by using that particular classroom to express those particular kinds of views, Goldwasser in effect undermined his ability to adequately perform his job. The factors taken into account were: (1) Goldwasser was employed by a military agency; (2) Goldwasser's views touched on questions of military policy and his views were contrary to the standard policy; and (3) of most importance, because of the nature of his students,

---

30. 312 F. Supp. 1105 (8th D. N.Y. 1970). Discussed extensively in chapter 2.
31. 417 F.2d 1169 (D. D.C. 1969), cert. denied, Goldwasser v. Seamans 397 U.S. 922 (1970).

the expression of those particular views in that particular classroom might well undermine the entire foreign officer exchange program.

The court went to extensive lengths to dispel any notions that this decision would in any way, manner, or form undercut *Pickering*. It distinguished the case from *Pickering* on the grounds that *Pickering* concerned statements made out of class, while this case concerned statements made in class, statements which affected the efficiency of Goldwasser's teaching.[32]

In my view, a total in class and out of class distinction is not valid. Many situations could occur in which off job expressions were so damaging as to constitute an interference, while many types of on job expressions would be perfectly permissible and therefore protected. *Goldwasser* was, in my opinion, correctly decided, but only because of the peculiar nature of the facts. If Goldwasser had made the same statements in front of a high school or college class or, in fact, in front of a military officers' class devoted to political affairs, such statements would probably have been protected even if they were contrary to the doctrine of his employer. However, the firing in *Goldwasser* was justified because the nature of this specific class was a particularly inappropriate forum for the expression of controversial public views. Goldwasser was hired to teach a technical subject devoid of any political content, and the students entered his class with the expectation that no matter of politics or government would enter into it (especially unsolicited expression of views on the part of the teacher). While the nature of the views may well have been the factor that provoked comments and complaints, nonetheless the same legal doctrine would have applied if he had made strongly right-wing views upholding military action, and another person in the class representing a socialist country made the complaint.[33]

---

32. "We note that the public school teacher in *Pickering* was not fired for what he said in class, but for writing a letter to a newspaper critical of the School Board and the School Superintendent in the allocation of school funds as between different educational programs. The efficiency with which Pickering taught Geography or Algebra to the pupils immediately in front of him was not affected by his expressions." 417 F.2d at 1177.

33. In Los Angeles Teachers Association v. Board of Education, 71 Cal. 2d 551, 78 Cal. Rptr. 723, 455 P.2d 827 (1969), at issue was a policy of the school board prohibiting the teachers from circulating certain petitions critical of school board policy during their lunch breaks. The California Supreme Court held that the teachers had the right to circulate these petitions and that there was no overriding school interest in preserving discipline, morale or teacher efficiency which would deny the teachers their First Amendment rights to circulate petitions. See also Roberts v. Lake Central School Corp., 317 F. Supp. 63 (N.D. Ind. 1970); Knarr v. Board of School Trustees of Griffith, Ind., 317 F. Supp. 832 (N.D. Ind. 1970).

Goldwasser, however, should be limited to its facts. As stated before, the Goldwasser statements would have been not only proper but constitutionally protected in almost any other classroom setting. Academic freedom is an aspect of the constitutional rights of public employees, and the *Goldwasser* case does not lessen it. *Goldwasser* differs because the setting was not academic in the generally accepted concept of the term. Because of the involvement with foreign affairs and the military, and the particularly nonacademic function that Goldwasser was hired to perform, concepts of academic freedom just did not apply.

However, before leaving this subject one hypothetical question should be answered. If Goldwasser was teaching English or another technical subject to American servicemen, would the result be the same? A legal distinction is present here, in that removal of the special facts involving the foreign officers, guests of the country who were legitimately offended by political statements, changes the entire picture. Under these circumstances even admittedly antimilitary statements made to a captive military audience by an employee of the Department of Defense would have to be judged not as to whether the employee had the right to make political statements, but rather whether these particular views could be so disruptive as to be subject to sanction. When the issue is the nature of the speech and the contents therein, the government has to meet a much higher standard in order to make such speech the basis of job action.

If, in *Pickering*, protected speech was the predominant reason for the job action and, in *Goldwasser*, allegedly impermissible speech was the basis, what would happen in a situation where the job action was based on a mix of protected speech and unprotected misconduct? This fascinating question was recently decided in the case of *Mt. Healthy Board of Education* v. *Doyle*.[34]

Fred Doyle was employed in 1966 as a teacher in the Mt. Healthy School District. He was given a series of one- and two-year contracts through 1971. In 1969, he was elected president of the Teachers' Association.

Beginning in 1970, Doyle became involved in a series of incidents not related to his role as teacher's union president. Once he got in a fight with another teacher, who slapped him. He refused to accept an apology, which resulted in joint reprimands and a teacher walkout. He became involved in an argument with cafeteria employees as to his portion of spaghetti. He also referred to some students in a disciplinary complaint as "sons of bitches" and made an obscene gesture to two girls who failed to obey his commands as cafeteria supervisor. At the same time these

34. 429 U.S. 274 (1977).

incidents occurred, the principal of his school circulated a dress code memorandum applying to teachers. When Doyle received this memorandum he immediately called a radio station in Cincinnati, which broadcast the news.

About a month later the school superintendent refused to recommend Doyle (he was not tenured) for reappointment. In response to Doyle's request for reasons he stated that it was due to his notable lack of tact in handling professional matters which "leaves much in doubt as to your sincerity in establishing good school relationships." He specifically mentioned the obscene gesture and radio station incidents.[35]

Doyle filed suit, stating that he was not retained because of an exercise of a constitutionally protected right of free speech. The district and circuit courts agreed, holding that a nonpermissible reason played a substantial part in the dismissal, despite the fact that the reason given for dismissal was independent of any First Amendment grounds.

The school board appealed to the Supreme Court; it agreed with their position, at least to the extent that the trial court could not ignore the importance of the independent grounds for nonretention.

What the Court held unanimously was that the trial court should have inquired as to whether, based on the teacher's conduct, he would not have been released even if the speech related incident had not occurred. If that was true his constitutional rights would have been vindicated "if such an employer is placed in no worse a position than if he had not engaged in the conduct."

> A border line or marginal candidate should not have the employment question resolved against him because of constitutionally protected conduct. But that same candidate ought not to be able by engaging in such conduct to prevent his employer from assessing his performance record and reaching a decision not to reappoint on the basis of that record simply because the protected conduct makes the employer more certain of the correctness of the decision.[36]

The Court then sent the case back to the district court to determine if the board, with a preponderance of the evidence, would have dismissed Doyle in the absence of the unprotected conduct.[37]

---

35. 429 U.S. at 279.

36. Ibid.

37. The Supreme Court cited several cases in which it found it necessary to formulate a test of causation which distinguished between a result caused by a constitutional violation and one not so caused. These were mostly when a criminal suspect confessed a second time voluntarily after having his first confession unconstitutionally coerced. Lyn v. Oklahoma, 322 U.S. 596 (1944); Wong Sun v. United States, 371 U.S. 471.

How should this case be assessed in terms of its impact on public employees? It actually represents a rather hopeful development, because it was a unanimous Court. Justice Rehnquist, the leading conservative voice, wrote a consensus opinion that reflected not only the conservative views of the Chief Justice and himself but the much more liberal views of Justices Kennan and Marshall.

This consensus held that in public employee personnel decisions, a continuous awareness of the relationship of actions to a protected constitutional right is necessary. If the employee probably would not have been dismissed, or no independent grounds legitimately existed at the time of the assertion of the right, the firing was therefore unconstitutional. At the same time the Court expressed the hope that an employee would not use the Constitution as a shield against responsibility for his own misconduct, which has no protection. In other words, the employee should not be able to fabricate a constitutional case to prevent a legitimate job action.

Based on my own experience with clients or potential clients this opinion, unlike some other, more recent opinions of the Supreme Court, truly comes to grips with what is really happening in public employment relationships. Employees do "go public" to try to immunize their behavior; at times they are forced into this action because they are the victims of a bad system or only they can alert the public.

Doyle extends to situations where First Amendment issues are present the system described in chapter 2 as to the basis of just cause or the requirement of a real factual inquiry into the circumstances of a dismissal based on arguably protected conduct. In those jurisdictions where the federal courts tend to favor the individual, this will require the employee to present more evidence than before in order to get reinstated. It also means that in other jurisdictions the government agency will have the burden of proving by the preponderance of evidence that, in the face of a charge of protected activity, its allegations of misconduct existed before the protected activity and were not derived from its own reaction to the protected activity.

On balance, *Doyle* is favorable to the employee, since the introduction of a strict evidenciary standard will require the litigation of close cases. If only in forcing settlements, this will be of great benefit to public employees. This also indicates that employees must become litigation minded in a different sense. The public employee who, because of his position (for example, a union activist) or holdings anticipates "going public" against his employers, must be sure that he does not engage in unprotected behavior that could get him in trouble. At the same time, the employee also realizes that, if he does engage in protected speech and it causes a job action against him, the courts must judge the validity of the employer's reasons for the action against a fairly rigid standard of evidence.

Special Legal Status of the Employee

The final area concerning those special interests of the employer which affect the right of employees to engage in speech pertains to the special legal standing of some public employees. The status of the public employee, rather than the nature of his job, is of concern here, especially if the employee has tenure or special contract prerogatives.[38]

This issue is of extreme importance because of United States Supreme Court decisions in the cases of *Board of Regents of State Colleges* v. *Roth*[39] and *Perry* v. *Sindermann*.[40] These cases, ostensibly concerning

38. A line of cases is not affected by the new Supreme Court cases, which holds that tenure rights do not affect First Amendment rights. What was discussed by the Court in the *Roth* and *Perry* cases was whether tenure or its equivalent affects rights of procedural due process. Albaum v. Cary, 283 F. Supp. 3 (E.D. N.Y. 1968), 310 F. Supp. 594; Pred v. Board of Public Instruction, 415 F.2d 851, 856 (5th Cir. 1969); Johnson v. Branch, 364 F.2d 177 (4th Cir. 1966); McLaughlin v. Tilendes 398 F.2d 287 (7th Cir. 1960); Bomar v. Keyes 162 F.2d 136, 139 (2d Cir.), cert. denied 332 U.S. 825 (1947): "The wrong is independent of any breach of contract. . . ."; Roth v. Board of Regents, 310 F. Supp. 972, affirmed 446 F.2d 806 (7th Cir. 1971).

39. 408 U.S. 564 (1972). In this case the respondent was a teacher at Wisconsin State University–Oshkosh, who was hired on a one-year contract. During the course of the year, as required in the contract, he was told his contract would not be renewed for the next year. He brought suit in the U.S. District Court claiming that: (1) the nonrenewal was in retaliation for his part in a racial dispute at the school; (2) that irrespective of the reasons for his nonretention, he was entitled to be afforded procedural due process, specification of charges, and a hearing prior to termination. The District Court, 310 F. Supp. 572 (W.D. Wisc. 1968), as per Judge Doyle, and the Seventh Circuit, 446 F.2d 806 (7th Cir. 1971), agreed with his second contention, holding that he was entitled to at least be afforded the reasons for his nonretention because of the implication and impact of his nonretention. The United States Supreme Court by a 6–3 vote reversed the circuit court.

40. 408 U.S. 593 (1972). In this case Sindermann, a teacher at Odessa College, Texas, who had worked four previous one-year contracts, was suddenly nonrenewed without any reason given. Sindermann claimed it was because of his role in a dispute over whether the school should be upgraded to a four year college. He brought suit in the United States District Court on the same basis as the *Roth* case, *supra*. In an unreported decision the district court ruled against him because Texas has no tenure system. The Fifth Circuit, Sindermann v. Perry 430 F.2d 939 (5th Cir. 1970), held that in situations where there was genuine First Amendment issue, the lack of tenure is irrelevant and the defendant is entitled to procedural due process, though in a somewhat different form than if he had an "expectancy" of reemployment. The difference is, if there is an "expectancy" of reemployment when a challenge is made, the college must come forward with reasons. When no "expectancy" is present, the teacher has

the related area of procedural due process of public employees, have great importance to questions of the rights of free speech of public employees; indeed the lack of procedural due process may well determine whether First Amendment rights are vindicated. Nevertheless, from a conceptual viewpoint, the issues are entirely different, with different rules governing them. This is especially true when the effect of contractual rights, or the lack of them, on both substantive and procedural due process rights of public employees is under consideration.

In both cases the Court held that a public employee does not have any rights of procedural due process with respect to nonretention (as opposed to dismissal within tenure or contract) unless he is entitled to such rights by virtue of contract, by state law, if the denial of due process would deprive him of an interest in "liberty," or if ". . . he had a 'property' interest in continued employment, despite the lack of tenure or a formal contract." This distinction between nonretention and dismissal, especially as it applies to procedural due process, can be critical.[41]

While the Supreme Court has stated that public employees do not have a right to procedural due process unless the employee has tenure or the equivalent or has the right guaranteed by contract, a different situation may exist if the employee, especially a teacher, is dismissed during the school year instead of having his contract expire without renewal.[42]

---

the burden of notifying the school of his claim so that the school can, if possible, show error. However, once this problem is resolved, the hearing given both types of teachers is the same. Interestingly, the Supreme Court seems to have misread the Fifth Circuit opinion. Its summary of the circuit court case stated that where a First Amendment claim is made, the district court must give an evidentiary hearing of the facts. It then said where the teacher had an "expectancy" of employment, he must be given full procedural due process rights, 408 U.S. at 601, 602. This separation between independent action on the First Amendment claim and procedural due process is what the Supreme Court eventually held, but it is not what the Fifth Circuit held.

41. The importance of procedural due process in vindicating First Amendment rights cannot be overemphasized. Van Alstyne has stated that "without question, therefore, the effective protection of the substantive constitutional rights of teachers and professors may critically depend upon the availability of pre-termination procedural due process." *The Constitutional Rights of Teachers and Professors*, 1970 DUKE L. REV. 866.

42. The question left open by the Court, though raised in these cases, is what constitutes minimum procedural due process, when the employee is entitled to some procedural due process. Involved are the questions of both form and time. In some excellent opinions concerning procedural due process, in areas other than employee rights, the Supreme Court has held that procedural due process must be given *before* the termination becomes effective. See Boddie v. Connecticut, 401 U.S. 371 (1971), right to counsel in divorce matters; Goldberg v. Kelly, 397 U.S. 254 (1959), withdrawal of welfare benefits; Bell v. Burson, 402 U.S. 535 (1972), withdrawal of

The Supreme Court apparently indicated in both *Roth* and *Sindermann* that state educational institutions have the right to decide who shall be permanent teachers. Because of the unique way in which faculties are developed, most employers understand that teachers not retained before completing their probationary period are let go for a multitude of reasons, most of which do not imply incompetence. Other employers accept this practice and generally do not hold it against the teacher. The reason may, of course, be retaliation for assertion of a protected constitutional right; if that can be proven the employee is entitled to reinstatement and damages.

Dismissal, however, especially for teachers on yearly contracts, is so unusual as to immediately raise questions of incompetence or worse. The allegation of stigma, which the court rejected in conjunction with nonretention in *Roth*, would be present in dismissal cases; thus, if the *Roth* rule is to be modified for nontenured teachers, it will be done to provide rights of procedural due process to employees dismissed during the term of their contract, even if the contract provides for dismissal for cause. This present Court will probably not change *Roth*. If a future, more liberal Court wishes not to throw out *Roth* entirely, this will be the change that will be made, since the reason for differentiating those with tenure is clearly stigmatizing. Accordingly, the same reasoning should apply to dismissals.

Of course this is primarily a problem in those jobs where employment is secured by renewable written contract. In situations in which employ-

driver licenses. The form to be followed is that the person whose rights are to be terminated must be given a specification of charges and an opportunity to respond to such charges. Goldberg v. Kelly at 261.

In the area of public employees rights, the approach has been similar, though by no means uniform. Some courts have held that not only are pretermination rights vital, but in addition, a hearing must be held in the matter. Board of Regents v. Roth, 408 U.S. 564 (1972), reversed. See also Olson v. Board of Regents of University of Minnesota, 301 F. Supp. 1356 (W.D. Minn. 1969). Other courts stress the pretermination aspect without putting any special value on a hearing. Drown v. Portsmouth School District; 435 F.2d 1182 (1st Cir. 1970); Lucia v. Duggan, 303 F. Supp. 112 (W.D. Mass. 1969).

Other courts have stressed the importance of some remedies either before or after the termination. Birnbaum v. Trussell, 371 F.2d 672 (2d Cir. 1966); Meredith v. Allen County Memorial Hospital Commission, 397 F.2d 33 (6th Cir. 1968); Goldsmith v. United States Board of Tax Appeals, 270 U.S. 117 (1923), practice before tax court; Dixon v. Alabama State Board of Education, 294 F.2d 150 (5th Cir.), cert. denied, 368 U.S. 530 (1961), students' rights; Murray v. Blatchford, 307 F. Supp. 1038 (D. R.I. 1968); Wilner v. Committee on Character and Fitness, 373 U.S. 96 (1962), practice of law; Parker v. Lester, 227 F.2d 708 (9th Cir. 1956); Slochower v. Board of Higher Education, 350 U.S. 551 (1956).

ment is made by schedule, and promotion or demotion is made unilaterally, different techniques will have to be developed.

By virtue of the citations used by the Court, the definition of the term *liberty* was not used in a First Amendment context, but rather with regard to daily activities, such as the right to education, marriage, employment, and the rest. This view of the concept of liberty without First Amendment implications was not shared by Justices Douglas and Marshall, who dissented in those cases.[43] Justice Douglas used the concept of liberty in terms of "important interest of the citizen." Included in this concept are teachers subject to disciplinary actions for asserting First Amendment rights. Other examples of "important interests of the citizen" given protection by the Court where First Amendment interests were involved included attempts to limit speech by withdrawing mailing privileges; conditioning tax exemption; and public accusation of immoral behavior.[44] In all these cases, Douglas concluded that when First Amend-

43. See Pierce v. Society of Sisters, 262 U.S. 390, 399 (1921):

> While this Court has not attempted to define with exactness the liberty . . . guaranteed by the [Fourteenth Amendment] the term has received much consideration, and some of the included things have been definitely stated. Without doubt, it denotes not merely freedom from bodily restraint but also the right of the individual to contract, to engage in any of the common occupations of life, to acquire useful knowledge, to marry, establish a home and bring up children, to worship God according to the dictates of his own conscience and generally to enjoy those privileges long recognized . . . as essential to the orderly pursuit of happiness by free men. [Quoted in Board of Regents v. Roth, 408 U.S. at 578.]

Justice Marshall, in his dissent in *Roth*, states:

> In my view, every citizen who applies for a government job is entitled to it unless the government can establish some reason for denying the employment. This is the "property" right that I believe is protected by the Fourteenth Amendment and that liberty—liberty to work—which is the "very essence of the personal freedom and opportunity" secured by the Fourteenth Amendment. [408 U.S. at 584.]

44. Justice Douglas uses the concept of liberty in terms of "important interests of the citizen." Included in that are teachers who are subject to disciplinary actions for asserting First Amendment rights. Sweezy v. New Hampshire, 354 U.S. 234 (1957); Keyishian v. Board of Regents, note 26 *supra*. Other examples of "important interests of the citizen" to which the Court gave protection where First Amendment interests were involved included Hannegan v. Esquire, 327 U.S. 146 (1946), attempt to limit speech by withdrawing mailing privileges; Speiser v. Randall, 357 U.S. 513 (1958), conditioning tax exemption on giving up First Amendment rights; Sherbert v. Verner, 374 U.S. 398 (1963), disqualification for unemployment compensation;

ment rights conflicted or could conflict with valid administrative needs, protection was given to the First Amendment interests. Furthermore, this protection should be given to nonrenewal of a teacher's contract as an entitlement equal in importance and dignity to those interests previously mentioned. The implication of the use of this definition of liberty, as opposed to the broader concept espoused by Justices Douglas and Marshall in *Roth*, is that the question of the right to procedural due process for public employees is entirely separate from the questions of their First Amendment rights.

That the Court makes this distinction can be discerned from the exceptions cited for the no procedural due process rule, namely: that such nonretention would substantially impair the employee's standing in the community, especially when it has implications of being based on allegations of dishonesty or immorality; or when the nonretention would impose on the employee a stigma harming his chances of further employment. Should such potential harm to the employee be present, the Court would hold that the employee should have procedural due process, his lack of contract rights or tenure notwithstanding.[45] While protection of public employees from this type of harm is important, the Court significantly refused to recognize the "chilling effect" on First Amendment rights of the nonretained employee as rising to the same level as purely personal harm.[46]

Wisconsin v. Constantineau, 400 U.S. 433 (1971), public accusation of immoral behavior. In all these cases, it was Douglas's conclusion that when First Amendment rights conflicted or could conflict with valid administrative needs, the Court gave protection to the First Amendment interests. And this protection should be given to nonrenewal of a teacher's contract as an entitlement of the same importance and dignity as those interests previously mentioned. Board of Regents v. Roth, 408 U.S. at 577.

45. Justice Stewart cites for this position: Wisconsin v. Constantineau, *supra*; Wieman v. Updegraff, note 2 *supra*; Joint Anti-Fascist Refugee Committee v. McGrath, 341 U.S. 123 (1957); United States v. Lovett, 328 U.S. 303 (1946); Peters v. Hobby, 349 U.S. 331 (1957). The last four cases are all loyalty-security cases. Senator Truax v. Raich, 239 U.S. 33 (1915); Schware v. Board of Bar Examiners, 353 U.S. 232 (1956); Wilner v. Committee on Character, note 42, *supra*. See also Cafeteria Workers v. McElroy 367 U.S. 886 (1961).

46. The "chilling effect" doctrine was first enunciated in Dombrowski v. Pfister, 380 U.S. 479 (1965). See also note, The Chilling Effect Doctrine in Constitutional Law, 69 COLUMBIA L. REV. 808 (1969).

This is not to say the Court is in any way overruling those prior decisions where a form of due process was required before a state was allowed to proscribe certain types of First Amendment rights. Carroll v. Princess Anne County, note 6, *supra*; Quantity of Books v. Kansas, 378 U.S. 205 (1964); Marcus v. Search Warrant 367 U.S. 717 (1961); Freedman v. Maryland, 380 U.S. 51 (1965); Bantam Books v.

The second exception cited by the Court was one in which an employee had a property interest in his job. This category was limited, however, in that such an interest could only arise from the contract status of the employee, not from the fact of public employment itself. In recent years many legal scholars and, indeed, the Supreme Court itself have begun to redefine the concept of "property," especially in the context of government actions and benefits.[47] The implications of previous decisions, especially *Goldberg* v. *Kelly*, indicated that the creation of new individual "property" interests in turn created concomitant constitutional rights arising out of those interests, especially rights of procedural due process of law.[48]

However, in *Roth* and *Sindermann* the Court specifically rejected this claim, holding that the property interest of a person in a government program or benefit is no greater than the rights created at the source of such a program; thus no new constitutional rights have been established.

With this extremely narrow definition of property established, the only property interest referred to by the Court as an exception to the contract or tenure rule is the interest arising in situations in which the conditions of a given person's employment would be tantamount to tenure, or in which the employee had an expectation of and a legitimate claim to reemployment.

The Court found such a situation in *Sindermann*. Under Texas law no tenure system was provided for junior college teachers and Sindermann, after four previous one-year contracts, was found entitled to due process of law before being terminated. While employee rights were upheld in this specific case, the effect of such decisions is to deprive due process rights to those public employees most in need of them, as the new employee rather than the established employee, is most likely to come into contact with his employers on matters of public utterances.

Sullivan, 372 U.S. 58 (1963). See Monaghan, *First Amendment "Due Process,"* 83 HARVARD L. REV. 518 (1970). Indeed, the Court specifically mentioned the above cases as being unaffected by the ruling. It distinguished these cases from Roth by holding:

> . . . the state has not directly impinged upon interests in free speech or free press in any way comparable to a seizure of books or an injunction against meetings. Whatever may be a teacher's rights of free speech, the interest in holding a teaching job at a state university, simpliciter, is not itself a free speech interest. [Board of Regents v. Roth, note 43 *supra* at 578.]

47. Reich, *The New Property*, 73 YALE L. J. 733 (1964); Van Alstyne, *The Demise of the Right-Privilege Distinction in Constitutional Law*, 81 HARVARD L. REV. 1439; O'Neill, *The Price of Dependency*.

48. See note 42, *supra*.

While the *Roth* and *Sindermann* cases ostensibly had no effect on the protected First Amendment rights of public employees, in practice these decisions created two classes of public employees, insofar as rights of free speech are concerned—differentiated only by their contract or tenure status.[49]

The Court went to great lengths to show that a public employee's lack of formal contractual or tenure security is irrelevant to any free speech claim he might have with respect to his loss of employment. Numerous cases were cited in which the Court had held that a government benefit could not be conditional upon the giving up of a protected constitutional right, especially the rights protected under the First Amendment.

Indeed, the Court was correct in asserting that First Amendment claims in a public employment context can be raised independent of any contract status. However, actions the Court said it would not take directly it took indirectly, by emasculating rights of procedural due process. Although this chapter concerns situations in which First Amendment issues are being litigated by both sides, asking whether an employee can assert such rights or the agency proscribe them, a common situation involves the agency's attempt to actually deny the presence of any First Amendment issue. In such situations the rights of procedural due process are not merely important, but absolutely crucial to the preservation of First Amendment rights.

The protection afforded by the Civil Rights Act of 1866 contains a great void, and it promises to get wider.[50] As long as the Supreme Court's decision to require minimum levels of procedural due process was open, many public employers either afforded some level of due process even if not required to by statute or contract, or held back on some possible actions. At present, however, employers choose to nonretain employees without any form of due process. Since the only remedy left to these

49. The Fifth Circuit has come down with a hybrid test containing elements of both theories. According to the Fifth Circuit, all tenured employees and employees with an expectation of continued employment would automatically have a right to procedural due process including notice, specification of charges, and a hearing. This would also apply to any other employees who, despite lack of status, raise a constitutional issue in challenging a dismissal. Pred v. Board of Public Instruction, 415 F.2d 851 (5th Cir. 1968); Ferguson v. Thomas, 430 F.2d 852 (5th Cir. 1970); Harkless v. Sweeney Independent School District, 427 F.2d 319 (5th Cir. 1970); Sindermann v. Perry, 420 F.2d 939 (5th Cir. 1970).

Sindermann v. Perry was affirmed only as to whether an employee without tenure could be considered to have the equivalency of tenure, and the validity of the above cases would seem to be in great doubt.

50. 42 U.S.C. §1983.

employees is independent action under the Civil Rights Act, any reasons given for dismissal or nonretention only serve to assist the employee in his court action.

The great benefit of procedural due process is that it places the burden upon the agency to justify its reasons for dismissing or nonrenewing a public employee. If the agency has to spell out the reasons for its actions in situations involving First Amendment rights, it either must clearly state that it is acting for these reasons, or concoct some others. In either case, an outside body (usually a court) looking at the matter can at least decide the matter within the context of the agency's own reasons. If the reason is concerned with the First Amendment, a jury can decide whether such speech is protected. If a non-First Amendment reason is specified, at least a definite claim is involved, one which can be justified as of the time of dismissal and not, as often happens, thought up and presented to the employee only in answer to his suit. The inhibitory effect of procedural due process is every bit as important as the aid to litigation it affords. Van Alstyne is rather emphatic in his feeling that lawsuits are disfunctional to the employee even if successful, and that the threat of lawsuits is equally upsetting to employers. Procedural due process serves as "the best check on arbitrary action in retaliation for the assertion of protected First Amendment rights."[51]

Without procedural due process, the burden falls upon the public employee to prove the nexus between his nonretention or dismissal and his engaging in First Amendment activities. This is often extremely difficult to do, especially if the agency is careful enough to never specify its reasons in any document or memorandum, or even to continually make public statements in support of the employees' right to speak.[52]

Thus, the Court in *Roth* and *Sindermann* certainly dealt public employees a bad blow, especially those employees without tenure or contract status. I predict that public employee organizations and unions will

51. *The Constitutional Rights of Teachers and Professors* 1970 Duke L. Rev. 860.
52. This is in conflict with the holding in Speiser v. Randall, 357 U.S. 518 (1958), which emphasized the importance of the government having the burden of proof where questions of First Amendment rights are concerned. While the presence of a valid administrative concern in personnel management would require some burden of proof on the nonretained employee, as pointed out by Judge Doyle in the district court decision in *Roth*, 310 F. Supp. at 979; the Court has made the independent 1983 action almost meaningless save in those situations where the government employer specifies a First Amendment reason for dismissal or where independent evidence, other than the "coincidence of time between speech and job action" is uncovered in the employee's claim. However, Mt. Healthy School Board v. Doyle may have helped in this regard.

now attempt to rectify the void left by the Supreme Court through collective bargaining and changes in state law concerning tenure rights.

This, of course, will have no substantive effect on the free speech rights of public employees, since such rights exist independently of contract or tenure. However, it will qualitatively affect the vindication of those rights, since procedural due process is so important and should not be the province of only those public employees with special standing. The issue of procedural due process will be discussed in more detail in a later chapter.

Nature of the Speech

Previous sections illustrated that the particular nature of a job limits a public employee's speech. So, too, may the particular nature of the speech itself be determinative of the employee's right of the employee to engage in it. Of the two types of speech, job related and non-job related, the latter is most protected. When such a speech does not concern, either in content or forum of delivery, anything directly affecting the job interest, it is actually an assertion of a First Amendment right by a citizen who also happens to be a public employee. Again, situations may exist in which job-connected speech would be limited because the nature of the job requires the employee to remain virtually anonymous under all situations.[53] A detailed examination of possible areas will indicate these nuances.

Non-Job Related Speech

A problem with non-job related speech may arise even if the content and forum are not in any way connected to the job, if the speaker identifies himself as a public employee even though no ostensible connection exists between the speech and the speaker's job. This is a rather subtle point, because here the public position is used solely to enhance the value of the private expression, and as such would not really affect the speaker's employment situation. However, the identification of public employment by the speaker might well have the effect, at least for some listeners, of

---

53. This problem was implicit in Murray v. Vaughan, note 20 *supra*, where the government was not only expressing an interest in keeping Peace Corps Volunteers apolitical with respect to politics of the host country, but also to avoid having the Peace Corps go on record as being opposed to the policies of the administration even if such policies were inimical to the mission of the Peace Corps.

attributing to the employing agency the views expressed in the employee's speech, and thus by implication attribute an endorsement of these views by the agency, when in fact no such connection could legitimately be made.[54]

In my opinion, when the associational connection is provided solely for identification purposes, especially if the person is, for example, a member of a public university faculty and this association in effect certifies the speaker as a person of competence, no such implication could legitimately be made, and any action taken against the employee would be totally illegal. Thus, if a professor of law from a large university writes a letter to the editor attacking the constitutionality of a given law, or any matter of public policy, and identifies himself as a professor of law at the university, the only implication permitted should be that because the speaker is a professor, such views may or may not be taken with a greater degree of seriousness than would another's views. These views should not be attributed in any way, manner, or form to the school in question.

A case on that very point has gained some notoriety in Virginia. A professor at a small women's college wrote a letter to the editor of *Redbook* magazine, in which he praised an article on premarital sex published in that magazine. The letter contained nothing offensive or unprotected, but the writer did sign his name and stated that he was a professor at this particular school. As a result of this incident, the professor argued that he was denied pay raises and other benefits that should have come to him by virtue of his rank, and thus was forced to go to court for restitution. The case dragged on for several years; the trial ended in a hung jury. Fortunately, the state of Virginia settled out of court rather than go through another trial.[55]

The school in question was rather notorious at that time for its administration's restrictive views toward expression by faculty members and was not representative of most state schools. Nevertheless, the incident caused the employee great harm both financially and mentally, indicating that public employees are still subject to attack for apparently innocuous and protected activities.

Note that if the expression was uttered in such a way as to imply that it formed a stated policy of the agency, I would think that the agency

54. American Association of University Professors recognized the problem of possible identification arising out of extramural expression of faculty member. The AAUP even concedes that failure to make this differentiation could be the basis of job action. See, 1964 Committee, "A Statement on Extramural Utterances," in Louis Joughin, ed., *Academic Freedom and Tenure at 64* (Madison: Univ. of Wisconsin Pr., 1969).

55. Jervey v. Martin, W.D. Va. (April 20, 1972).

would have the right to at least have the employee retract any such implication from his expression. The degree to which any kind of job action might be taken by the agency against the employee for such action would depend entirely on the facts of the case. If proof was found to indicate that the employee had attempted to grossly misuse his position of trust as a public employee to further a private idea or belief, possible action could be taken, not because of the belief itself but because of the misuse of a public trust for private gain. However, unless the issue in question somehow bears a close resemblance to the nature of the agency's work, any attempt to attribute to a large agency, such as a university, an official position on a topic in no way concerned with its function would be difficult. Thus, any case brought under such circumstances probably involves more than just speech. Likewise, if the speech does tend to border on the agency's work, the matter would be entirely different, concerned with job-connected speech and involving a different set of pertinent rules and rights.[56]

Similarly, the question of institutional identification can lead to the analogous problem of the violation of a public trust resulting from unconnected speech. One case involving the issue of an employee using or misusing his position of trust was the *Murray* case.

While this case turned on later actions of the petitioners in publicly protesting the suppression of the petition, the original act of petition itself presented an interesting question which could have been decided either way, depending on the predilection of the judges. The more liberal view held that, since the subject matter of the petitions did not bear upon any aspect of their work nor was it critical to the host government, the right of the Peace Corpsmen to write and publish their petition remained protected. If one presumed role of the Peace Corps was to export the basic tenets of democracy, and if the members of the Peace Corps supposedly exemplified the best of America, the sight of these members being prohibited from asserting their First Amendment rights would be somewhat incongruous. Fortunately for Murray, the judge in his case took this expansive view of First Amendment rights and, as a result, he prevailed in his litigation.[57]

---

56. I think that the AAUP has conceded far too much in its statement on extramural utterance. Only when there is a deliberate attempt to imply that the statement has an institutional basis and such statement would be contrary to the previous public position of the institution, should such an act be the basis of job action.

57. The statement in *Pickering*, that at certain times, certain employees have almost an obligation to speak would be an analogous situation to the problem of institutional identification. If the speech of certain public employees is especially valued because

The opposite view, which is also plausible, holds that this situation did not involve the individual views of a large number of persons employed by the government on an issue not concerned with their jobs, but a concerted attempt by a group of public employees, all with a common employer and common employment goals, to use their positions (or at least their job identification) for the purpose of undermining their superiors, rather than merely giving credence to their personal views. In this view the effect of their petition was not merely to show that individual government employees hold different views on certain government policy, which would clearly be protected speech; but rather, because of the concerted nature of the action, to show, especially to foreign governments, that a deep cleavage existed in the government between young, nonpermanent employees and those in more permanent positions, or at least those in policy making levels of the government. The interpretation the government put on the matter was that the real purpose of this petition was not simply to express beliefs about the war in Vietnam, but rather to inform the governments of South America (and the world, when their petition was publicized) that government policy does not represent the feelings of all, or even a great many, employees, but is really subject to internal challenges. As a result, great suspicion could be cast upon government policy.

My feeling is that the government's characterization of the petition's purpose was absolutely correct, but that the Court was equally correct in recognizing that allowing the government to suppress this petition would also allow the government to suppress each and every type of policy dissent by its employees. Thus, the Court in effect treated this as job-connected speech and simply held that in these circumstances job-connected speech was protected, since the government cannot be allowed to suppress each and every bit of criticism that an employee may have with each and every policy. This problem will be discussed in greater detail in the discussion of job-connected speech.

Another problem involves use of the employment situation as the forum for speech, rather than the presence of any job-connected content. The *Goldwasser* case, previously discussed, featured a forum obviously inappropriate for the speech, leaving the employee subject to discipline. However, situations do exist in which the employment forum is used indirectly rather than directly, creating new problems.

---

of the expertise and knowledge of that employee, then it is necessary in some cases for the employee to identify himself as a public employee. The effect of this identification would not be to equate the views of the employee with the agency, but rather to give added value to the views expressed by virtue of the position of the speaker.

One interesting case came from the Chicago area, and concerned Carolyn Kiiskila, a civilian employed at the Fort Sheridan Military Reservation. She was a former member of the Women's Army Corps and was a member of the Veterans for Peace organization.[58]

One activity scheduled by the Veterans for Peace was a rally to be held in Chicago in October of 1968. Several days before the rally Kiiskila, in a casual conversation on the post, mentioned the rally to a lieutenant. She informed him that she would be a chairwoman at the rally and gave him a ticket to attend it.

The next day the plaintiff distributed literature concerning the rally at locations near, but not on, the Great Lakes Naval Air Station. That evening she returned to Fort Sheridan, accompanied by a serviceman. Upon entering the post she was stopped by military police; her car was searched and about fifty pounds of anti-Viet Nam War literature was discovered in the trunk. Much of the literature had allegedly been in Kiiskila's car for several months. The plaintiff was interrogated and escorted off the base. Several days later, the commanding officer of Fort Sheridan issued an order permanently excluding Kiiskila from the post. No hearing was held prior to the issuance of this order. The basis of this order was that the events occurring on those two days, mainly the conversation and the distribution of literature, violated a Fort Sheridan regulation which prohibited picketing, demonstrations, sit-ins, protest marches, political speeches, and similar activities to be held on the base. As a result of the exclusion from the post, Kiiskila was obviously unable to perform her duties, and her civilian employment was terminated.

The plaintiff went into federal court to seek reinstatement. At the lower level she lost the case, with the court holding that the Army had the power to exclude her from the base without a hearing, that it was not a violation of due process to do so, and that this exclusion did not violate her First Amendment rights. The court of appeals, however, reversed that decision.

The basis of the court of appeals decision was that the Army failed to show any peculiar interest that would give it the right to punish the plaintiff in the way it did for the assertion of her constitutional rights. It held that all citizens have a right, indeed almost a duty to engage in criticism of governmental policies, including the use of assemblies to do so. Of most importance, it held that the fact that the person happens to be a government employee is irrelevant to a citizen's right to engage in that particular speech. The reason for this is that dismissal from government employment, like criminal sanctions or damages, might in-

---

58. Kiiskila v. Nichols, 433 F.2d 745 (7th Cir. 1970).

hibit the propensity of the citizen to exercise his right to freedom of speech and expression. It was the court's feeling that the defendants "used the plaintiff's status as a civilian employee at Fort Sheridan to discourage plaintiff and others like her from exercising their rights. . . . In the absence of any overwhelming countervailing governmental interest peculiarly pertaining to the plaintiff's job at Fort Sheridan, we think her exclusion from the base and the concomitant loss of her job are unconstitutional under the First Amendment."[59]

One point raised by the government and specifically knocked down by the court was that the exclusion was not because of her antiwar activities, but because of the commander's fear that she would engage in similar conduct on the base in violation of the regulation. The court held emphatically that this was not a valid reason to exclude in the manner she had been excluded, and that something more substantial than the fears of a military commander that a person would engage in prohibited activity must be present.

The important point in this case is that the court provided a very narrow construction of job-related speech. By excluding from the definition such incidents as Kiiskila giving a ticket to the rally to a fellow member of her base and her petitioning in the area of another military base, the court gave full breadth to the assertion of First Amendment rights.

In the last few years, however, the Supreme Court has heard cases that both affirm and modify Kiiskila.[60] In *Flower* v. *United States*, the Court overturned the conviction of a civilian who had been distributing leaflets on an open street of a military base after having been previously fined. The Court, in that case, held that the military had abandoned any claim to a special interest on that street and that the case was more one of leafletting on a public thoroughfare.

In *Greer* v. *Spock*, however, the Court upheld a refusal by federal and state authorities to allow Benjamin Spock and some other candidates to hold a rally on the military base, citing the special character of military bases.

59. 433 F.2d 745, 749 citing New York Times v. Sullivan, 376 U.S. 254 (1964); Bond v. Floyd, 385 U.S. 116 (1966):

> An essential corollary of this principle [of New York Times v. Sullivan] is that a citizen is permitted, even expected to criticize the policy decisions of his government. This includes expressions in opposition to national foreign policy in Vietnam. . . . Indeed because plaintiff is a former WAC and because she comes into contact with many members of the Armed Forces, her criticism of military policy may be especially valued by society.

60. Flower v. United States, 407 U.S. 197 (1972); Greer v. Spock 424 U.S. 818 (1976).

Both these cases arose in the context of nongovernment employees seeking access to a military base for First Amendment purposes. They did not involve an employee, as in *Kiiskila*, which has a unique fact situation. Based on these cases I think that if a *Kiiskila*-type case reached the Supreme Court, it would hold that in areas not basically public the speech could be prevented, but the employee could not be dismissed without a specific warning that certain types of activity were not to be permitted on certain areas of the base. This is a moderation of the Seventh Circuit rule, but each order would probably have to be examined as to scope.

While the court states, as it must, that incidents could occur in which off-base or off-job activity could lead to a job prohibition, it takes the interesting position that the issue of whether speech could be prohibited if it conflicts with the job has still not been determined by the United States Supreme Court, and was intentionally left open in the *Pickering* case. While the Court stated that it would not be necessary for it to decide that particular issue, since in this case the speech was neither job-connected nor of a type that would interfere with the job, the implication of its particular position was that situations may exist in which speech that conflicts with the job may nonetheless still be protected and the employee not punishable for engaging in the same.

One final item: in practice in the field the employing agency often, with great sanctimony, says that it would never try to punish the employee for protected speech. It may, however, try to get around that particular issue by dismissing the employee for a violation of some kind of administrative rule conveniently found at the time the plaintiff engaged in this controversial speech.

A fine example of this is the case of Ellis Hodgin.[61] Ellis Hodgin was a librarian in the small southern city of Martinsville, Virginia. A dedicated librarian, Hodgin nonetheless incurred a great deal of controversy in the community because of his belief that the library should be used in a certain way, plus the fact that he grew a beard. The dispute between Hodgin and the city fathers became very strained when Hodgin became active in a movement to forbid city public schools to engage in a religious education program, a program by all standards unconstitutional. Hodgin had a daughter in school at that time who was affected by this program. Finally, when as a parent Hodgin could no longer secure relief from the school board, he went into federal court and brought suit challenging the constitutionality of the program. The suit eventually was successful, but four days after filing, Hodgin was asked to resign by the

---

61. Hodgin v. Noland, 435 F.2d 859 (4th Cir. 1970).

city manager. No reason was given for the request. When Hodgin refused, he was again brought before the city manager several days later and summarily fired with no cause given.

At the time of his firing, Hodgin was afforded no reasons. However, when he went into court to seek reinstatement and damages, he was given an administrative reason for his firing; he had violated a regulation concerning overspending his budget. This case was appealed to the Supreme Court; it was held for nine months before being denied certiorari in the wake of *Roth* and *Sindermann*.

In summary, in respect to statements and other First Amendment activities, a public employee has a broad right to engage in activities which have no real connection to his job. Difficulty arises not because of legal limitations, but because of the peculiar situation of the employee. He may work for a government employing agency unusually harsh in its attempts to deal with its employees; in such a situation, the employee is faced with a difficult matter peculiar to himself. Or he may work in an area in which the courts are unresponsive to his action, leaving him unable to get relief afforded in other parts of the country. However, as a matter of doctrine, a speech made without any job connection is made as if by a private citizen, and thus is protected.

Job Related Speech

To what degree are First Amendment assertions made by a public employee which concern some aspect of his employment protected by the Constitution? This question is important, because a public employee engaging in a First Amendment activity concerning his employment is in a very special position with respect to the impact of his speech. Whereas an educator talking about the Vietnam war will be listened to neither more nor less than any other educated person, an educator talking about an aspect of the administration of the school district in which he teaches would *indeed* be listened to with great attention, and his words would have a much greater impact than another's. Concomitantly, the effect of his speech on the employing agency would thus be much greater because it was based on knowledge of position, rather than on mere opinion. In such situations the agency will obviously attempt to limit such speech, because its impact would be considerably greater than if the speech was made on a subject totally irrelevant to the employment situation. Because of the countervailing factors of the necessity for expert and informed opinion to be given to the public, and the equally great desire on the part of the employing agency not to be subject to public criticism by its own employees, the legal factors involved in such speech are equally controversial. In this area all absolutes disappear. The public employee has no absolute right to engage in public criticism of his employer or aspects of his employment; the public agency has no absolute right to prohibit employees from engaging in such types of activities.

In short, this area is one of evolving law, with important questions of public interest in the matter of the public's right to know versus the agency's interests in functioning without public disclosure. This issue converges in a discussion of the employee's right to engage in public discussion about his employment, especially if such discussion is derogatory in nature, as far as agency interest is concerned.

Job-connected speech can be broken down into two general categories —internal and external communication. External communication will necessitate a further breakdown into petition and outside dissemination to the general public. These areas will be discussed separately.

Internal Communication

Speech can occur even if the expression itself is not disseminated to an outside source. A private memorandum or an oral discussion made by an employee within the context of his agency is as much speech as a letter to a newspaper editor or a petition to Congress. An internal communication is speech because the employee is attempting to assert his particular point of view or criticism of others, and asserts it in such a way as to influence others to accept it. Thus, in the context of the First Amendment an internal communication is treated the same as other forms of communication.

While internal memorandums are considered speech in a technical sense, the usual agency interest with respect to this type of speech nevertheless tends to be much higher than it would be with respect to a public communication. The reason for such higher governmental interest is ironically due to the very fact that the employee used an internal rather than an external forum. Clearly the government has an absolute right to set up departmental regulations and general conditions of work. These could naturally be challenged when they limit protected constitutional rights that an employee would have as a citizen, or when administrative irregularities are involved.

If the administration of a given agency tends to frown upon internal criticism and the employee chooses internal criticism as his means of speech, he has in effect waived his opportunity to challenge the constitutionality of his limitations by choosing to operate within the framework of the administrative setup. He is therefore subject to that type of setup. Thus, in a situation in which an employee might freely have engaged in public criticism of his employer, internal criticism could result in both punishment and a limited legal standing.[62]

An interesting example of this situation involves a case from Minnesota.[63] In that case, the plaintiff was a welfare caseworker who had made allegedly defamatory statements in his official case reports. The material was inserted in these reports contrary to official instruction governing the form and content of such reports. The plaintiff's aim was to challenge the right of welfare officials to proscribe the form for official use. In finding against the plaintiff, the federal circuit court of appeals made the following statement, which rather distinctly provides the reason why a public employee stands in great danger of having job action taken when he makes internal statements which displease his superiors:

> The plaintiff asserts a right to make any criticism or charges he deems warranted under the protection of the First and Fourteenth Amendments. Within the bounds imposed by the laws of libel and slander no one would deny the plaintiff has this right. Plaintiff, however, has no right to public employment. He may speak as he pleases and level charges at all suspects. But if the exercise of this privilege disrupts his own work and reduces the efficiency of the department he is subject to discharge for cause. The plaintiff has an absolute obligation to satisfactorily perform the duties and work inherent in his position. One of these duties is to conform to departmental regulations in making his investigations and reports. He may speak as he wishes but he must also be responsible for his statements. When speech is disruptive of the proper functioning of the public's business the privilege of government employment may be withdrawn without it being said that he was denied his freedom of speech.[64]

While certain statements made by the court echo the old Holmes doctrine, nonetheless when dealing with internal communications, the factors that the government may assert to limit speech, such as the nature of the

---

62. See Emerson, *The System of Freedom of Expression*, pp. 570–74. Hilton v. Sullivan, 334 U.S. 323 (1948); Scott v. Macy 349 F.2d 182 (D.C. Cir. 1965), affirmed 402 F.2d 582 (1963), cert. dismissed 379 U.S. 904 (1964); Carter v. United States, 417 F.2d 384 (D.C. Cir. 1970). These cases deal with the illegality of dismissal of government employees for lack of administrative cause, rather than violation of constitutional rights. However, the same standard of fitness for and interference with the particular job are used in both instances.

63. Jenson v. Olson, 353 F.2d 825 (8th Cir. 1965).

64. 353 F.2d at 829.

job and administrative necessity, play a much more important role and, indeed, can become paramount.[65]

Even when such statements are made within proper channels set up to handle them, the employee could find himself dismissed if his information is either wrong or not totally accepted by his superiors. In one case, the plaintiff made defamatory statements to an investigator, in which he charged two of his superiors in the field office with dishonesty and incompetence, saying that one was communistically inclined and the other failed to report a sexual pervert. The investigator exonerated the two persons so charged, and as a result the plaintiff was dismissed from his position immediately. The dismissal was affirmed on the grounds that no constitutional rights of the plaintiff had been violated.

Thus, if an employee wishes to take advantage of his constitutional rights to criticize his superiors, he is surprisingly better advised to make such criticism in a public or semipublic fashion, rather than through a form of internal communication, although this, too, has its hazards.

External Communication

External communication includes both petition and public dissemination. In a legal sense these are two different types of speech with different legal consequences. Public dissemination is simply the act of a public employee making his beliefs known to the public in general through the means of public media, rather than government channels. Such dissemination could be in the form of a letter to an editor, a speech on television, or one of a multitude of other ways. Petition is the making of a formal protest to another government body.

Petition. Petition refers to the act of a public employee making statements to another public body regarding conditions of his employment. The public body can be either legislative or administrative, but differs from the area of internal communication in that the body resides outside the normal working relationship and the normal channels of communication. Petition also differs from public dissemination in the audience and the intent of the speaker. These differences have a substantive impact in determining the validity of the speech.

The right of a public employee to petition government bodies other than his own agency to redress his personal grievances or to correct a situation he found to be wrong within his agency is one which preceded the general application of constitutional principles to public employees. The right of public employees to petition Congress has a long legislative history.

65. Arnett v. Kennedy, 416 U.S. 134, discussed previously, bears this out.

All cases which have arisen concerning the right of public employees to petition for redress of grievances have arisen in the context of federal employees.[66] The dearth of law concerning state employees petitioning their state legislatures or state executives can be explained in a number of ways. For instance, no state statutes in any of the fifty states give state public employees the right to petition. In addition, state employees have traditionally believed that state legislatures and state administrators would tend to be less responsive than Congress to the demands of public employees. Therefore, while state employees have hardly been quiet, their protests tend to be through the use of public dissemination rather than petition as such.[67] Accordingly, this discussion will concentrate exclusively on the question of the right of federal employees to petition Congress, the administrative branch, or the executive branch of government. The principles which have evolved out of the cases to follow can be considered applicable to state employees as well, should such cases arise.

In 1912, when the doctrines of Holmes in the *McAuliffe* case were in effect, public employees were deemed to have no constitutional rights. Congress then passed Section 7102 to the Civil Service Laws, better known as the Lloyd-La Follette Act of 1912. The section stated:

> The right of employees individually or collectively, to petition Congress or a member of Congress, or to furnish information to either House of Congress, or to a committee or member thereof may not be interfered with or denied.[68]

The passage of Section 7102 was in reaction to certain executive orders issued by Presidents Theodore Roosevelt and William Howard Taft, better known as the "Gag Rules," which were designed to limit, if not entirely prohibit, the right of civil servants, especially post office em-

66. Houston v. United States (156 Ct. Cl. 38) 297 F.2d 838 (1962); cert. denied 371 U.S. 815 (1962). See also Krennrich v. United States, 340 F.2d 653 (1965), cert. denied 382 U.S. 570 (1965) (anonymous letters to superiors, fellow workers).

67. Brukiewa v. Police Commissioner of Baltimore, 257 Md. 36 (1967); 263 A2d 210 (Md. Ct. App. 1967).

68. The Lloyd-La Follette Act of 1912 was primarily a postal administrative statute. The particular provision which has erroneously become known as the act was simply a rider added to protect the postal employees in particular and federal employees generally in the exercise of their right to petition Congress. For an exhaustive study of the area of rights of federal employees to petition Congress, see note, The Right of Government Employees to Furnish Information to Congress: Statutory and Constitutional Aspects, 57 VIRGINIA L. REV. 885 (1971).

ployees, to petition Congress.[69] The executive order formulated by President Taft read as follows:

> No bureau, office, or division chief or subordinate in any department of the Government . . . shall apply to either House of Congress or to any committee of either House of Congress, or to any Member of Congress . . . for Congressional action of any kind, except with the consent or knowledge of the head of the department; nor shall any such person respond to any request for information from either House of Congress, or any committee of either House of Congress, or any Member of Congress, except through, or as authorized by the head of his department.[70]

The uproar caused by these rules, especially by organized postal employees, led to the passage of the rider to the Lloyd-La Follette Act, Section 7102.

The primary issue concerning the nature of this particular law is whether or not this is merely an administrative remedy statute, or if it grants to public employees certain constitutional rights. Legislative history can provide some answers. Another purpose of the law was to allow Congress to find out what the executive branch was doing by encouraging petitions from federal employees, a problem of prime importance today. In language which could easily have been spoken by Senator Proxmire or any other current congressional "watchdog" of the executive branch, Representative Lloyd, coauthor of the amendment, stated that government employees should be encouraged to speak their mind: "This government will be more popular when its official proceedings are an open book and the conduct of its officials continuously subject to scrutiny and investigation."[71]

---

69. Executive Order No. 163, Jan. 31, 1902, reprinted in 48 *Congressional Record* 5223 (1912):

> All officers and employees of the United States are hereby forbidden, either directly or indirectly, individually or through associations, to solicit an increase of pay or to influence or attempt to influence in their own interest any other legislation whatever, either before Congress or its committees, or in any way save through the heads of the departments in or under which they serve, on penalty of dismissal from the Government service.

70. Executive Order No. 1142, Nov. 26, 1909, reprinted in 48 *Congressional Record* 4513 (1912).

71. 48 *Congressional Record* 10671. The purpose behind the section seems to be twofold. First, there was the desire to grant substantive rights to public employees. Remember that this was the height of the Progressive Era and the beginning of the

In addition to legislative history, a look at the judicial interpretation of the section can be helpful in defining the scope of the problem. Unfortunately, however, apparently few cases were involved with the problem.[72] In *Turner* v. *Kennedy*, an FBI agent petitioned various congressmen after being denied a transfer of offices, claiming his talents were being poorly used by the FBI. His letters were critical of the FBI and some of its policies. He was dismissed from the bureau, and his dismissal was ultimately upheld by the circuit court of appeal.[73] In dissent, Judge Fahy said that Section 7102 does protect the First Amendment rights of the plaintiff, with the limitations on that right being the same limitation put on freedom of the press in *New York Times* v. *Sullivan*, a famous case concerning whether or not a public official could sue a newspaper for libel. In that case, the Supreme Court held that a public official could not sue for libel unless actual, malicious intent upon the part of the newspaper to destroy the reputation of the public official by the publication of false and misleading information was proved. Since one of the allegations against Turner apparently was supposed falsehood or misrepresentation in his petitions, within its own terms *Turner* v. *Kennedy* might be decided differently today, since *Pickering* implied that mere mistake would not limit constitutional protection, provided the statements were not purposefully false or misleading. However the *Arnett* case, involving the OEO employee who made allegedly libelous statements, puts a premium on the employee showing that any misinformation was simply a mistake.[74]

Wilson administration. With labor unions, especially public unions, beginning to show some muscle, an obvious target was the "Gag Rules." The natural tenor of the arguments in favor of the rider would be to give the employees a voice, not simply a remedy.

72. Steck v. Connally, 199 F. Supp. 104 (D. D.C. 1969); Meehan v. Macy, 392 F.2d 822 (D.C. Cir.), modified 425 F.2d 469 (1968), vacated 425 F.2d 472 (1969) (en banc per curium); Levine v. Farley, 107 F.2d 186 (D.C. Cir. 1939), cert. denied 308 U.S. 622 (1940); Eustace v. Day, 198 F. Supp. 233 (D. D.C. 1961); Ruderer v. United States 412 F.2d 1285 (Ct. Cl. 1969), cert. denied 398 F.2d 857. The major cases in this area are: Turner v. Kennedy, 332 F.2d 304 (D.C. Cir. 1964), cert. denied 379 U.S. 901 (1964), and Swaaley v. United States, 376 F.2d 857 (Ct. Cl. 1967).

73. Neither the district court nor the circuit court discussed the applicability of 1702, apparently assuming that the statute didn't apply to Turner's actions.

74. 332 F.2d 307, quoting Mr. Justice Story in his *Commentaries on the Constitution*, 5th ed. (1891), vol. 2, §1895, p. 645, note b:

> The statements made in petitions addressed to the proper authority, in a matter within its jurisdiction, are so far privileged. That the petitioner is not liable, civilly or criminally for making them; though they prove to be untrue and injurious, unless he made them maliciously.

In *Swaaley* v. *United States,*[75] the United States Court of Claims accepted the view of Judge Fahy and held that the standard to be applied in cases of dismissal of public employees was the standard of *New York Times* v. *Sullivan.* In the *Swaaley* case, a mechanic at the Brooklyn Navy Yard, was dismissed after he petitioned the secretary of the Navy complaining that promotions in his department were made on the basis of favoritism and bribing. His letter to the then secretary of the Navy claimed that the promotion policy of his department was, "usually made in an unfair and prejudicial manner."[76] Swaaley gave the names of certain shop personnel most responsible for these alleged discriminations and then cited various incidents of alleged favoritism and wrongdoing at the shipyard. He specifically mentioned an incident in which he asked his supervisor why he did not get a job promotion, stating that the promotions were going to less qualified people. The supervisor allegedly responded, "You do not get a promotion because you deserve it, you must pay for it. When you are ready, I will let you discuss the terms with [name omitted]." After a series of administrative hearings, Swaaley brought suit for back pay in the court of claims.[77] The court held that Swaaley was dismissed solely for petitioning his superiors, and that such petition is protected by the First Amendment to the Constitution and Section 7102.[78]

75. 376 F.2d 857 (Ct. Cl. 1967).

76. 376 F.2d at 858.

77. After dismissal, a Hearing Advisory Committee was convened by the base commander. This committee upheld the dismissal on the grounds that "plaintiff failed to demonstrate either that his statements are true or that there was a reasonable basis on which an employee might make such statements." (Ibid.) The case was then appealed to the Director, New York Region, Civil Service Commission's Board of Appeal and Review, which reversed the previous findings and ordered reinstatement on the grounds that many of the plaintiff's allegations "were essentially true and that the shipyard made no investigation" except as to one charge. (Ibid.) However, the Navy got a rehearing and the Commission sustained the dismissal on the grounds that the investigation of the one charge (the statement of bribery) was sustained and this ground alone was enough to justify the removal. (Ibid., p. 860.)

78. The Court decided that petitions of this type were protected by the First Amendment and were subject only to the limitation which Judge Fahy derived from New York Times v. Sullivan. In Turner v. Kennedy the Court stated:

> No statutes or regulations are cited to us specifically delimiting the form and content of petitions for redress of grievances by Federal employees to the heads of their departments. There seems to be no reason, in the inherent nature of Federal employment, or otherwise, why *New York Times v. Sullivan, supra,* should not be deemed in the absence of legislation or regulation, to state the limits a Federal employee may go towards defaming supervisory officials in the course of a petition, without loss of First Amend-

Thus, while the law interpreting Section 7102 is still somewhat unclear because of *Turner* v. *Kennedy*, the trend of recent decisions can lead to no other conclusion than that Section 7102 gives federal employees substantive rights which have, at their base, a constitutional standard.

One final subarea of the right to petition Congress is the situation in which a federal employee is compelled to testify by a congressional committee as to certain policies of his agency. Section 1505 of Title 18 of the United States Code makes interference with any witness before a congressional committee a federal crime.[79] Some doubt has been expressed, however, that this statute protects federal employees whose testimony is compelled.[80] The problem is that the statute talks about injury to person or property of the witness, and in 1940 government employment was not considered to be property. While the law has changed sufficiently to allow a reading of property to include employment, the fact that no equivalent civil remedy to the basis of the criminal charge makes the statute virtually unenforceable.

However, a recent, very publicized case illustrated the extreme difficulties the public employee has in enforcing his rights when he has been dismissed, or at least suffers harm, through the use of the petition.[81] It also shows that First Amendment rights do pertain to the petition power. This is the case of Ernest Fitzgerald, a force analyst for the Air Force. In 1968 he petitioned and testified before a congressional committee,

---

ment protection. . . . Therefore, we hold that a petition by a Federal employee is covered by the First Amendment and if it included defamation of any Federal Official, protection is lost only under the circumstances in which a newspaper would lose protection if it defamed such official. [376 F.2d at 864.]

79. U.S.C. §1505 (1964) provides that:

. . . whomever threatens to influence, intimidate, or impede any witness in . . . connection with any inquiry or investigation being had by either House or any committee of either House, or any joint committee of the Congress: or

Whoever injures any party or witness in his person or property on account of his testifying of having testified to any matter pending therein; . . . shall be fined not more than $5000 or imprisoned not more than five years or both.

80. The legislative history would seem to indicate that Congress was considering physical threats against witnesses called to testify before one of its committees. The subject of federal employees didn't enter into the mind of the congressman drafting the statute. See note, The Right of Government Employees to Furnish Information to Congress, 57 VIRGINIA L. REV. 885, 897.

81. Fitzgerald v. Hampton, 467 F.2d 755 (1973).

disclosing vast cost overruns on the C-5 cargo plane contract running into billions of dollars.

While the effect of his testimony was to ultimately result in a saving of money for the government, his Air Force superiors, both military and civilian, were so incensed with his testimony that he was taken off his job as a force analyst on questions of airplane contracts, given the job of studying the course of bowling alleys on Air Force bases in Thailand, and eventually dismissed from government service.

He sued; after protracted litigation the Court of Appeals for the District of Columbia ruled that he was dismissed solely because of his testimony before a congressional committee, that his right to do so was protected both by the Constitution and the writer to the Lloyd-La Follette Act, and as such the dismissal was illegal. He was reinstated with back pay and at present is still employed by the Air Force.

Public Dissemination. The most important area concerning public employee's freedom of speech is the public dissemination of information by the public employee which involves a job-related matter. This is difficult because, in this particular area, all the conflicting interests between the right of the public employee to assert his First Amendment rights and the interests of the governmental body come to a head. First Amendment rights are brought into conflict with the right of an agency (1) to prevent criticism by its own employees, and (2) to keep disputes involving the agency within the bounds of the agency, with strong arguments being raised by both sides in favor of their respective positions.

The starting point for discussion is naturally the *Pickering* case, which has been discussed previously in some detail. In *Pickering*, the Supreme Court upheld as constitutionally protected the act of a public school teacher in writing a letter to the editor of his local paper complaining about certain actions of the school board with respect to a bond issue. However, the Court refused to grant a blanket protection to public employees, holding rather that: "the problem in any case is to arrive at a balance between the interest of the teacher, as a citizen, in commenting on matters of public concern in the interest of the state, as an employee, in promoting the efficiency of the public services it performs to its employees."[82] Thus, while the Court spoke in terms of weighing various balances and interests, the important issue remaining with regard to the *Pickering* case, one which must be examined closely, is the free speech interests present in this case which would constitute the balancing factor in Pickering's favor.

82. 391 U.S. at 817.

In determining the outcome of the *Pickering* case the Supreme Court weighed four particular elements involved in the speech; by resolving these in favor of Pickering held that his dismissal was unwarranted. These elements are: (1) confidentiality of information; (2) First Amendment interest in this assertion; (3) confidentiality of working relationships involved, and (4) impact of the speech.

With respect to confidentiality of the information, the key factor to be determined is whether or not the information upon which the assertion of the public employee is based was discovered solely as a consequence of his employment. While *Pickering* does not answer the question of the degree of protection the speech of a public employee may have when it is based upon information solely learned as a public employee, nevertheless the Court emphasized that in this case Pickering's statements were based upon his interpretation of the public's reaction to the school board; indeed, this accounts for certain errors in his statements.

Van Alstyne raised the fascinating question of a situation in which "the information released in a deliberate breach of confidence pertained to a subject that school authorities were falsely representing to the public, that involved an undisclosed policy of the school which itself was illegal, or that was clearly a matter, which viewed objectively, was reasonably subject to the influence of public judgement and review concerning the operation of schools."[83] No easy answer is available for that particular question; indeed, *Pickering* does not seek to answer it. However, as a result of the Pentagon Papers case this has become a matter of great public interest.[84]

While the Pentagon Papers case[85] had certain special ramifications with respect to the means by which the information was obtained and disclosed and the nature of the information itself; conceivably and inevitably a situation will develop in which the public employee makes a

83. *The Constitutional Rights of Teachers and Professors*, 1970 DUKE L. J. 851.
84. The Supreme Court specifically hedged in this situation, stating:

> It is possible to conceive of some positions in public employment in which the need for confidentiality is so great that even completely correct public statements might furnish a permissible ground for dismissal. Likewise, positions in public employment in which the relationship between superior and subordinate is of such a personal and intimate nature that certain forms of public criticism of the superior by the subordinate would seriously undermine the effectiveness of the working relationship between them can also be imagined. We intimate no views as to how we would resolve any specific instance of such situations, but merely note that significantly different considerations would be involved. [391 U.S. at 567, note 4.]

85. New York Times v. United States 403 U.S. 713 (1971).

public statement by way of letter or otherwise, accusing his agency of violating the law, giving the specifics of the violations, and as a result of either being dismissed from the job, subject to criminal prosecution, or more likely both.[86] While to predict how such a case would go would be too difficult, nonetheless I think that any court facing such a case should assume that as a part of his job, the public employee is not only protected but almost has a duty to inform the public of situations in which the agency is violating the law and no relief can be obtained through normal agency channels. This is an aspect of the right to petition of federal employees; yet, as in the *Ellsberg* case, in which Congress refused to act upon the information given to it, the public employee may be left with no alternative but to go to the public itself. In such a situation, a degree of protection should be afforded to the public employee.[87]

The second aspect the Court discussed in the *Pickering* case was whether or not the employee had a First Amendment purpose in his assertion, as opposed to a simple attempt to air a basically private dispute. The facts indicate that the purpose of Pickering's letter had nothing to do with his own personal situation directly, but rather was an attempt to bring to the public an issue which he considered to be important, one in which his particular expertise would be of value. This is in contrast to a situation in which the public employee was seeking some advantage on a personal grievance in his dealing with his employer by the fact of public disclosure. In the latter situation, the agency would have a greater interest in prohibiting the speech, at least until the mechanics of the internal grievance procedure have been exhausted.[88]

However, even if the problem is an intramural one, a total and absolute ban against public dissemination is not called for. If, in a specific

---

86. See S. Ungar, *The Papers and the Papers* (New York: Dutton, 1972), pp. 62–70.

87. According to newspaper accounts, Ellsberg first tried to bring the papers to Senator Fulbright, but he refused to make them public. Later, during the initial furor over the publishing of the "papers," Senator Gravel of Alaska received a copy and proceeded to read portions into the *Congressional Record*. This, in turn, spun off a new constitutional crisis when a federal grand jury in Boston, investigating possible criminal violations occurring from the release (as opposed to copying and dissemination) of the papers, subpoenaed Senator Gravel's legislative assistant, Leonard Rodberg, and representatives of Beacon Press, which subsequently published the grand version of the papers, and asked them if Gravel obtained the papers from Ellsberg. They refused to answer, citing Gravel's congressional immunity. They were cited for contempt. The case was appealed to the Supreme Court, which held 5–4 that they did not have immunity.

88. The court in *Pickering* alluded to the possibility that in certain situations the public's need for information might require that certain public employees, such as teachers, who possess the expertise and facts vital to such debate, must be afforded the right to speak in public. 391 U.S. at 571–72.

situation, the mechanics for resolving internal grievances were inadequate or had been exhausted without satisfaction to the employee, the employee might then seek to "go public." When the issue involves something other than the capability of the employee to perform his job, as in a dispute over policies or an action of the agency in which the public has an interest beyond that of seeing that the employee gets treated fairly, additional First Amendment factors are present which would weigh heavily in the protection of the speech.

Another factor weighed by the Court was whether or not the speech involved the public airing of a disagreement between the employee and his working colleagues or subordinates. The fact that the confidentiality of working relationships issue was not present in Pickering's case was in his favor, but did not affect the fact that this was an important issue. As the Court stated:

> Appellants' employment relationships with the board, and, to somewhat lesser extent, with the superintendent are not the kind of close working relationships for which it can persuasively be claimed that personal loyalty and confidence are necessary to their proper function.[89]

The fourth part of the *Pickering* test concerns the Court's evaluation of the impact of the speech on certain types of protected governmental interests. An unfortunate aspect of the *Pickering* case is not that it used impact as a test, but rather that it found that the speech, in this case, was protected because there was very little impact, because nobody would believe the plaintiff in his assertions, especially those parts that happened to be false. What is most disturbing about this is the implication, which may or may not be valid, that the speech's slight impact gave it added protection; taking this one step further might indicate that if a speech has a definite impact on policy or community action on policy, it will be less protected. Again a further implication might show that if a speech has great impact but also contains false information, the combination of the two might lead to the conclusion that the public employee might not be fit to perform his duties because of this particular activity.

While the assertion that the purposeful falsifying of facts done to change policy could be the basis for action on unfitness for the job, nevertheless the making of a mistake in a public utterance, even a gross error, should hardly be the basis of judging the competency of a public employee, especially when the mistake was based on facts outside a particular field of competence.[90] Anything less than a purposeful misuse of

---

89. *Ibid.* at 570.
90. The problem could be resolved by the use of the New York Times v. Sullivan test as was done by Judge Fahy in his dissent in Turner v. Kennedy. See note 78 *supra*. See also Time Inc. v. Firestone 424 U.S. 448 (1976).

position by virtue of a public utterance should not be the basis of a disciplinary or other type of action when the only basis for the action is use of misleading false statements in public utterance. To hold a public employee to that kind of standard, in effect basing his job on his accuracy, has a chilling effect on his assertion of First Amendment rights. Rather than risk making statements based on honest beliefs, even if some facts are wrong, the public employee will inevitably not speak for fear of losing his job. While the Court presumably did not intend this type of impact in its rule, nevertheless in future decisions the Court should clarify the proposition, or even better, drop the test entirely because of its susceptibility to misuse.

The *Pickering* case was extremely important, if for no other reason than that the United States Supreme Court was the deciding court in the case. However, the principles which went into the making of the *Pickering* case did not originate in that case, but rather had been principles used by other courts and dealt with in similar problems prior to the *Pickering* decision. *Pickering* is crucial because, when the Supreme Court came out on the side of the employee using the balancing test, the effect was a subtle shift in the balancing test in favor of the employee, rather than the governmental body.[91] To see how the *Pickering* case has worked in this regard two cases will be examined, both of which involve similar types of fact situation, one decided before *Pickering* and one afterward.[92] While certain key differences exist between the two cases, these differences are subtle; if not for *Pickering*, the first case would probably be controlling in the second. However, because of the intervening *Pickering* case, the Court in the latter case found that the public employee was protected.

---

91. Subsequent to *Pickering*, the Supreme Court used a similar balancing test in several cases in which the issue was whether public employees could be made to waive immunity before a grand jury upon pain of losing their job. In those cases, the Supreme Court per Justice Fortas held that public employees could not be forced to surrender their First Amendment rights as a condition of their employment, but at the same time public employees are subject to a public trust and they "subject themselves to dismissal if they refuse to account for their performance of this public trust, after proper proceedings, which do not involve an attempt to coerce them to relinquish their constitutional rights." Garner v. Broderick and Uniform and Sanitation Men's Association v. Commissioner of Sanitation, 392 U.S. 273, 284, 285 (1968). See also Spevack v. Klein 385 U.S. 511 (1967); Garrity v. New Jersey, 385 U.S. 453 (1967); Slochower v. Board of Higher Education 350 U.S. 551 (1956).

Following the *Roth* and *Perry* cases, that part of Mr. Justice Fortas's opinion which assumes procedural due process would no longer seem to be valid.

92. Meehan v. Macy, note 72 *supra*; Brukiewa v. Police Commissioner of Baltimore, note 67 *supra*.

Private Meehan was a member of the police force of the Panama Canal Zone and president of the patrolmen's union. In 1964, following the severe rioting in Panama which became a matter of international concern, attempts were made to alleviate or prevent any further situations by changing the makeup of the Panama Canal Police Force. Up to that time, no Panamanians served on the police force, but it was proposed that, in order to prevent future rioting, Panamanians would become members of the force. Meehan, as both a policeman and the president of the union, was called to a meeting with many of the leaders of the Canal Zone; he was told that Panamanians must be placed on the police force to prevent further rioting. Meehan was opposed to the plan, but because of the volatile situation he was told to avoid any press disclosure of this plan and to restrict his protest to regular channels.

The next day, however, Meehan went to the press and voiced his opposition to the plan; one week later he had published five thousand copies of an anonymous letter and two enclosures which consisted of a poem written by another person and an excerpt from the *Congressional Record*, all of which savagely attacked the government, which "recruits the foreign nationals/rejects the native sons." The letter further charged that the governor "refutes the wish of Congress/by subterfuge and lies/twists knives of propaganda/which factual heart beats dies." The letter itself urged the readers to write their congressman and protest the governor's plan, with the strongest paragraph stating:

> We do not intend to perpetrate a personal attack on the Honorable Governor of the Canal Zone, we are aware that he is only a Major General and in reality only an instrument of the boys in the black strip [sic] pants in the State Department whose major goal since the time of Alger Hiss is to implement the policy of New Americanism and erase all opinions opposed to their policies.[93]

On the basis of the arranging for the publishing of this material, Meehan was discharged from the department on the grounds of "conduct unbecoming an officer." He filed suit in the district court asking for reinstatement on the grounds that his dismissal was in violation of his constitutionally protected right of freedom of speech. The district court upheld the dismissal.[94] The case was then appealed to the United States Circuit Court for the District of Columbia which affirmed the dismissal although, in the process, gave an extremely important opinion in terms of its close and subtle analysis of the problem.

93. Meehan v. Macy, at 833.
94. District Court action by summary judgment for defendant, no reported opinion.

Even though this case was decided before *Pickering*, the court found that public employees do in fact have First Amendment rights which cannot be abrogated simply by virtue of their public employment. However, it also introduced the balancing test, which in a sense predicted the form of *Pickering*, though it came out with a different result. The court held that certain circumstances can arise in which the government employee engages in activities incompatible with effectiveness and discipline in administration, and in such situations his constitutional rights may be more limited than those of the ordinary citizen. It found that this particular situation was one in which a limitation of Meehan's constitutional rights was justified.[95]

The court found three factors present in this case which allowed Meehan to be dismissed: (1) the fact that Meehan was aware that the situation in Panama was extremely inflammatory; (2) the fact that Meehan was given direct orders not to go to the public, but to proceed through regular channels to voice his disagreement; and (3) while the court did not use quite this phrasing, the speech went beyond a First Amendment situation, and was in effect an attempt to undercut a governmental policy.

In discussing the situation, the court spoke not only of an inflammatory situation, but also of the confidential information given to Meehan, information which could have an incendiary effect upon the public. Thus, when Meehan made this information public, he not only acted on a situation which was itself inflammatory; but his action was based upon the use of confidential information which the government had a right not to disclose prematurely, and which affected the situation more seriously. This concept was later used by the Supreme Court in *Pickering* when it spoke of one of the tests as being whether or not information on which the assertion of First Amendment rights is based is learned solely as a consequence of employment. In this situation Meehan's action was clearly a deliberate and direct breach of confidence, in which the information used was solely learned from his employment.

The second test used by the circuit court was that Meehan was given direct orders not to make these statements, and told to confine his dis-

95. Meehan was originally charged with (1) conduct unbecoming an officer, (2) failing to obey instructions, and (3) failure to obtain clearance for publication. While the court upheld dismissal on count 1, it remanded the case back to the Civil Service Commission because of uncertainty whether the charges were separate or cumulative and because the warning given Meehan was inadequate. After *Pickering* was decided, the court ordered the Civil Service Commission to reexamine the first count, though it clearly implied that this case was distinguishable from *Pickering* and its original opinion was still valid. See 425 F.2d at 471.

agreement to official channels. The court considered significant the fact that he did have official channels in which to express his disagreement, that he was not faced with an absolute ban on his speech. The court considered this a justification of his dismissal.[96]

Under the unusual fact situation found in *Meehan*, the use of this particular ground as a basis for dismissal was justified, though not for the reasons given by the court. Taken in conjunction, the order not to disclose confidential information, combined with the need to prevent public disclosure of confidential information, could be justified on the basis of confidentiality alone. Meehan did disclose confidential information to the press, the day after he was expressly requested to keep the matter confidential. However, the order to use official channels rather than public dissemination to express displeasure would be subject to severe limitations. I would think that a very different situation would have prevailed had Meehan waited until the plan was officially released by the government and had then gone to the press to attack it. Under such circumstances, I do not think that a ban on public speech by Meehan, especially since Meehan held the public position of president of a policemen's union, could in any way be justified.[97]

A third factor found to be significant by the court was a discussion of the type of speech itself, although I think that too much emphasis was placed on this factor. The court described the documents in the following way:

> In our view, appellant's conduct in printing and beginning distribution of the letter and poem was a legitimate basis for discharge to promote the efficiency of the service. These documents, especially the poem, were intemperate and sarcastic, contemptuous and defamatory lampoon of the governor and his policies. This invective by a police-

96. *Ibid.* at 834. Some weight must be given to the fact that Meehan was a policeman. Judge Leventhal alluded to that in his opinion; when a policeman disobeys a direct order, the balance would tend to come out on the side of the government.

97. The court only briefly discusses the issue of whether Meehan's position as the leader of his policemen's union local put him in a different situation than another policeman without a union position. As a policeman, Meehan was clearly wrong in releasing the documents, but as a union official, he would be acting within the scope of his duties, especially since the dispute was over the inclusion of native Panamanians on the force, which was certainly of interest to the policemen's union. Indeed, the local officials gave the information to Meehan not because he was a policeman, but because he was the head of the local union. When they told him to confine his complaints to official channels, they were not only limiting his speech, but also limiting his effectiveness as a union leader. If the court had put the issue in these terms, they might have still concluded that Meehan's firing was justified, but it could have been decided the other way.

man, charged under the circumstances with special responsibilities and requirements of discipline, against the official ranking as chief of the force, is such a flouting of elemental loyalties to his employer and their common enterprise as to provide cause for discharge, except as the employee's act may be necessary to preserve his own protected rights. Loyalty to the government employer cannot be held to compel servility of thought and expression, but it does set a limit on channels and methods available to indicate disagreement with a superior official.[98]

Thomas I. Emerson, professor of law at Yale, in commenting on this case, made what I believe to be a sound statement. He said that the court in *Meehan* made the mistake of placing primary emphasis on the form and style of communication, because the impact of communication should not be a proper basis of limitation of expression.[99] Thus the *Meehan* case in effect anticipated the other two tests of *Pickering*, namely whether the speech was for a First Amendment purpose, and the impact of the particular speech, especially in the presence of erroneous information.[100]

In my opinion, if this particular information had not been released as part of Meehan's plan to break his order of confidentiality, the information itself should not have been the basis of any type of dismissal. Had he waited until the information concerning the proposed plan was made public through official release rather than by his statement, even if he had issued the very same statement, I do not believe a basis for dismissal would have existed. The information in the statement, while opinionated, was not deliberately false in the sense of publishing misleading information, and its only purpose would have been a First Amendment purpose had it been published after official disclosure. In effect, it would have been an expression using very strong, rather bitter invective by the president of the policemen's union attacking an official government plan which was having a strong effect on the union. Since *New York Times* v. *Sullivan* had already been decided by the Supreme Court at this time, had the other factors not been present, I think Meehan would have been protected by *Sullivan*.

Because this case came down before *Pickering*, I think it should be considered an extraordinary opinion. It anticipated all the issues discussed in *Pickering* and came to the correct conclusion, that Meehan should have been dismissed though for reasons not having to do with the con-

98. Ibid. at 833–34.
99. *The System of Freedom of Expression*, p. 577.
100. See note, The First Amendment and Public Employees—An Emerging Right to Be a Policeman, 37 George Washington L. Rev. 409 (1968).

tent or form of the speech. In addition, it set down rather broad protections for the constitutional rights of public employees and tests which in effect were adopted by the Supreme Court in *Pickering*, fortunately with somewhat greater protection for the employee.

Another case, one with a similar fact pattern to *Meehan*, though with enough differences to allow a court hearing the case after *Pickering* to come to a different conclusion, will now be discussed. The contrast between these cases provides excellent illustrations of how the various competing concepts come into play in an actual case.[101]

Eugene Brukiewa was a member of the Baltimore Police Force for over thirteen years. He was, in addition, the president of the Baltimore City Police Union local. In 1968, in the midst of a public controversy concerning some new reforms instituted by the city police chief, two policemen went on local television to discuss this controversy. During the course of the discussion, the policemen complained that, among other things, the new changes in the rules had caused a loss of morale in the ranks, were a criminal waste of money, and endangered the lives of the policemen. Indeed, they even called the police commissioner an incompetent administrator.[102]

As a result of these statements made on the television show, the two policemen were charged with conduct unbecoming a member of the Baltimore Police Department and conduct prejudicial to or tending to undermine good order, efficiency, or discipline of the department. Ironically, this was the very same charge leveled against Meehan after his statements.

---

101. Brukiewa v. Police Commissioner of Baltimore, 257 Md. 36 (1967).
102. The statements which were the basis of the charge were answers to specific questions. The text of the statements was as follows:

> Q. Do you think Commissioner Pomerlian is a competent effective administrator?
>
> A. (Woodcock) No.
>
> Q. Do you think the union should be in a position criticizing public policy?
>
> A. (Brukiewa) We feel that it's gotten to a point when definitely we have to start criticizing public policy due to the fact we have tried to get together with Commissioner Pomerlian to explain problems that still exist with patrolmen, the reporting system, other issues, but Pomerlian sticks strictly to the I.A.C.P. [International Association of Chiefs of Police] report and we feel definitely that this is nothing to this city.

In addition, Brukiewa stated that morale was at a low ebb because of this report because without a foot patrol people would not be met, and at this point of time he felt that "the bottom will fall out of the city at the rate things are going." Ibid. at 39.

A hearing was held before the Police Department Disciplinary Board and each officer was found guilty of the charge, suspended, and put on probation for a period of twelve months; however they were allowed to go back on duty. The policemen then appealed the matter, first to the commissioner, as a matter of legal requirement; of course the finding was affirmed. Brukiewa then went into the Court of Maryland, where he eventually scored a substantial victory in the Maryland Court of Appeals.[103] The basis of the court's holding was as follows:

> Nothing that Brukiewa said has been charged, shown or found to be false or even inaccurate, nor may it be presumed to be. His personal fitness to perform his daily police duties obviously was not impaired by what he said for the Commissioner kept him on regular active duty. His statements were not directed toward a superior with whom he would come into daily or frequent contact. His statements were not charged, shown or found to have affected discipline or harmony or the general efficiency or effectiveness of the police department. There is no basis in the record and no basis in permissible judicial notice for Judge Godar's statements; that the utterances were in fact corrosive of confidence in the police department and tended to widen the breach between the police and public and that the morale and discipline of the Department obviously had to suffer from the divisive effect of the statements. The burden is on the state to establish that public utterances make the utterer unfit for public service or adversely affect public services to a degree that justifies their restriction. As *Pickering* said, effect or conditions that permissibly inhibit or hamper the exercise of free speech are not to be presumed. Here, neither the police disciplinary board nor the Commissioner made any findings which would support the state's right to inhibit or hamper Brukiewa's right to speak freely on matters of public importance, particularly matters as to which he had experienced expertise.[104]

The court analyzed this case correctly, because it first established that policemen have basic First Amendment rights, and only after giving a presumption of validity to the speech did it begin to weigh the possible countervailing factors such as interference with his ability to do his job, and so on. Indeed, the *Brukiewa* court adopted a "compelling interest" test rather than a strict balancing test and thus found for the policeman in what was otherwise a close case.

To see how the use of this test allows a result different than *Meehan*, a careful study of how the *Brukiewa* court distinguished this case from *Meehan* is in order. It found three main distinctions between the cases:

---

103. Only Brukiewa appealed. Woodcock chose to accept the discipline.
104. Ibid. at 52.

1. In *Meehan* the letter and poem were correctly found to be "intemperate and sarcastic invective and a contemptuous and defamatory lampoon of the Governor of the Canal Zone." In contrast, this court found the statements in this case to be simply an honest belief that some of the commissioner's policies were unsound and not good for the police department or the public.

2. The philosophy and reasoning of *Meehan* was not in accord with *New York Times* v. *Sullivan*, and later *Pickering*.

3. *Meehan* itself was in effect vacated after *Pickering* and thus had no real precedental value.[105]

Unquestionably, the facts in this case and the facts in *Meehan* were different, and the case probably could have been decided the same way even if *Pickering* had not added extra weight to it.[106] First of all, in *Meehan* the speech not only had First Amendment purposes, but also was an attempt to undercut, rather than influence, a policy at its inception by the disclosure of confidential information.[107] Here, the purpose of the speech was purely for First Amendment purposes, namely the expression of an opinion. That the opinion happened to be a strong policy disagreement with the police chief would not in itself be grounds for disallowing the speech.

Second, to disqualify speech the *Pickering* test requires that the speech would have to interfere with the ability of the policeman to do his job or violate confidential relationships or confidential information. In this case, none of these factors were present. The fact that Brukiewa was allowed to go back to work after being put on probation showed that the penalty was not invoked because his speech had interfered with his ability to do his job. Rather it was invoked because the police commissioner felt that a police officer should not publicly criticize the policies of the police department. I also think that the special fact that Brukiewa was a leader of the policemen's union, and in effect was speaking not only as an individual policeman but as a union leader, contributed to the deci-

---

105. Meehan v. Macy, note 72, *supra*, at 56–57. I would argue that the facts are distinguishable. Though, as stated previously, the quality of the speech per se should not be determinative of the validity of the speech; only its effect on interests or the effect of certain interests on the speech should be the basis of the decision on which the speech should be proscribed or lead to job action.

106. The first and second distinctions the court made between *Meehan* and *Brukiewa* would have been valid according to general analysis, once the old Holmes doctrine was no longer assumed valid. By using the loyalty-security cases (see chapter 5) as the basis of the holding, *Brukiewa* could have been decided the same way without *Pickering*.

107. As distinguished from *Meehan*, when the purpose was to undercut policy before it was implemented.

sion. Because of his union position, it would be expected that he would make public utterances on questions which are of great importance to the union, and certainly the reforms instituted by the police commissioner, whether correct or incorrect, were a matter of great interest to the union.[108]

Thus, when he spoke as a union leader any questions of confidences or, for that matter, the ability to do the job would not be present as a disqualifying factor. True, Meehan was a union leader and he also spoke as a leader of the union, but the critical difference between the two cases was that, as explained before, Meehan did not speak in criticism of the policy (allowing the public eventually to decide right or wrong or to allow another governmental body to act), but rather for the purpose of making a disclosure to prevent the policy from being implemented. Thus, Meehan's speech was action rather than speech, while Brukiewa's speech was speech in the classical sense.

The remaining question arising from *Brukiewa* involves the public employee making a speech highly critical of his employer without speaking in a capacity such as that of a union leader.[109] I think *Pickering*

108. According to Emerson, the proper way to determine the validity of a given expression is by applying a speech-action test, with speech being presumptively protected in the absence of a compelling governmental interest, and action likewise unprotected. The difference between the two is not simply between verbal and physical, but is rather based on intent and impact. Thus, expression, verbal or physical, which has a First Amendment intent and impact, is speech; while expression, verbal or physical, which has a non-First Amendment intent or impact, is action.

For example, Emerson would hold that such physical acts as wearing arm bands or burning draft cards are speech; while verbal expression designed to induce criminal activity or to interfere with a valid governmental function ("Let's take over the building") is action rather than speech.

Emerson would hold that Meehan's activities constituted speech, though I believe that since the purpose of his releasing the information was to undercut a policy before implementation, this was action rather than speech; and since he did not have a right to undercut policy, his actions were wrong. See Emerson, *The System of Freedom of Expression*, pp. 17–18, 575–78. See Emerson, Haber and Dorsen, *Political and Civil Rights in the United States* (3rd ed.; Boston: Little, Brown, 1967).

As to the expression-action distinction, contrast Tinker v. Des Moines School District, 303 U.S. 305 (1969) with United States v. O'Brien 391 U.S. 367 (1968). See also Schacht v. United States 398 U.S. 58 (1970); United States v. Berrigan, 437 F.2d 750 (4th Cir. 1971).

109. Courts have now established that there is a constitutional right to unionize, though not to strike. Atkins v. City of Charlotte, 296 F. Supp. 1068 (W.D. N.C. 1969); McLaughlin v. Tilendes, note 38 *supra*; American Federation of State, County and Municipal Employees v. Woodward, 406 F.2d 137 (8th Cir. 1969). Case Comment, 55 VIRGINIA L. REV. 1151. See generally NAACP v. Alabama, ex rel Patterson 357 U.S. 449 (1961); DeJonge v. Oregon 299 U.S. 353 (1937).

shows that the fact of union leadership or official position among public employees is really not a relevant factor in the sense that it must be present to guarantee speech; rather its presense only adds extra weight to the legitimacy of the speech. Pickering had no official position, and spoke solely as an individual teacher expressing his personal views. Thus, where no union position or similar situation is present, the validity of the public employee's speech should be determined strictly according to the *Pickering* test.[110]

In 1974, the United States Supreme Court decided a case that contained certain elements of the cases previously decided in this section and, though it found against the public official, the impact this case had on substantive rights of public employees was probably less than its impact on the procedural issues. The case, *Arnett* v. *Kennedy*,[111] concerned a field representative in the Office of Economic Opportunity charged with making slanderous public statements accusing his superiors of bribery. He was dismissed from federal service on the basis of the just cause provision. Several issues before the Supreme Court concerned the nature of the hearing he was to be given or the lack of such; substantively, however, the issue was whether or not the standard of just cause had become so broadened in its ramifications that it would have an inhibiting effect upon the rights of free speech of public employees. The Court, with Justices Douglas, Brennan, and Marshall, found the statute was not unconstitutional, holding instead that it was not designed to limit the protected expressions of public employees, but rather to cover situations like the fact situation in question, in which the employee made false accusations which had a devastating impact on the efficiencies of the service.

I think the real impact of this case is not that it strips away protected constitutional rights of public employees with respect to freedom of expression guaranteed by *Pickering*; indeed the Court specifically held that *Pickering* was not in any way overruled. The case did indicate that in those close situations discussed previously where speech may have some impact on the job or job-connected things and the just cause standard is applied, the government could now be given the benefit of the doubt in close cases, whereas under *Pickering* alone the employee would be

110. Wellington and Winter, *Securing Collective Bargaining in Public Employment,* 79 YALE L.J. 805 (1968); Khul, *Strikes and Public Employment* 67, MICHIGAN L. REV. 931 (1969). See Rankin v. Shanker 23 N.Y. 2d 111, 242 N.E. 2d 802 (1960); School District for City of Holland v. Holland Educational Association, 380 Mich. 314, 157 N.W. 2d 206 (1968), where courts gutted the application of strong anti-strike laws because of questions of public policy.

111. 416 U.S. 134 (1974).

given the benefit of the doubt. This, to some degree, indicates a narrowing of rights in the gray areas which are in many ways the areas of greatest public concern, where the employee is, in effect, "blowing a whistle" on his employers. I think that the *Arnett* case places a burden on the employee to be absolutely correct factually; wild allegations, no matter how well-intended, if not supported in whole or at least in substantial part by facts, will probably now be the basis for dismissal.

As a matter of policy, full vent must be allowed public employees in their assertion of First Amendment rights. The recent rise in the militancy of public employees through unions or as individuals, especially among teachers, policemen, and firemen, makes absolutely imperative the concept that no reasonable limits should be put on First Amendment rights. To prohibit public employees from making full use of First Amendment rights would encourage them to engage in much more militant tactics. As long as they are denied the right to strike, they must be allowed to have the alternate right of strong public expression of their particular grievances. Strikes of public employees, especially with underlying bitterness, are extraordinarily destructive of the fabric of public life; witness the continuing scars resulting from the 1968 teachers' strike in New York City.

Conclusion

As of this writing, the law regarding the rights of freedom of expression for public employees has been settled; witness *Mt. Healthy* v. *Doyle.* I believe that the law is clear and will not be changed; an unconnected expression by a public employee, barring any special circumstances, will be clearly protected. As for job-connected speech, whether external or internal, as long as the employee has the constitutional right to engage in such activities, the decision of the Court clearly places a burden on him to be factually correct; any employee who chooses to take on his employer through a forum other than his own agency is running a severe risk of finding himself subject to some kind of job action unless he can support his allegations.

Finally, decisions in *Roth, Sindermann,* and later in *Arnett* bearing upon the question of procedure of due process have had an additional substantive impact. At present the employer, except where the employee is tenured or has specific rights to proceed to due process under law (as most federal employees do), does not have to give reasons for any kind of job action; the employee subject to such actions will thus find it increasingly difficult to vindicate himself. If the employer has to give reasons, these reasons can be subject to scrutiny; if obviously unsupportable, the employee will find vindication easier.

In short, the law is now reduced to a case-by-case basis, with each situation decided not in any broad, sweeping terms, but simply on the facts. Thus, public employees anticipating conflict with their employers through public statements will find that exact knowledge of the law is absolutely imperative; if necessary they must seek legal advice prior to engaging in these activities so as to enhance their chances of success, should something happen as a result of their speech.

Chapter 4

Political Activities

While *Pickering* and other cases have now guaranteed that all public employees may freely engage in protected First Amendment rights so long as such rights do not interfere with their ability to perform their public jobs, nevertheless one area of activity, akin to First Amendment activity, exists in which public employees are under far greater restrictions than any private citizen. This area is the right to engage in partisan political activities; the Supreme Court has recently not only affirmed but increased restrictions on political activities of public employees.

Historically, a recurring theme in American political life has been the conflict between public officials, who wish to use their government jobs as the basis for establishing and maintaining their political positions, and other elements in society who wish to completely detach the Civil Service from partisan political activity. While utilization of government positions as a means of maintaining political power actually originated with the founding of the Republic, nevertheless, for the nation's first forty years, a kind of merit system based on background and breeding prevailed, so that government jobs were usually filled by persons qualified to perform them. In addition, the concept of government held by both Federalists and Republicans tended to downgrade the importance of government in the affairs of the country, except insofar as its role in performing certain vital functions such as national defense and banking.

However, with the election of Andrew Jackson in 1828, a vast change occurred as to the government's role in the life of the country. Not only did Jackson and the Democrats view the government as a means for the average citizen to assert his influence in national affairs, but in addition Jacksonians looked upon the government as a means of perpetuating their power through the process of creating government jobs and filling them with political appointments. This, of course, is commonly referred to as the "spoils system," although the term is somewhat misleading. The importance of the spoils system was not that government jobs would be filled by political appointments, but that jobs were actually created for the very purpose of being filled with political appointments; existing Whig jobholders were purged.[1]

Jackson, indeed, did not invent the political spoils system; all presidents since Washington had been filling government jobs with their friends and supporters. The so-called Jacksonian revolution was also not the origin of political parties; the Democratic party could be traced back to Jefferson, Aaron Burr, and the original Tammany Hall. The election of 1828 was unique because it marked the first time that a political party was used as a vehicle to both elect a candidate and form a base from which supporters of the party's candidate could expect to obtain government jobs as their reward.

The political party became a permanent institution in 1828, a source for government jobs and offices. The prospective elective officeholder petitioned the party for support in the general election; in return for that support he in effect pledged to fill those government offices and jobs which he would control with party faithful.

Indeed, the separation of interests in the 1828 election has endured to this day. The same broad elements that elected Jackson in 1828 elected Carter in 1976, and the elements which constituted the Whigs in 1828 were an integral part of GOP support in 1976. This is true despite the fact that in 1828 comparatively few foreign born, and almost no black voters participated in the election. Development of the law restricting the political activity of public employees should, therefore, be set against the backdrop of a political system that has functionally remained the same for almost 150 years. This is true for both federal and state governments, both before and after the Civil War.

The fear of politicized government services has always been strong and has caused a continuous interest in limiting the rights of government workers to engage in politics. This is similar to the traditional fear of a standing military, a fear which lasted through World War II, and a

---

1. See Claude G. Bowers, *The Party Battles of the Jackson Period* (Boston: Houghton Mifflin, 1924), on the background of the spoils system.

fear of unnecessary entangling foreign engagements, which also lasted through World War II.

Prior to the Civil War, the concept of states rights was so strong a doctrine that the federal government had a much smaller role to play, and so most federal jobs were in effect political jobs, with the assumption that the holder of the federal job would engage in politics to further the ambition of the party or the particular president that appointed that person to office. Likewise, state governments had a concomitantly larger role to play and since, as in *Barron* v. *Baltimore*,[2] the Bill of Rights was held to be inapplicable to the states, the Tenth Amendment was paramount.[3]

The federal government had little continuity with the exception of the Civil Service. Thus on the federal level the distinction between an employee and an official was almost meaningless, since all posts were subject to political appointment. Likewise, states were so insulated from outside control that no precedent could be established from individual state law. Only after the Civil War and the concurrent emergence of a unified national law and economy did the national government begin to expand at such a rate that a permanent Civil Service became a necessity. State governments also established their own civil services to meet the additional burden incurred by a developing industrial society.

Of course the Civil Service was not ignored by the political parties, but because of the vast technical jobs given to it, a purge of the entire Civil Service, as Jackson had done in 1828, was no longer possible. Instead politicians sought two ways to influence the Civil Service: first, by limiting the size of the permanent Civil Service so as to cover mostly technical jobs, not especially coveted by large numbers; second, to influence the individual civil servant by establishing a system in which individuals could be replaced for political reasons, a form of mass intimidation. While mass replacement may have been out of the question, the individual employee never knew his status; thus the intimidation factor. This situation naturally caused a reaction among those who thought that

---

2. Barron v. Baltimore, 7 Pet. 243 (1833).

3. This marked a complete turnabout for Chief Justice Marshall since, in his previous opinion, he championed a strong central government especially as to fiscal affairs. It would have been a short jump from a position held in McCulloch v. Maryland 4 Wheat 316 (1816) holding that the state could not tax a constitutionally established national bank to a holding that states could not abrogate a constitutionally guaranteed personal right. However, this was not to be; by 1833 states rights was in the ascendancy in both the Jacksonian and Whig parties. See also Gibbons v. Ogden, 9 Wheat 1 (1824).

a Civil Service should be established to take certain continuing functions of government out of politics, as much as possible.

The eventual establishment of the Civil Service has had a legal effect on the political rights of public employees. This chapter will discuss whether or not the government has gone from one extreme to another, from a politically motivated Civil Service to one in which a citizen's basic political rights have been unjustly prohibited for public employees.

Because the impetus for the regulation of political activities of public employees occurred with federal employees, most of this study will be devoted to the area dealing with the control of political activities of federal employees. Federal law has indeed been the leader in this particular area and, generally speaking, state laws are simply small-scale versions of federal statutes. In addition, because the federal government has major control over state and local governments, state laws on this matter are in many cases required by federal law.

Statutory History

The first attempt to regulate the political activities of federal employees occurred with the Civil Service Act of 1883, the so-called Pendleton Act.[4] This act was a culmination of many years of political debate over the necessity of putting a part of the federal bureaucracy under Civil Service, rather than having it subject to presidential appointments. Among its provisions was a section which forbade federal employees in the Civil Service from using their official authority or influence to coerce the political action of any person, or to interfere with federal elections. This attempted to prohibit the practice, still common in many state and local jurisdictions, in which a public employee used his official position to coerce others either into contributing to his party or voting for certain candidates under threat of removing certain government benefits. Usually the main target for this type of activity was other federal employees working under the person in question, although, as the history of local political machines has shown, this same coercion could also be used against large numbers of persons, all of whom were dependent upon someone for political favors for their livelihoods or subsistance.

However, this act did not prohibit public employees from engaging in political activities, such as working for a political candidate. Thus, this

4. 22 Stat. 403. The first regulation on the Civil Service Commission was in 1884. Besides the limitation on coercion, the rule protected applicants by prohibiting inquiries concerning the political or religious opinions on applications of any applicants. That prohibition lasted sixty-four years, until the loyalty program of 1948.

statute only prohibited situations in which the employee used his privileged position as an employee to assert an influence on an election or political activity which he would not have otherwise been able to do as a citizen. It did not prevent him from acting as a citizen with respect to the assertion of his own political beliefs.

For almost twenty-five years after its passage, this particular statute and the rules formulated by the Civil Service Commission interpreting the statute were the only legislative limitation on political activities of public employees. However, sparked mainly by the growth of large political organizations on the state and local levels, many elements in society, typified by the so-called progressive movement, urged greater control over the political activities of public employees. As a result of this campaign, in 1907 President Theodore Roosevelt, by virtue of his own executive order, placed the following limitations upon political activities of public employees: "Employees in the classified service while retaining their right to vote as they please and to express privately their opinions on all political subjects, shall take no part in political management or in political campaigns."[5]

While the 1883 act only limited those activities of public employees clearly beyond the scope of First Amendment type activities, this particular executive order was quite a different matter. It was concerned with the exercise of normal political activities guaranteed to all citizens by virtue of the Constitution, rather than abuse of position and fraud. While the executive order was somewhat open ended and vague, in that it did not define either political management or political campaigns, nevertheless it formed a limiting factor on the rights of public employees.

Because this limitation was by executive order rather than statute, its enforcement was a matter of predilection on the part of the particular administration in power. Likewise, because no legislative support was behind this executive order, enforcement of the rule was also a desultory affair. Thus, during the period when this particular executive order was the only regulation, the political rights of public employees were not actually circumscribed in any way, merely because the rule lacked strong legislative support.

The New Deal, featuring a greatly expanded role and size for the federal bureaucracy, brought about the development of a real movement to have the 1907 executive order reenacted in the form of a statute and to provide strong disciplinary sanctions for violations of these rules. Because the size of the federal bureaucracy had expanded so much during

---

5. Executive Order 642 (June 3, 1907) presently codified in 5 USC § 1101 et seq. and Civil Service Rule 5 CFR §1101.

the first term and a half of Franklin Roosevelt's administration, to the point where Roosevelt's federal appointees constituted the largest number of all Civil Service employees, a great fear arose among his opponents that this large number of federal employees could be used by Roosevelt to insure his continued election and the election of successor government. This fear of the federal bureaucracy's political power culminated in 1939 with the passage of the now-famous Hatch Act, which provided strong limitations on the political activities of public employees in the classified Civil Service.[6] The most important section of the Hatch Act read as follows:

> It shall be unlawful for any person employed in the Executive Branch of the Federal Government or any agency or department thereof to use his official authority or influence for the purpose of interfering with an election or affecting the results thereof. No officer or employee in the Executive Branch of the Federal Government or any agency or department thereof shall take any active part in political management or in political campaigns. All such persons retain the right to vote as they may choose and to express their opinions on all political subjects and candidates.[7]

While the language of the Hatch Act was merely a reiteration of the language of the Civil Service Act of 1883 and the executive order of 1907, the fact that the two were combined in a single statute, one which also provided for enforcement powers, made limitation on political activities of public employees not a matter of executive desire but one of national law which could not be disobeyed by any member of the executive branch, even if they so desired, unless they were willing to subject themselves to punishment. A year later, Congress amended the 1939 act by extending its prohibitions to certain employees and offices of state and local executive agencies employed in connection with activities financed in whole or in part by loans or grants made by the United States or federal Civil Service Commission; to this day the statutory scheme remains the law concerning political activities of federal employees. Indeed, all employees of the federal government and those most explicitly exempted by law are covered by this statute and have their political rights circumscribed in accordance with the regulation.

---

6. The pertinent parts of the Hatch Act are codified in 5 U.S.C. §§7324, 7326 as to federal employees; state and local employees are covered by similar provisions in 5 U.S.C. §§1501–3.

7. This is the famous §9(a), now 5 U.S.C. §7324.

Scope of the Limitation

The statute states very clearly that public employees may not engage in certain prohibited types of political activities. Since the statute itself states that the employee retains the right to vote as he may choose and to express his opinion on all political subjects and candidates, the determination of those other types of activities now prohibited becomes a matter of some difficulty.

In attempting to grapple with this problem, the Civil Service Commission has issued elaborate regulations which attempt to delineate what is and what is not prohibited activity. An examination of what the Civil Service Commission considers to be prohibited and nonprohibited activities is instructive; and so a close look at the court decisions on the issue follows, allowing for the anticipation of possible future changes.[8]

According to the Civil Service Commission, the act is "designed to prevent those subject to it from assuming general political leadership or from becoming permanently, prominently identified with any political movement, party or fraction, or with the success or failure of any candidate for election to public office." In interpreting this particular concept the commission has listed a series of activities which can and cannot be performed by public employees.

According to the commission, public employees cannot: run for public office; distribute campaign literature; organize or speak at a political meeting; circulate nominating petitions; attend political conventions except as a spectator; solicit or handle political campaign funds; publish letters or articles soliciting votes; or hold office in a political organization.[9]

Also according to the commission, the following activities can be entered into: voting; joining political organizations and attending meetings; contributing to a campaign; signing nominating petitions; and wearing campaign buttons.[10]

A set of regulations also concerns activities of state and local employees covered by the act. Particular state and local employees covered by the Hatch Act are those whose salaries are partly or wholly subsidized by federal funds, especially in the areas of education and welfare, and to a lesser degree in the area of law enforcement. However, since these regu-

8. See United States Civil Service Commission, *Political Activities of Federal Officers and Employees* (Washington, D.C.: U.S. Government Printing Office, May, 1968).
9. 5 CFR §733.122.
10. 5 CFR §733.111.

lations nearly parallel in total that of the main body of regulations, they do not need to be fully differentiated; all discussions and regulations that apply to federal employees apply equally to state and local employees covered by the statute.

Rather than treating individual parts of the regulations at this time, first the main Supreme Court cases concerning the Hatch Act which upheld its constitutionality will be discussed. In view of the great changes which have recently occurred with respect to the constitutional rights of public employees, the continuing validity of either the act or the regulations or the cases at the present time will be questioned.

The Mitchell Case

The first major question of the Hatch Act's constitutionality was the case of *United Public Workers* v. *Mitchell*.[11] This suit asked for an injunction and declaratory judgment against the enforcement of the statute by a group of federal employees and their union to prevent the Civil Service Commission from enforcing the Hatch Act.

Of all the plaintiffs, only one had actually engaged in activities contrary to the regulations. He was an employee of the Federal Mint in Philadelphia who also held the position of a precinct leader in the Democratic party. All the other plaintiffs, plus the union, joined the suit to enjoin the commission from applying the act to them on the grounds that they were being prevented from engaging in protected political activities for fear of being subjected to the sanctions under this statute.

The Court, by a vote of four to three, upheld the constitutionality of the statute. Justice Reed, writing the majority opinion, held that the statute did not violate either the First, Fifth, Ninth, or Tenth Amendments, while recognizing the limit on congressional power to regulate the conduct of government employees. The Court held that the matter of determination of the extent to which political activities of government employees could be regulated rested primarily with Congress; the courts would only interfere when such regulations "passed beyond the generally existing conception of governmental powers, as developed from practice, history, and changing educational, social, and economic conditions."[12] The Court further noted that, since the statute only prohibited activity with respect to partisan political actions, any activity of the government employee with respect to nonpartisan political activity would not be prohibited.

Three justices dissented. Justice Black and Rutledge expressed a dissenting opinion (written by Black) which concerned the First Amend-

11. 330 U.S. 75 (1947).
12. 330 U.S. at 99–100.

ment issue directly. Justice Douglas wrote another dissenting opinion based upon the difference between certain types of federal employees.

Justice Black held that, in his opinion, the statute violated the First Amendment; it was uncertain in its consequences and overbroad in its restrictions. He believed that statutes such as the 1883 statute concerning political coercion were perfectly proper, but that when such matters as those covered by the Hatch Act were involved, in effect no benefit accrued to the public administration by the denying several million citizens their right to play a part in campaigns which might have the effect of changing their lives. Justice Black's opinion should be quoted, because its language in many ways anticipated language later employed by the Court in invalidating certain limitations on public employees which were previously discussed in the context of loyalty oaths. Justice Black stated:

> Legislation which muzzles several million citizens threatens popular government not only because it injures individuals muzzled, but also because of its harmful effect on the body politic and the depriving of the political participation and interest of such a large segment of our citizens. There is nothing about federal and state employees as a class which justifies depriving them or society of the benefits of their anticipation in public affairs. They, like other citizens, pay taxes and serve their country in peace and war. Taxes they pay and wars in which they fight are determined by the elected spokesmen of all the people. They come from the same homes, communities, schools, churches and colleges as do the other citizens. I think the Constitution guarantees them the same rights that other groups of good citizens have to engage in activities which decide who their elected representatives shall be. The section of the act here held valid reduces the constitutionally protected liberty of several million citizens to less than a shadow of its substance. It relegates millions of federal, state, and municipal employees to the roll of mere spectators of events upon which hinge the safety and welfare of all the people, including public employees. It removes a sizable portion of our electorate from full participation in affairs destined to mould the fortunes of the nation. It makes honest participation in essential political activities an offense punishable by proscription from public employment. It endows a governmental board with the awesome power to censure thoughts, expressions, and activities of law abiding citizens in the field of free expression, from which no person should be barred by a government which boasts that it is a government of, for, and by the people—all the people. Laudable as its purpose may be, it seems to me to hack at the roots of government by the people themselves; and consequently I cannot agree to substain its validity.[13]

13. 330 U.S. at 110–11.

In many ways the Hatch Act is not so much venal as it is naive. It reflects a belief that politics are by nature corrupting and evil, and that civil servants who should be above the battle must be spared or prevented from every opportunity to get themselves entangled in partisan politics for fear that they might become corrupted. While the need to prevent public employees from abusing their offices for corrupt purposes is indeed of paramount interest and a legitimate concern of Congress, the Hatch Act is much too broad in view of the limited necessity for preventing corruption.

When the ten prohibitions listed by the Civil Service Commission concerning the political activities public employees cannot engage in are examined, most appear to be no more likely to lead to corruption in a person not already so inclined than the act of voting itself. In fact the real end of the Hatch Act is the same as that found in various loyalty programs; namely the reform has poisoned the entity it sought to preserve as much or more than the evil it was trying to prevent. In both situations the evil was certain criminal activities easily definable and subject to traditional legal remedies. Espionage and sabotage were the targets of the loyalty program, while the Civil Service Acts attempted to prevent the selling of an office for political or personal gain. In both cases limited legal remedies would have sufficed. In the loyalty program, an investigative program designed to uncover aberrant behavior (alcoholism) or events in an individual's life (criminal conviction) which could lead to blackmail would have been more than sufficient. A Civil Service program prohibition against employee exposure to large sums of money, such as found in managing a political campaign, would have sufficed.

What has happened in both loyalty programs and Civil Service protection statutes is that a new element has been added to the narrow basis of regulation, one designed to prevent public employees from becoming a political force through the expression of ideas which might be in contravention of existing political dogmas. This is not the same as preventing employees from organizing for the betterment of their working conditions. In short, these statutes and regulations were aimed at preventing the emergence of public employees, especially federal employees, as a political force, and not because of their numbers, but because of their expertise.

The loyalty program emerged in its final form because the opinion held by many politicians about communism was subject to challenge by civil servants, especially in the State Department. This is something of an oversimplification and the next chapter will discuss it in greater detail. The argument that the loyalty program had as its major cause a fear of the intellectual force of a segment of the Civil Service cannot, however, be questioned.

Likewise, while Civil Service protection acts go back to 1883, not until 1939 did they really become tough. I submit that fear of corruption had no or little role in the passage of the Hatch Act. Rather it was primarily the emergence of the New Deal bureaucracy as an intellectual force that scared many politicians. Remember that many of the strongest supporters of the Hatch Act were conservative Democrats, including Hatch himself. If strictly partisan politics were involved, a heavily democratic Congress in 1939 would not have passed this legislation, and Roosevelt would certainly not have signed it.

The act prohibited so many speech related activities simply to limit civil servants from access to the public, where they could criticize Congress or the administration, and where their positions would give their views credibility.[14] Indeed, these civil servants had the facts, and with access to the public could be an extremely potent force in the public debate, acting either as individuals or in groups.

Ironically the basis of present complaints about the government's bureaucracy may be due to an unintended effect of the Hatch Act. Because public employees have been prohibited from going public, at least in the context of the election process, they have turned inward and have resorted to secrecy, obfuscation, and so on as a counterweight to politicians. Surely this is no better than exposing themselves to the electorate. If fear of an organized monolith was a factor in the Hatch Act, then this fear was obviously misplaced, because a large government is extremely resistant to the formation of a consensus of belief or action, much less an organized force, from within.

If a governmental employee can be trusted with so much authority, surely no one really believes that his power would become dangerous if he becomes part of the political debate. While I have tried to avoid any polemics in this book, I think that in this instance, as in the case of the loyalty program, the general public has been hoodwinked by a creation of primarily conservative politicians who feared the effect of the infusion of primarily liberal ideas into political life from a group that could muster real evidence to support such ideas. Fear of the ideas of public employees, not their acts, prompted the Hatch Act, and that is why I consider it a violation of the First Amendment.

14. *Pickering* is a perfect example of an individual public employee going public through a personal appeal to the media. How much more powerful his voice would have become if he could have channeled his ideas through a political party.

To be fair, the Hatch Act does not completely lack redeeming qualities. Watergate shows that some individuals would indeed turn the Civil Service to their own personal political ends, and that certain types of activities which, if engaged in by public employees, could lead to their placement in compromising or tempting positions (witness Henry Peterson). The most serious possibility would involve placing a public employee in a situation where he could solicit or handle a large campaign fund. If one activity in our political sphere is the antithesis of a Civil Service concept, it would be the methods used to raise and distribute money for political campaigns, as Watergate has so clearly shown. Even in the most aboveboard, legitimate campaigns, the inducements used to get people to contribute large sums of money to political campaigns is not a matter for pride. If a public employee was involved in a government activity which would include the dispensing of large sums of money in contracts or other benefits, to allow him to be a leader in political functions, with the possibility of connecting political inducements of campaign contributions to government contracts as such, becomes too obvious to the sanctioned.

The second type of activity which needs to be closely examined is the allowing of a public employee to hold a political office, even a party office, when the office engages in the dispensation of patronage. The havoc that might be caused by allowing a public employee to hold a position in which he could pass upon, or at least make recommendations concerning the appointment of persons to government service, even if the jobs were not covered by the Civil Service, could be serious. Nevertheless, the question of which offices would or would not be involved in the dispensation of patronage must be answered on a case-by-case basis through the promulgation regulations, just as the income tax service and other government agency regulations stand covering individual fact situations; a blanket prohibition would seem to be overkill. Also, do not forget that these prohibitions refer to employees receiving favors, not politicians attempting to subject employees to such pressure.

Aside from the holding of political office involved in patronage or the handling of political campaign funds, most of the other activities on the prohibitive list should not be prohibited, because to do so actually implies that the holding of strong political beliefs would be corrupting per se. Obviously, if a person's job as a civil servant is to be affected because of his ideological slant, such job will be affected whether or not the person is active in venting his views in a political form. The real point of the prohibition is explained only in those circumstances in which the employee can actually use his office or job as a means of promoting his political views, such as soliciting funds, running for office, or holding another political office. In such cases, I think the prohibition would be valid.

In the mid-1960s, both state and federal courts had been making decisions severely limiting the effect of the *Mitchell* case. Indeed, a three judge federal court in the District of Columbia declared certain portions of the Hatch Act to be unconstitutional. However, when this case, a test case brought by the National Association of Letter Carriers and other organizations against the Civil Service Commission, reached the Supreme Court in 1973, the Court upheld the constitutionality of the challenged portions of the Hatch Act. Thus, this whole area concerning political rights of public employees seemed frozen, barring a change in the statute.[15]

The particular kinds of activities which the letter carriers and their employees wished to engage in included running in local elections for such offices as school board member, city council member, or mayor; writing letters on political subjects to newspapers; participating as a delegate in political conventions; running for office in a political party; and campaigning for candidates for political offices. The lower three judge federal court deciding the case held that the *Mitchell* case was not conclusive on the subject, because it left open the definition of political activities, and political activity as defined in the section of the Hatch Act in question was vague, overbroad, and therefore unconstitutional. By "overbroad," the court intended that the prohibitions covered by the statute were far in excess of the legitimate interests of the government, namely, the prohibiting of corruption of public employees through involvement in certain types of political activities. By "vague" the court indicated that the term "political activities" could have so many interpretations that a person seeking to comply with the statute would not know from reading it which activities are or are not prohibited. This was the form in which the Supreme Court received the *Letter Carriers'* case.

The heart of the Supreme Court ruling in the *Letter Carriers'* case was based on that balancing test, previously discussed with regard to the freedom of speech of public employees in *Pickering*. The Court stated:

> The restrictions now so far imposed on federal employees are not aimed at any particular party, groups or points of view, but apply equally to all partisan activity of the type described. They discriminate against no racial, ethnic or religious minorities, nor do they seek

15. United Civil Service Commission v. National Association of Letter Carriers, 413 U.S. 548 (1973).

to control political opinions or beliefs or to interfere with anyone's vote at the polls.

But as the court has held in *Pickering* v. *Board of Education*, the government has an interest in regulating the conduct and speech of its employees that differs significantly from those it possesses in connection with the regulation of speech of citizenry in general. The problem in any case is to arrive at a balance between the interest of the [employee] as a citizen in commenting upon matters of public concern and the interest of the [government] as a employer promoting the efficiency of the public services it performs through its employees. Although Congress is free to strike a different balance than it has . . . we think the balance that it struck so far is sustainable by the obviously important interest thought to be served by the limitations on partisan political activities now contained in the Hatch Act.[16]

In the discussion of the *Pickering* case, the conclusion reached was that, while the spirit of *Pickering* allowed a broad extension of rights to public employees, the language contained some unnecessarily narrowing clauses concerning the balancing of the interest between the employee and the employer, which in the hands of a different court with a different set of perspectives could lead to a diminution, rather than an extension, of rights of employees, which was the intent of *Pickering*. In the *Letter Carriers'* case, in the paragraph just quoted, the worst fears over the use of *Pickering's* language were fulfilled. The Court indicated that even though the restrictions placed by the Civil Service Commission on political activities of public employees may have been unnecessarily narrow and restrictive, the interest of government in having a nonpartisan Civil Service was so great that the Court would allow these restrictions to stand even if unnecessarily narrow.

As for the construction of the statute itself, the Court held that the use of the term "political activities" to refer to the prohibitive act had to be read in terms of the Civil Service regulations themselves; since these regulations covered in great detail and with great specificity acts which were prohibited, the statute would not be vague.

In regard to the question of overbreadth, the Court held that the act itself allowed public employees to "express opinions on political subjects and candidates as individuals." This question of speech became difficult

---

16. 413 U.S. at 565. The court also stated that one prime concern of the government is to prevent a rapidly expanding work force becoming a "powerful, invincible, or perhaps corrupt" political machine. This neatly sums up the inherent fear in conservative circles which lies behind the Hatch Act and the loyalty-security program.

in that part of the regulation which forbade the endorsement of a partisan candidate for public office or political party office in a political advertisement, broadcast, campaign literature, or similar material. A similar paragraph prohibited the addressing of a convention, caucus, rally, or similar gathering of political parties in support of or in opposition to partisan candidates for public office or political party office. These provisions should have caused grave constitutional questions, one of which, in my reading of the philosophy of *Pickering*, would render them unconstitutional. However, the Supreme Court, using the balancing test, simply held that these restrictions were really on political acts normally performed only in the context of partisan campaigns, not on speech per se, and thus were sustainable for the same reasons that the other acts of political campaigning are constitutional.

The Court, however, held in the next paragraph that these acts might well be overbroad and thus constitutionally impermissable. But they agreed that this whole statute would still be valid.

The danger of overbroad statutes is, as the justices stated, that if someone does not know what is or is not prohibited, and if severe sanctions are attached to violations, the employee might simply refrain from action rather than risk punishment. This is known as the chilling effect and, in the context of public employees, the chilling effect is very much a deep freeze on their activities. The dissenting justices rather sensibly suggested, in view of the hopeless conditions and confusion involved in the area, that the whole statute and regulation should be scrapped, save for those prohibitions against obvious corruption, and the law be redrafted, allowing those political activities normally available to any citizen to be given to the public employee, rather than taking them away from him arbitrarily.

However, in view of the scope of this case and the present makeup of the Supreme Court, apparently at least for the next decade, unless the Supreme Court undergoes a rather drastic personnel change, the *Letter Carriers'* case will be the law and the Civil Service Commission will probably tighten up and expand prohibitions, rather than loosen any of their hold on public employees. For the federal public employee, evidently partisan political activity of any kind will doubtlessly be totally banned.

Movement in Congress to revise or repeal the Hatch Act has been noted. President Ford said he would veto such an action, which is why it had not passed before 1977. Undoubtedly President Carter would sign such a change. Thus, Congress's willingness to reverse the Hatch Act without the excuse of a presidential veto is, at the moment, suspect.

State and Local Employees

The *Letter Carriers'* case applied only to federal employees; nevertheless, the effect of that case is going to be felt on a state and local level.

In a case decided the same day as *Letter Carriers, Broadrick v. State of Oklahoma*,[17] the Supreme Court upheld, by a five to four vote (rather than six to three in *Letter Carriers*), the constitutionality of an Oklahoma statute which is, if anything, more constitutionally suspect in terms of the language than the Hatch Act and its regulations.

The paragraph in question in the Oklahoma statute provided that no such employee shall belong to "any national, state or local committee of a political party or be an officer or member of a committee of a partisan political club or candidate for any paid political office or take part in management affairs of a political party or campaign except as to exercise his right as a citizen, privately to express his opinion and vote."[18]

The Supreme Court majority even conceded that this statute moved beyond the Hatch Act and prohibited activities which would have been allowed under the old *Mitchell* case. However, it states that, since the activities of the Oklahoma employees in question, namely their soliciting of political funds from coworkers for the benefit of a superior, would be prohibited under any statute, the employees cannot avail themselves of the overbreadth of the argument to challenge their dismissal from punishment.[19]

The Supreme Court simply limited its ruling on the Oklahoma statute to the particular point in which the activities constitute the so-called hard core activities which all Hatch Act-type statutes wish to prohibit; activities, in effect, which would constitute a form of extortion. I would have no qualms about this decision. Indeed, strong precedents from other decisions were written by the Warren court which used the pro-

17. 413 U.S. 601 (1973).

18. Section 818 of the Oklahoma Merit System of Personnel Administration Act (Okla. Gov. Annuals, Title 74 §801 et seq.).

19. See generally note, The First Amendment Overbreadth Doctrine, 83 HARVARD L. REV. 844 (1970), for an exhaustive study of this aspect of First Amendment law through the Warren court. The Burger court has used this doctrine on several occasions, though judging from the Broadrick case, it is not a particular favorite of the new court. See Coates v. Cincinnati, 402 U.S. 611 (1972); Cohen v. California, 403 U.S. 15 (1971), "FUCK THE DRAFT" on the back of a jacket; Grayned v. City of Rockford, 408 U.S. 104 (1972), prohibition on picketing near school. Since 1973 the Court has not invoked the doctrine, which is very ominous. See Laird v. Tatum 408 U.S. 1(1972); Parker v. Levy 417 U.S. 733 (1974). Bigelow v. Virginia 421 U.S. 809 (1975) would have invoked overbreadth, but a change in the Virginia abortion advertisement statute removed the "chilling factor" prior to decision.

cedural device of refusing, as a matter of policy, to declare statutes unconstitutional where the complaining parties are clearly in violation of the legitimate portions of the statute, no matter how many illegitimate aspects the statute might have.[20]

If the Court had simply stopped at that point I would see no problems; but it went beyond that point, or at least seemed to go beyond it. In a somewhat confusing statement, the Court held that, as to statutes of the type where strong government interests exist with regard to the maintaining of an effectively functioning Civil Service, in order for a court to find such a statute unconstitutional for overbreadth reasons, the statute must be substantially overbroad, rather than merely overbroad. This would seem, if it is in fact a change of law, to wipe out a whole large body of law which developed during the late 1950s to 1960s in the area of civil rights statutes and the loyalty security cases which used the overbroad test to invalidate many statutes.[21]

Obviously, more than imagination indicates that a Court which says that having a completely nonpartisan Civil Service system could not also mean that the state has an equally high interest in having a "loyal" Civil Service system; thus the loyalty oath statutes, which have been wiped off the books one at a time, could be revived and sustained by this Supreme Court.

Patronage Dismissals

If this Supreme Court has shown a consistently conservative trend by upholding various forms of limitations on political activities of public employees in the Hatch Act cases, it has absolutely and unexpectedly surprised most legal scholars with its opinion concerning the practice of patronage dismissals.[22]

This case involved a situation in the city of Chicago. Until the early 1970s, the Cook County Sheriff's Department, as opposed to all other branches of the Chicago and Cook County government, was in the hands of the Republican party. In December of 1970, the Democrats won the

20. See Cox v. Louisiana 379 U.S. 536 (1965); Cameron v. Johnson 390 U.S. 611 (1968).

21. Discussed in great detail in chapter 5.

22. Elrod v. Burns, 427 U.S. 347 (1976). This decision was not a complete surprise because it is consistent with *Letter Carriers* and *Broadrick*, in so far as a nonpolitical civil service is the goal. Surprising was the use of the unconstitutional conditions doctrine, 360 U.S. 362 (the Hatch Act, discussed on 370).

office of Sheriff of Cook County, and all previous employees of the department who were Republicans and who refused to swear allegiance to the Democratic party were immediately dismissed from office. The dismissed employees filed a class action suit against the Sheriff of Cook County, Mayor Daley, and the head of the Democratic organization, charging that these dismissals violated their constitutional rights, even though they had no civil service or entitlement to the job. The Supreme Court agreed with them.

The plurality opinion, as an opinion representing the opinion of the whole Court but not agreed to by five justices, was written by Justice Brennan, joined by Justices White and Marshall. A concurring opinion, an opinion presenting the same belief as the majority but for different reasons, was written by Justices Blackman and Stewart. Dissenting opinions were written by Chief Justice Burger and Justices Powell and Rehnquist. Justice Stevens did not sit on the case because he had been a member of the Court of Appeals for the Seventh Circuit, whose opinion, upholding the employees, was affirmed in this case by the Supreme Court.

Taking the plurality and concurring opinion, the single common position was that, as a matter of law, a public employee in a nonconfidential position cannot be discharged from a job that the employee is satisfactorily performing upon the sole grounds of his political beliefs. This is the direct holding of the case and the only single position on which all five of the justices of the majority can agree. I specifically emphasize this, because the plurality opinion by Justice Brennan is extremely wide-ranging in its scope; but, nevertheless, the full ramification of that opinion is that it does not represent the thinking of five members of the court, but rather only three.

First of all, Brennan took the position that patronage dismissals have the effect of severely restricting political belief and association, which are protected by the First Amendment, in that the government cannot force a public employee to relinquish these rights to political association as a price of holding public jobs.

This, of course, is what the concurring judges agreed to and constitutes the rule of the case. Justice Brennan expands this rule in his supporting argument for that position. He first takes the position that First Amendment rights are not absolute, but may be curtailed only by the showing of interests of vital importance on the part of the state;[23] also, in this

23. This is the compelling state interest test which I have urged as being the proper test to apply to First Amendment rights rather than a balancing test. Discussed in chapters 3 and 5 in detail.

particular case, the government must show that the need for patronage dismissals serves some vital government function that cannot be done by a means less drastic than dismissal of satisfactorily performing employees. Justice Brennan goes on to discuss the question of inefficiency and the need for the government to deal with inefficient employees. He holds that since unproductive employees may always be discharged and merit systems are available, a less drastic means than patronage dismissal is available to insure that the people working for a government are in fact efficient and effective.

Likewise, Brennan dismissed the idea that these patronage dismissals could be justified by their contribution to the proper functioning of the democratic process through their assistance to partisan politics, since whatever assistance they may have afforded partisan politics still does not override the encroachment on First Amendment freedoms.

Finally the remaining idea states that under the terms of the old right-privilege doctrine, since the government did not have to create these positions originally, it could fire people holding these positions for this or any other reason. This book has discussed in great detail how the right-privilege doctrine is now disused and overruled, with the high-point being the case of *Keyishian* v. *Board of Regents.*[24] Brennan, in his opinion, pointed out that this doctrine had been rejected in *Keyishian*, that this is the law today, and that the right-privilege doctrine cannot be used to justify these patronage dismissals.

While this is not, of course, new law, the real issue here is why Brennan felt compelled to discuss what was seemingly an accepted doctrine. In my opinion he did so because, with the Court eroding so many Warren court philosophical and administrative holdings in the area of rights of criminals and of public employees, Brennan felt that he should reinforce the fact that the right-privilege doctrine is no longer law. When the Court, in the *Sindermann* and *Roth* cases, talked about dismissals for protected constitutional rights as the basis of federal court action, it also meant that the right-privilege doctrine was truly no longer viable. Other rulings of the Supreme Court in the last few years limiting the rights of public employees also have not revived the right-privilege doctrine in the area of assertion of constitutional rights. The fact that Brennan felt compelled to state what was already the law shows how far this new Supreme Court has gone in eroding guarantees given to public employees during the Warren court years. His statement indicates that this was the philosophy of the Warren court and that some justices consider this to be not only the law, but also correct from a philosophical point of view. It

24. 385 U.S. 589 (1967).

tends to preserve the position for the time when a new Supreme Court, one more responsive to public employee claims, will be in office and obviates any possible claim that somehow the doctrine overruling the right-privilege doctrine has been lost through attrition.[25]

The effect this new decision will have for public employees is hard to say. Clearly it reinforces constitutional protection in areas other than simply patronage dismissals, but also dismissals for public utterances similar to that of *Pickering*. While of course it does not restore the loss of rights of public employees from the destruction of their jurisdictional interests which has occurred during the most recent term of the Supreme Court, it at least opens up the federal courts for protection of rights of public employees on the state and municipal level (and also on the federal level) which had not been previously recognized. This alone is reason to be grateful.

However, ultimately the real value of *Elrod* v. *Burns* is that in a period of entrenchment it provided not only a brake to the slide, but also a base for later courts to expand or reaffirm rights. Indeed, *Elrod* v. *Burns* may eventually provide the basis to reverse or severely limit Hatch Act cases. If political party application is labeled a protected First Amendment right, how then can the broad range of prohibitions on these rights by the Hatch Act be justified? They obviously cannot be justified, and thus perhaps in time the law will be changed either by statute or court decision.

---

25. Justices Powell, Rehnquist, and Burger in dissent take the position that patronage has real value to the body politic which overcomes any limitations on First Amendment rights. Since this position is so inconsistent with the holding in *Letter Carriers* and *Broadrick*, it proves that the conservative justices are not motivated by a desire to limit partisan interference in the Civil Service but rather wish to destroy any chance the Civil Service has of becoming a nonpartisan independent political force.

Chapter 5

Belief and Association

Previous chapters have discussed first the limitations placed on First Amendment rights of public employees by virtue of their employment, with actual expression being the focus of the inquiry, and second, the limitations placed on the political activity of public employees, with political activity being defined as participation in the election process. The focus of discussion was the special legislative scheme that is designed to limit partisan political activities of public employees, such as the Hatch Act.

This chapter will explore the degree to which a public employee may maintain private associations and beliefs unacceptable to his employer, keeping the existence of such associations and beliefs from him. In the United States, at least, this problem is peculiarly one affecting public employees. A popular assumption holds that intellectual unorthodoxy among government workers will hamper their ability to execute their mandate. Thus, their beliefs are thought to need monitoring.

Whereas private citizens persecuted or prosecuted for their personal beliefs and associations are generally harmed only after these beliefs and associations receive a certain degree of publicity, public employees, alone among citizens of the United States, have been subjected to systematic attempts by their governmental employers to uncover their beliefs and associations. Such inquiries have been made across the board without any attempt to link a particular employee with a particular type of belief or association, or more especially an association which might be illegal.

The legal questions surrounding the types of beliefs and associations which may or may not be limited by the government is an extremely complex subject, which will be discussed with the question of the conflict between public employment and the public employee's right to belief and association. The significant general proposition which should be explored is: To what degree have the methods used by the government to attempt to discover the beliefs and associations of its employees destroyed the peculiar status that the public employee maintains in this country?

Earlier, theories concerning the legal relationship of the public employee and his employer were discussed, with the conclusion that until the 1960s, the public employee was generally powerless, in the absence of a specific statutory protection, from governmental intrusions on his constitutional rights. Nevertheless, he was generally not subjected to any broad assault on his constitutional rights because a unique "mystique" protected him, because persons who became public employees did not usually maintain unpopular beliefs or associations in any event, and because a presumption of correctness of belief and behavior attached to the public employee. In short, generally public employees received little or no criticism concerning their advocacy of unpopular or even illegal beliefs and associations.

Ironically, however, the same historical development which led to the constitutional protection of public employment also destroyed the mystique protecting it, thus making legal protection a necessity. Before 1938, as Alan Barth explains in his book *The Loyalty of Free Men,*[1] government employees were assumed to be loyal to the country, and the only oath administered to them was a general oath of allegiance similar to that taken by the president or military inductees. The idea that tests of political orthodoxy need be administered (I use *political* in the broad sense, not as in partisan politics) were unknown and indeed proscribed by an 1884 Civil Service rule.

However, the shock of the United States' conflict with giant totalitarian states, first Nazi Germany then the Soviet Union, did something to the American psyche. (Japan was a traditional and quite understandable foe, such as Mexico in 1848. The war with Japan was purely military and involved no ideological conflicts; thus it was infinitely more popular than the war against Germany.) The reaction in the country to the events of the post-war era, especially the lack of a 1919-style peace and the presence of a new and, in the opinion of many, more ominous foe, led to a search for scapegoats.

1. New York: Viking, 1951.

At the same time the Democratic administration was in its fourteenth year; for purely partisan political reasons, the more conservative elements in the country labeled the domestic programs of the New Deal "communistic" or "socialistic." As explained earlier, the great revolution brought by the New Deal was the conversion of the central direction of the country from private business to the federal bureaucracy. This combination of a political party seeking to regain power (in this case Congress in 1946) and an inherent dislike of public employees, especially those who came to Washington after 1933 and the change in the world situation, transformed the question of the loyalty of public employees into a political issue in the 1946 Congressional races.

When the Republicans won both Houses of Congress, their victory was based, to a great extent, on the "communism in government" issue, and public employees became fair game. This resulted in the loyalty-security program, started in 1947 by President Truman, partly as a reaction and partly to (unsuccessfully) head off worse legislation. The impact of this program was greatest on public employment simply because traditional laws governing public employment limited the constitutional rights of public employees as opposed to those of private individuals, thus allowing the institution of procedures and mechanisms not possible against the general public, but, nevertheless, legally permissable against public employees.

While, at the time of this writing, much of the impact of the loyalty-security program on public employees has been lessened either through judicial action or the passage of time and the lessening of fear, nevertheless, the fruits of the program are still present in one form or another, and do present problems. Likewise, in a period of rising tension, a moribund program could be reinstituted. A possible increase in judicial conservatism might succeed in the reinstitution of the program, as certain recent Supreme Court cases have indicated. Thus, the loyalty-security program should be discussed in some detail so that the protections that must be sought against it can be formulated.

The Loyalty-Security Programs

After World War II, the loyalty-security program was introduced first on the federal level, followed quickly on the state and local levels. While the historical reasons for the introduction of such a program arose from factors of foreign and military policy completely unrelated to any issues of the performance or loyalty of the public service, the decision to introduce such programs at the level of the public employee must have been shaped by the decision makers' knowledge that public employees had no legal standing or power to object to the imposition of any kind of program.

As a result, these programs subjected public employees to increasingly repressive measures covering such constitutionally protected areas as the right to hold political beliefs, the right to join organizations, and the right to express ideas, no matter how controversial. The loyalty-security program in fact weakened constitutional guarantees at all levels of society, not just the public employment sector. Whether those who sought to repress rights met no initial resistance from their targets at the outset, or because their activities were judicially sanctioned, based on the public employee's lack of legal standing to object, their tactics became legitimatized and inevitably spread beyond the confines of public employment, until these criteria of loyalty became a factor in all aspects of the country's business.

If the federal government could justify use of informants and kangaroo courts, as in *Bailey* v. *Richardson*,[2] local police could likewise justify their use. If the need to protect the country could be used as justification for prohibiting speech which, though not actually seditious, had "bad" tendencies, the same need could be used to justify stifling political opposition.

Today, this period is viewed somewhat placidly, an aberration. Yet a real loss of rights might well have occurred had not the most famous demogogue of the era, Senator McCarthy of Wisconsin, not attacked the one sector of the public service able to defend itself from such political attack: the military. McCarthy had already seriously weakened such vital agencies of government as the State Department, and the idea that he could take on the Army did not seem so farfetched at the time. The so-called Army-McCarthy hearings proved the high point of the loyalty-security programs. Finally, following McCarthy's censure by the Senate, the climate was set for a change in judicial attitudes toward the programs, which followed inevitably on the heels of the political change.

However, the damage this era caused to the standing of public employees is still present. If public employees now have legal rights they did not previously possess, they no longer have their intangible assets, often as useful as legal rights. This does not mean that public employees were better off when they had mystique instead of rights, but in the fight to secure their rights for protection against future onslaughts like that of the loyalty-security programs, public employees lost something

2. 182 F.2d 46 (D.C. Cir. 1950), affirmed by an equally divided court, 341 U.S. 918 (1951).

that will never be regained. The public service has always been a proud and honorable profession, and today the public employee is much more secure in his job; but I venture to say that the job does not have the same significance it once had.

The effects of an era of fear and distrust are not easily erased. If the public employee has more rights today, it is because he needs more rights. He must be more distrustful of the public he serves; if it once subjected him to the onslaught of the McCarthy era, it could do so again. While most of the charges of disloyalty and subversion made against public employees were completely false, their effects still linger in the mind of the citizen. When for years the highest public officials of the country raised grave doubts about the loyalty of public employees, a feeling of distrust for public employees and their motives is doubtless left with the people they serve.[3]

Fear breeds repression. Fortunately, however, many of the nation's greatest institutions realized that an attack on public employees was an attack on all American citizens who dared to speak or believe in a manner different from the prescribed orthodoxy. Inevitably, the courts realized that public employees were under attack because of their weak standing and not because of any propensity on their part to engage in subversive activities. They also realized that the activities for which public employees were being attacked concerned the most vital constitutional rights held by *all* citizens. As a result of this belated judicial realization, public employees have, over the last fifteen years, reclaimed rights of free expression and freedom from unconstitutional conditions being attached to their employment to a degree heretofore never experienced by this group.

The fight over the loyalty program is so legally important because, even though it developed in the context of governmental attempts to protect the country from subversion and sedition, the issues involved the most basic rights of free speech and association. Thus, the legal principles which have evolved out of the loyalty program are applicable to many aspects of public service employment beyond that of the loyalty program. Indeed, the discussion of the substantive aspects of public employee rights shows that the issues and principles either now applicable or being attempted, were first developed and raised in cases involving the security program. To this end, a more detailed look at the development of programs at both the federal and state levels will be discussed, as there are significant differences between the two programs.

3. See Hacker, "Freedom in the Campus," in *The Price of Liberty*, ed. Alan Reitman (New York: Norton, 1961), pp. 104–6.

The Federal Program

The federal loyalty-security program originated in the late 1930s through the efforts of the forerunners of the House Un-American Activities Committee (the present House Internal Security Committee). This committee was started in 1934 by Rep. Samuel Dickstein of New York to ferret out Nazi elements; it was soon taken over by Rep. Martin Dies of Texas, who turned its focus from Nazi activities to the activities of left wing groups.

While the activities of the committee were not focused on public employees, nevertheless the effect of the committee's activities was to sensitize the House as to real or imaginary dangers from public employees engaging in activities which were considered in some circles to be subversive.[4] Thus, when Congress in 1935 sought to deal with activities of public employees in the context of their political activities in the Hatch Act, it included in that statute the provision to make unlawful any federal employee "to have membership in any political party or organization which advocates the overthrow of our Constitutional form of government in the United States."[5]

Later, in 1941, Congress began to include in all appropriations act provisions a statement to the effect that such funds could not be used to pay the salary or wages of "any person who advocates, or is a member of an organization that advocates the overthrow of the Government of the United States by force or violence."[6]

In 1942, the Civil Service Commission issued regulations which would disqualify or remove a person from public employment if "reasonable doubt" were found regarding the "loyalty [of the person involved] to the Government of the United States by force or violence."[7]

The effect of these provisions was to divest the federal employee of the special status and immunity he had enjoyed since 1884, protecting him from interference with his political beliefs. This divesting was compounded by a lack of constitutional guarantees; thus public employees were left open to real onslaughts against their rights when the political climate changed after World War II.

When the end of World War II did not bring an era of absolute peace, but instead one of conflict with the forces of international communism,

4. For the best overall study of the House Un-American Activities Committee, see Walter Goodman, *The Committee* (New York: Farrar, Straus, 1968).

5. 53 Stat. 1147, 1148 (1939), now 5 U.S.C. §7311.

6. 55 Stat. 5 (1941).

7. Civil Service War Regulation §18.2(c); 7 Fed. Reg. 7723, now Civil Service Regulations §731.201, 5 CFR §731.201.

a movement developed in this country that this situation did not occur because of historical consequences, but rather because of perfidy in the country.[8] Adding to this uneasy feeling was the development of military uses of atomic energy, which completely destroyed the feeling of absolute immunity from harm that had previously given the country such psychological comfort. And, since the government had a monopoly on the knowledge of atomic weapons, a feeling pervaded the country that the most vital task for national security was to prevent the Soviet Union from acquiring atomic weapons. A widely held belief maintained that the Russians were incapable of developing such weapons on their own, so that the only way the security of the country could be compromised

---

8. Alan Barth in *The Loyalty of Free Men* aptly described the effect of the loyalty-security program on the public service and its image. Writing in 1951, before the program had reached its most virulent form, Barth stated:

> Before 1939, the American People took it for granted that the Fellow-Americans they employed as government servants were loyal to the United States. They set certain standards for appointment to the Classified Civil Service designed to exclude the criminal and the incompetent. They endeavored to have government jobs awarded on a merit basis rather than through political patronage. They established a number of checks and regulations, sometimes referred to as red tape, to prevent abuses and irregularities and to assure a reasonable amount of industry on the part of employees. But so far as loyalty was concerned, they asked only that federal workers take an oath on assuming office to support and defend the Constitution of the United States against all enemies, to bear true faith and allegience to the same, and to discharge all their duties well and faithfully.
>
> Tests of political orthodoxy are repugnant to the American Tradition. So far as government employees are concerned, indeed, they were expressly banned by a Civil Service Rule promulgated in 1884. The rule stated: "No question in any form or application or in any examination shall be so framed as to elicit information concerning the political or religious opinions or affiliation of any applicant, nor shall any inquiry be made concerning such opinions or affiliations, and all disclosures thereof shall be discontinued."
>
> Once the government of the United States assumed that it could set standards to determine the loyalty of its employees, the development of the whole complex machinery of investigation and trial now known as the loyalty program became inevitable. If "subversives" were to be kept out of government, inquiry into belief and affiliation became necessary. If persons who responded to such inquiry falsely were to be detected, investigation of the most searching character had to be undertaken. If investigation was to be genuinely effective, it had to resort to the use of informers. If the continued effectiveness of informers was to be assured, their identity had to be concealed and their information had to be kept confidential. If individuals were to be safeguarded from the errors incident to investigation conducted in such a manner, an elaborate system of hearings and reviews and appeals had to be contrived. [p. 97]

was through espionage and subversion. The government had the knowledge; therefore the focus of attack had to be on governmental employees, with a weeding out of those persons who could supply this information to the Russians.[9]

The rise of international communism and the development of atomic weapons came at a time when domestic politics were also undergoing great changes. The New Deal years saw the development of governmental programs in areas heretofore reserved for the private sector. The New Deal provoked a strong reaction among the more conservative, business oriented segments of society, with the public employee, evident in greater numbers, as one target. The war suspended the bitter political fighting over the wisdom of such programs, but anti-New Deal feelings were not forgotten. In the postwar years, a common interest developed between business interests and professional patriots who, for different or even similar reasons, saw the public employee as the greatest enemy to their particular dreams, ambitions, or fears. That the public employee was only the servant of change, not its creator, was irrelevant; he was the target.[10]

The attack came swiftly. In 1945, Rep. Rankin of Mississippi, through legislative sleight of hand, was able to revive the old Dies Committee as a permanent committee of the House of Representatives, renaming it the House Un-American Activities Committee. In 1946, the cold war deepened and the country moved to the right and elected a Republican Congress, the now-famous 80th Congress.

With control of the Congress, business and patriotic interests joined together in open warfare on public employees. President Truman gave in quickly to the clamor for an investigation of subversion in government and with Executive Order 9835, promulgated on March 21, 1947, the loyalty-security program was instituted. This order called for an investigation of all applicants for federal employment and all existing employees

9. This, of course, had some kernal of truth, since much of the work on the design and assembly of the atomic bombs at Los Alamos was made available to the Soviet Union by the actions of Klaus Fuchs, a member of the British scientific exchange team assigned to Los Alamos. See A. Alex Moorehead, *The Traitors* (rev. ed.; New York: Harper and Row, 1963).

10. Despite all the smoke and furor, the only employee of the federal government definitely shown to be a Soviet agent was Judith Coplon, an employee of the Justice Department. This is not to say that there were not others, but it is obvious that any agent under such deep cover would never be uncovered in a loyalty-security program. To get a feeling of the impact with respect to one of the most famous cases covered under the loyalty-security program, see Phillip M. Stern, *The Oppenheimer Case: Security on Trial* (New York: Harper and Row, 1969).

in the executive branch. The basic standard was whether, "on all the evidence, reasonable grounds exist for the belief that the person involved is disloyal to the United States Government." The standard, while stated to be "reasonable," still involved inquiry into "belief." Investigation, because the focus was on the concept of loyalty, had to involve subjective factors.[11]

The only way such a program could be prevented from becoming a witch-hunt among public employees was the presumption that basically public employees were loyal. If this presumption existed, doubts could be resolved in favor of the employee, and activities and associations that could raise questions, even if they were harmless, would be accepted for what they really were, not for what the investigators thought they might be.

Until the middle of 1948, the loyalty program was still more of an administrative burden on the public employee than the instrument of terror it was to become. At this time, employees of the federal government, unlike their less fortunate counterparts in state and local governments, still maintained, in the public view, a measure of immunity. The presumption still existed that public employees, by and large, were loyal. But this feeling was very tenuous and needed only one small incident to destroy it.

In 1947, when the Republicans took over Congress, they naturally also took control of all committee chairmanships. The House Un-American Activities Committee now came under the control of a Congressman for the 7th District of New Jersey, J. Parnell Thomas. While Rankin was certainly no liberal, he at least came from the old populist school, which saw in governmental action good things for the people. His definition of

---

11.   . . . the order provided that the "activities and associations" to be considered in determining loyalty were to include (a) sabotage, espionage or knowingly associating with spies or saboteurs; (b) treason or sedition or advocacy thereof; (c) advocacy of revolution or force or violence to alter the constitutional form of government; (d) intentional, unauthorized disclosure of confidential documents or information; (e) performing duties or acting so as to serve the interests of another government in preference to the interests of the United States; and as the most far-reaching, (f) Membership in, affiliation with or sympathetic association with any foreign or domestic organization, association, movement, group or combination of persons, designated by the Attorney General as totalitarian, fascist, communist, or subversive, or as having adopted a policy of advocating or approving the commission of acts of force or violence to deny other persons their rights under the Constitution of the United States, or as seeking to alter the form of government of the United States by unconstitutional means. [Emerson, *The System of Freedom of Expression*, p. 216.]

people may have been narrow and his idea of who should be in government limited, but at least he saw the relationship, to some extent, between governmental action and progress. Thomas was entirely different. He was bitterly anti-New Deal and saw governmental bureaucracy as the ultimate enemy, both for patriotic and economic reasons. Soon after assuming the chairmanship, the committee, under Thomas's direction, announced an eight-point program, the most important points in regard to public employees being:

1. To expose and ferret out the Communists and Communist sympathizers in the Federal Government
6. Investigation of Communist influences in education
8. Continued accumulation of files and records to be placed at the disposal of investigative units of the government and armed forces.[12]

Other targets included Hollywood figures and labor unions. In fact, the first group Thomas attacked was the movie industry, with well-publicized hearings in which many of the leading lights of Hollywood appeared before the committee either to denounce other members of the industry or, in certain celebrated cases, to take the Fifth Amendment. However, this was just a sideshow, amusing to all but those involved.

In 1948, however, the committee hit pay dirt, and the lives of public employees have never been the same since. The committee had been holding hearings into the loyalty of public employees with inconclusive results when Richard M. Nixon, a freshman member of Congress from California (who was given a seat on the committee as a reward for defeating a leading member of the New Deal, Jerry Voorhees), made the shattering public announcement that he had been contacted by a former Communist named Whittaker Chambers (later editor of *Time* magazine) who was willing to testify under oath that Alger Hiss, a leading foreign affairs advisor of the Roosevelt administration, and presently chairman of the Carnegie Endowment for Peace was, during the 1930s and probably all during his time with the administration, a member of the Communist party and quite possibly an agent of the Soviet Union.

For public employees, no worse catastrophe could have occurred. That Hiss was not actually a public employee, but rather a high ranking official, was irrelevant. In the public mind, if an official as important as Hiss was a spy, what about the millions of lesser governmental employees? How much more susceptible would they be to such influences? Hiss had been involved, to the further misfortune of public employees,

12. Walter Mills, "Legacies of the Cold War," in *Individual Freedom and the Common Defense* (New York: Fund for the Republic, 1955), p. 57. The Thomas program is discussed in detail in this article.

in those public events and organizations most under attack for being centers of Communist subversion or examples of Communist victories. Hiss was at Yalta; he was a delegate to the San Francisco organizational meeting of the United Nations. In 1948, Yalta was the rallying cry for rabid anticommunists.

Making the situation worse was the fact that Nixon and the committee made a good case on the facts. Chambers was a very persuasive witness and, while the truth of his accusations cannot be proved, Hiss was also hardly the victim of some monstrous frame-up. Quite possibly he was guilty of all charges.[13]

Hiss eventually went to jail; with him went the last hope for millions of loyal public employees of preventing the institution of a truly repressive loyalty-security system. During World War II, Congress had passed a series of laws allowing the heads of so-called sensitive agencies the right of summary dismissal (without a hearing) of employees deemed to constitute a threat to the war effort. Physical acts, not beliefs, were the criteria for dismissal and, under the circumstances of the war, this legislation was entirely reasonable.

Such power had never been given to the government for reasons other than physical interference with its legitimate effort to conduct a war, however. An entirely reasonable law for public employees in time of war became an instrument of terror when applied to questions of belief and association, rather than physical interference.

The Hiss case clearly tipped the balance against the public employee and made more restrictive legislation and regulation inevitable. In 1950, Congress passed Public Law 733, which allowed the heads of certain agencies to suspend summarily and then terminate the employment of any employee "whenever he shall determine such termination necessary or advisable in the interest of the national security of the United States."[14] The act further stated that the employee was to be given the reasons for termination only to the extent the agency head "determined that the interests of national security permit." The law applied to eleven named agencies, including the Departments of State, Justice, Defense, and Commerce; but the president was given the power to apply it to other agencies as he deemed necessary in the name of national security.

This law placed many federal employees at the mercy of their employers. The concept of national security was so broad that almost any reason for firing an employee could be made to fit under such a rubric.

13. James Arthur Wechsler, *Confessions of a Middle Age Editor* (New York: Random House, 1960).

14. 5 U.S.C. §§22.1–22.3. See Emerson, *The System of Freedom of Expression*, p. 217.

The passage of 733 predictably occurred almost simultaneously with Senator McCarthy's first appearance in the national spotlight with his Wheeling, West Virginia, speech.

With the intensification of the cold war during the last years of the Truman administration, the position of the public employee in the federal government deteriorated, although examples of arbitrary action were still isolated rather than widespread occurrences. However, the advent of the Eisenhower administration marked the beginning of a period in which public employees came under assault from their own employers.

Almost as soon as the Eisenhower administration took office, the Truman order was superseded by Executive Order 10450, which provided that Public Law 733 should be applied to *all* agencies of the federal government.[15] It listed as its criteria for retention the same criteria set out by the Truman order, but also added a major change, in that the agency head not only had to consider matters of loyalty, but also whether the employee was reliable or trustworthy.

This transformed the existing loyalty program, which at least obstensibly focused on actual activities on behalf of a foreign government, into a program in which the concept of national security included insuring that public employees not only did not belong to disapproved organizations, but also did not hold beliefs incompatible with the accepted orthodoxy as to ideas and policies.

This development was ominous in the extreme; at least under the Truman policy the employee was faced with known limitations, such as the organizations he could not join or the extremes allowed in advocating his causes. This, of course, did not make it constitutional, since even in its own terms Executive Order 10450 was subject to great abuse (see *Bailey* v. *Richardson*). The Truman program was also limited to certain agencies and obviously focused on so-called extremest groups. Again, I

15. A special committee of the New York Bar Association found procedures under Executive Order 10450 not only to be haphazard and inconsistent, but also to be stacked against the employee. It held:

> Each of these programs has its own set of standards and procedures. In most of these programs once a question is raised as to the fitness of an employee, the burden of proof is placed on the employee to establish his fitness. Thus, under President Eisenhower's Executive Order of 1953, the burden rests upon the individual to demonstrate that retention in employment is clearly consistent with the interests of national security. If any doubt remains in the mind of the hearing officer, the employment must be terminated. [L. Green, "The Right to Know and Communicate," *Constitutional Freedom and the Law* (St. Louis Bar Association, 1958), p. 119.]

am not defending the program but stating that it was much more limited in intent and scope than the Eisenhower program.

The Eisenhower program was a different matter. It not only covered all agencies but allowed subjective factors to be the determinant of loyalty, such as reliability or trustworthiness. This made the program not only open-ended, but in fact constituted a total suppression of the First Amendment rights of public employees, since an employer did not need to limit action to advocacy or the joining of groups. Under the rubric of trustworthiness or reliability, the employer could now punish for belief. Since belief is private and need not be expressed, the only way an employee could protect himself was to remain totally silent. And, because of the mechanism established to probe disloyalty, the employee never knew if a statement or even an internal complaint could not be the subject of a loyalty complaint; his only answer was total aquiescence, since a complaint once made could easily get out of hand and have disastrous consequences. This was true not only on the federal level but at state and local levels as well. Many, if not most, states set up their own loyalty programs and the problems at the federal level were often repeated at the local level as well.

Thus, with the rights of public employees under assault, the courts inevitably had the ultimate responsibility to decide the controversy in all its ramifications. In doing so courts, especially the United States Supreme Court, have not only severely limited, if not eliminated, loyalty-security programs, but in the process have greatly expanded the First Amendment rights not only of public employees but of all citizens.

Indeed, it can be truthfully said that with the possible exception of the civil rights movement, no legal controversy has had as major an impact on the fabric of public life as the fight over the loyalty-security program. The history of the judicial reaction to the program will next be explored in detail.

Judicial Reactions

The first case tried under the loyalty program was the notorious case of *Bailey* v. *Richardson*. Dorothy Bailey had worked for the government for fourteen years with an exemplary record. She lost her position because of a reduction in manpower after World War II, and reapplied for another position with the government. However, the request was held up and she was required to be interviewed about some unfavorable allegations made against her to the effect that she was a Communist. She appealed an adverse finding by the original interviewer to the then Loyalty Review Board. She presented evidence in the form of affidavits to the effect that she was not a Communist and never had been. However, the charges against her were vague and the evidence unknown; at the hearing the board kept referring to statements made against her by five unidentified informants, which the board characterized as being reliable on the basis of an FBI report so stating. The board would not tell Bailey who these informants were, nor the exact nature of the charges made against her. On this basis of evidence, she was found disloyal and barred from federal service.[16]

She brought suit in the federal courts to have the determination of disloyalty removed. She lost. Both the Court of Appeals for the District of Columbia and the United States Supreme Court, affirming by a tie four to four vote with one justice not participating, held that the government was not held to any standard of sufficiency or reliability of evidence in a noncriminal determination of suitability for government employment.

Since the Supreme Court failed to write an opinion, with the dissenting judges adopting opinions in another case decided the same day, the only opinion which stands is that of the court of appeals.

The majority opinion, written by Judge Prettyman, deals with the lack of rights of public employees and more particularly the lack of rights of one not protected by Civil Service status.[17] The question of the sufficiency of the evidence was never reached, as the court assumed that public employees had no rights and therefore the question did not warrant discussion.

In dissent, Judge Edgerton made an impassioned plea for justice for Miss Bailey, saying that in effect she had been the subject of a "lynching." He stated:

> The Loyalty Review Board made an adverse finding. It is indisputable from the record that this finding was based entirely on the assertions of five unidentified, unsworn informants characterized as "reliable" by the F.B.I. Not only was Miss Bailey denied an opportunity to confront and cross-examine these accusers; but the board itself was denied any independent means of checking their reliability. It did not know if they were disinterested in point of fact, it did not know if they were real and living persons.
>
> To brand Miss Bailey disloyal to her country on such evidence alone —and despite an abundance of sworn testimony as to her trustworthiness by known, reputable witnesses, supported by a record of fourteen years of service in Government was to fly in the face of the President's order that eligibility should be determined "on all the evidence." More

16. Barth, *The Loyalty of Free Men*, pp. 114–15.
17. 182 F.2d at 58.

it was to fly in the face of every standard of fairness that has gone on to make up the American concept of due process. It was immaterial whether Miss Bailey was actually a Communist or not. A lynching is a lynching no matter whether its victim is innocent or guilty.[18]

The minority did express their view in the Supreme Court in another case decided the same day as *Bailey*, known as *Joint Anti-Fascist Refugee Committee* v. *McGrath*.[19] In this case, which limited the power of the attorney general to place groups on his list of subversives, the minority held that the entire loyalty program violated the First Amendment.

The Prettyman rule that held that the First Amendment did not apply to public employees was so extreme as to be untenable, and was quickly relegated to oblivion. However, the effect of *Bailey* was long-lived. It was not until 1967, in the case of *United States* v. *Robel*,[20] that any portion of the substantive basis of the federal loyalty program was held to be in violation of the Constitution.

The first limitations on the federal loyalty program occurred in cases in which the issue was procedural under the program, or where the applicability of the program to certain employees was in doubt. The first of these cases was *Cole* v. *Young*,[21] involving the dismissal under Executive Order 10450 of a food and drug inspector employed in the New York District of the Food and Drug Administration. Cole was allegedly a security risk, based on his past associations with persons and groups reported to be communists.

The Supreme Court held that Public Law 733 authorized dismissal of an employee in a summary, arbitrary fashion only where the dismissal is "necessary or advisable in the interest of national security."[22] However, "national security" was intended to refer only to the protection of sensitive activities, and thus an employee could be discharged under the provisions of 733 only if he occupied a sensitive position.

This decision made Executive Order 10450 void insofar as it exceeded the authority given to the president by Congress in Public Law 733. Thus, while persons deemed to be security risks could still be summarily dismissed, only those employees in sensitive positions would be subject to such action. Since the overwhelming number of federal employees were not employed in sensitive positions (Public Law 733 only applied to eleven agencies and not all employees of those agencies had "sensitive"

18. 182 F.2d at 72.
19. 341 U.S. 123 (1951).
20. 389 U.S. 256 (1967).
21. 351 U.S. 536 (1956).
22. 351 U.S. at 540.

positions), the effect of the decision was to relieve millions of federal employees from the danger of summary dismissal on that most serious of all grounds—loyalty.

Cole v. *Young* was followed in quick succession by a series of cases which further limited the power of the federal government to summarily dismiss on loyalty grounds. However, in none of these cases was the issue of constitutionality of the federal loyalty-security program directly brought into question, though this, of course, was the real issue even if the case was based on another issue.

In *Peters* v. *Hobby*,[23] Dr. John Peters of the Yale Medical School challenged his removal as a special consultant in the U.S. Public Health Service on loyalty grounds. In this case the agency loyalty board of the Public Health Service cleared Peters and declared him fit to serve. However, the Loyalty Review Board, the chief reviewing agency for loyalty cases under the Truman loyalty-security program, reopened the case on its own motion and conducted what it called a "post-audit." The result of this post-audit was a determination of reasonable doubt as to Peters's loyalty; he was therefore dismissed from his consulting position.

When the case finally reached the Supreme Court, the Court held that the Loyalty Review Board was not authorized to review cases on its own motion and decided in favor of the employee. While the ruling was based on rules of administrative procedure, in effect the Court applied the double jeopardy standard on loyalty proceedings. In this case the Court used a time-honored technique of deciding a case on the narrowest possible issue. Since an administrative alternative was present upon which the case could be decided, the Court so used it, thus avoiding the need to declare part of a federal statute unconstitutional. However, the effect of the decision was constitutional; from this case on, all administrative agencies were told that their personnel policies would be subject to a standard of due process, similar to that of the courts, at least insofar as a finding in favor of the employee would be a final "verdict" based on the given charge.

The *Peters* case had a very interesting sidelight which has great significance today. Traditionally the Solicitor-General of the United States signs all briefs which the United States government presents in cases before the Supreme Court. In 1956, when this case was to be argued, the solicitor-general was Simon Soboloff of Baltimore. A liberal Republican, Soboloff was opposed to the position held by the Department of Justice on the issue of the right of the Loyalty Review Board to review, on its own motion, findings in favor of the employee. Because of his feelings, he refused to sign the government's brief, or to argue the case.

23. 349 U.S. 331 (1955).

Because the case was such a distasteful one to argue from the government's side, most of the senior officials of the department refused to touch it. Finally an assistant attorney-general in the criminal division agreed to sign the brief and undergo the ordeal of having to argue the point in the Supreme Court. His name was Warren E. Burger. As a reward for doing his duty, Burger was given a promotion in the department and was soon thereafter appointed to the United States Court of Appeals for the District of Columbia. The rest of his rise to the Supreme Court bench is history. Later, Soboloff was also given a judicial appointment to the Court of Appeals for the Fourth Circuit, where he has served since, although he is now in semiretirement.

Following *Peters*, the Court rendered a series of decisions dealing with rights of procedural due process with respect to the employee's right to be told of the reasons for his dismissal.[24] But not until the late 1960s did the Supreme Court finally decide cases which raised substantial constitutional doubts about the loyalty-security program on substantive, rather than procedural, grounds

The landmark case was *United States* v. *Robel*, involving a section of the Internal Security Act of 1950 (the McCarren Act), which provided that once an organization was ordered to register with the Subversive Activities Control Board, it then became unlawful for any member of that organization to engage in any employment in any defense facility.[25] Robel, a member of the Communist party, was employed as a machinist in the Todd Shipyards in Seattle. He was employed before the Supreme Court upheld the registration provisions and before the Secretary of Defense had designated the Todd Shipyards a defense facility. After those events occurred, Robel continued to be employed at the shipyards and because of this was indicted for violation of the section. The district court dismissed the indictment because Robel was not an active member of the Communist party with an intent to further the goals of the party. The government appealed this ruling (double jeopardy was not present, since Robel was never actually brought to trial) and the Supreme Court upheld the district court on different and much broader grounds.

The majority decision, written by Chief Justice Warren, held that the district court's contention that the statute applied only to known active membership (not applicable in Robel's case) could not be read that narrowly. Rather, this statute was a broad, all-inclusive statute which

24. Service v. Dulles, 354 U.S. 363 (1957); Vitarelli v. Seaton, 359 U.S. 535 (1959); Greene v. McElroy, 360 U.S. 474 (1959); Cafeteria and Restaurant Workers Union v. McElroy, 367 U.S. 886 (1961).

25. The statute provided that the secretary of defense was vested with the power to designate certain facilities "defense facilities" and the statute would be applicable to these specifically designated facilities.

"sweeps indiscriminately across all types of association with Communist-action groups, . . . and thus, . . . runs afoul of the First Amendment."[26] In even sharper terms, Warren stated: "The statute quite literally establishes guilt by association alone, without any need to establish that an individual's association poses the threat feared by the Government in proscribing it." The Chief Justice then went on to set down a series of tests for such statutes. Significantly, the rules he espoused had been developed in cases involving state and local loyalty programs, but had never yet been applied to federal loyalty-security legislation. He stated:

> It has become axiomatic that "precision of regulation must be the touchstone in an area so closely touching our most precious freedoms," [cites omitted]. Such precision is notably lacking in §5(a)(1)(D). That statute casts its net across a broad range of associational activities, indiscriminately trapping membership which can be constitutionally punished and membership which cannot be so proscribed. It is made irrelevant to the statute's operation that an individual may be a passive or inactive member of a designated organization, that he may be unaware of the organization's unlawful aims, or that he may disagree with those unlawful aims.[27]

> It is also made irrelevant that an individual who is subject to the penalties of §5(a)(1)(D) may occupy a nonsensitive position in a defense facility. Thus §5(a)(1)(D) contains the fatal defect of overbreadth because it seeks to bar employment both for association which may be proscribed and for association which may not be proscribed consistently with First Amendment rights [cites omitted]. This the Constitution will not tolerate.[28]

Warren, later in his opinion, recognized the interest that Congress had in preventing sabotage and espionage in national defense industries and stated that "Nothing we hold today should be read to deny Congress the power under narrowly drawn legislation to keep from sensitive positions in defense facilities those who would use their positions to disrupt the Nation's production facilities."[29]

Implicit in this decision is the simple factual issue of Robel's long tenure at the shipyard. The fact that he had been employed in a nonsensitive position for a long time, without evidence of his engaging in any truly disloyal or subversive activities, undoubtedly weighed heavily on the minds of many of the justices. His situation dramatized how broad and widely sweeping the legislation was, as well as its misapplication. To declare at that late date that Robel was a security risk based on

26. 389 U.S. at 262.
27. Ibid., at 265.
28. Ibid., at 266.
29. Ibid., at 266–67.

associational activities present at the time of hiring and predating the statute comes dangerously close to accusing Robel of actual criminal behavior. A well-known doctrine states that criminal statutes must be construed more strictly than noncriminal prohibitions (unless something is called a conspiracy, in which case the loosest allegations of criminal behavior can be made—and they will stick); to allow a loosely drawn statute to apply retroactively to employed workers would almost constitute a bill of attainder.[30] When the U.S. Constitution was adopted, the term bill of attainder was used to describe any act of Congress or the states which provided for punishment or loss of rights to an individual rather than defining given types of activity and letting the judicial system be the vehicle for any kind of individual punishment arising under such law. This is in contrast to an ex post facto law, which is a criminal law with retroactive effect, that is, no legislature can pass a law prohibiting such acts and then punish persons for having done such acts at a time when they were still legal. A bill of attainder was a criminal law aimed at a specific individual or individuals (not a class of persons).

Indeed, in a case decided several years previously in the related field of control of subversives in the labor movement, the Supreme Court found a provision of the Labor-Management Reporting and Disclosure Act of 1959 (Landrum-Griffin) to constitute a bill of attainder. In that case the statute made it a crime for a member of the Communist party to serve as an officer or as an employee, except in clerical or custodial positions, of a labor union while a member of the Communist party.[31]

30. Article I, §9, cl. 3 of the U.S. Constitution provides: "No Bill of Attainder or ex post facto law shall be passed by Congress."

Article I, §10 of the U.S. Constitution provides: "No state shall pass any Bill of Attainder, ex post facto law or law impairing the Obligation of Contract."

Historically, a bill of attainder was a Parliamentary act sentencing to death one or more people. Acts providing for lesser penalties were called bills of pains and penalties. When the U.S. Constitution was adopted, the term bill of attainder was used to describe any act of Congress or the states which provided for punishment or loss of rights to an individual rather than outlawing a given type of activity and letting the judicial system be the vehicle for any kind of individual punishment arising under such law. See Fletcher v. Peck, 6 Cranch 87, 138 (1810); Cummings v. Missouri, 71 U.S. 277 (1867) and Ex Parte Garland, 71 U.S. 333 (1867); United States v. Lovett, 328 U.S. 303 (1946).

31. United States v. Brown, 381 U.S. 437 (1965), interpreting §504 of the Act: 73 Stat. 536, 29 U.S.C. 504 (1958 ed. Supp. 10). This statute provides:

> (a) No person who is or has been a member of the Communist Party . . . shall serve—
>
> (1) as an officer, director, Trustee, member of any executive board or similar governing body, organization or other employee (other than as an employee performing exclusively clerical or custodial duties) of any labor

The primary target of this statute was Archie Brown, an avowed Communist for more than a quarter of a century, and a member of the Executive Board of Local 10 of the Warehouseman's Union in San Francisco. He was indicted under the statute and convicted. The court reversed the indictment on the grounds that the statute violated Brown's First and Fifth Amendment rights. The government appealed and the Supreme Court found the statute to be a bill of attainder and thus unconstitutional.

This act constituted a bill of attainder because it was clearly aimed at an identifiable person or persons, and the statute was framed in such a way as to make it impossible for Brown and possibly others to avoid being classified in violation of the statute. Thus, in effect, it was a legislative punishment of an identifiable person for an identifiable act.

Robel might have been decided on the grounds of bill of attainder considering the nature of the statute, except that when the McCarren Act was passed many members of Congress were under the delusion that the defense industries were honeycombed with Communists.[32] This made it a general application statute based on facts, albeit nonexistent facts, rather than legislative punishment of an identifiable person for an identifiable act. A general application statute is simply a term for normal laws which have applicability to everyone in the class covered by the law, rather than a specific application to an individual or group.

Another complication was that, even if the secretary of defense qualified a given facility as a defense facility for the purpose of eliminating an identifiable Communist (as might well have happened in *Robel*), the bill of attainder section applies only to legislative acts and not administrative discretion. This is because a bill of attainder is historically a legislative act and cannot be stretched to include administrative tools. However, the equal protection and due process clause of the Constitution can be used to remedy such actions.

---

organization . . . during or for five years after the termination of his membership in The Communist Party. . . .

32. Other cases in which the Court was presented with a claim that a statute was a bill of attainder but found otherwise include: Communist Party v. Subversive Activities Control Board, 367 U.S. 1 (1961), all "Communist action organizations" must register; Board of Governors v. Agnew, 329 U.S. 441 (1947), no officer of a securities issuing organization shall serve as an officer, director, etc. of a federal bank; American Communication Workers Association v. Douds, 339 U.S. 382 (1949), in which the predecessor statute to 29 U.S.C. 504 (1958 Fed. Supp. 10) was upheld because there was no five-year provision and one could get free of the statute by resigning from the Communist party and signing an affidavit of disavowal.

The problem of administrative discretion was raised in the concurring opinion of Mr. Justice Brennan. He would not grant that this particular statute was overboard per se, but he thought the statute to be unconstitutional on the grounds that "the congressional delegation of authority to the Secretary of Defense to designate defense facilities creates the danger of overbroad, unauthorized, and arbitrary application of criminal sanctions in an area of protected freedoms and therefore, in my view, renders this statute invalid."[33]

In the constitutional sense, overbreadth means that the statute, ordinance, or regulation in question is so broad in its scope of coverage that it covers not only activities within the legitimate area of regulation, but also could be extended to prohibit or inhibit constitutionally protected activities.[34] A prize example of a law allegedly having overbreadth effect is the Hatch Act. While the Supreme Court has held that this act is not overbroad, the controversy over it raises classic issues of overbroad application and provides an excellent guide for the issue.

Brennan's opinion in the *Robel* case is interesting because he certainly was not one to shy away from using the overbreadth concept, as he literally invented the doctrine. In many ways his view is close to the heart of the problem of federal loyalty-security programs. Unlike most state cases involving a statutory oath, the problem in the federal program evolved from the enforcement machinery, rather than statutory language. In *Robel*, not only did the secretary of defense make the decision as to what facilities were "defense facilities," but also decided the organizational membership on which the sanctions would be imposed. The decision as to employment of individuals designated as illegal was made not by legislative action as much as by a decision of an administrative body, the Subversive Activities Control Board. By allowing administrative boards to set standards which could have criminal repercussions, Congress had abdicated its responsibility and also tried to immunize the program from real judicial scrutiny. Interestingly, the last time, previous to *Robel*, that the Supreme Court declared a congressional statute unconstitutional on the grounds of excessive delegation of power to an administrative body was in the famous *Schecter* case, in which the National Recovery Act of 1933 (usually referred to as the Blue Eagle case) was held to be unconstitutional on just such grounds.[35]

However, the Brennan theory remains an anomaly in the law. Even though *Schneider* v. *Smith*,[36] which followed *Robel*, involved a statutory

33. 389 U.S. at 257.
34. See especially Dombrowski v. Pfister, 380 U.S. 479 (1965).
35. Schecter v. United States, 295 U.S. 495 (1935).
36. 390 U.S. 17 (1968).

scheme not too dissimilar to that found in *Robel,* the Court shifted gears somewhat and focused on the problem of legislative standards and administrative discretions rather than testing the extent to which the statute impinged on protected First Amendment freedoms. This constitutes a departure; when the focus is placed on legislative standards and administrative discretion rather than on use of the test of overbroad applications, this action in effect concedes the right of Congress (or any legislative body, for that matter), to legislate as to a given subject. *Robel* rather strongly questioned the whole concept of the loyalty and security of public employees as a class as being a fit subject for legislative activity. This did not guarantee, of course, that individual public employees would not commit activities such as sabotage and espionage which would be in violation of the national interest, but such actions would be covered by criminal penalties with long historical precedents. However, the general concept of loyalty and security of public employees based on a general standard in the absence of any specific activity was a relatively new concept, and *Robel* severely questioned its validity.

At issue in *Schneider* was the constitutionality of the Magnusen Act, which authorized the president to issue regulations "to safeguard against destruction, loss, or injury from sabotage or other subversive acts" all vessels in the territories or waters subject to the jurisdiction of the United States.[37]

Based upon such regulations, Willard Smith, commandant of the Coast Guard, refused to process Schneider's application for validation of his mariner's certificate on the grounds that he had refused to answer certain questions in a questionnaire as to his attitude toward the U.S. form of government, or whether he had contributed to or attended functions of any of the groups on the attorney general's list. Schneider admitted that he had once joined the Communist party, but had quit because of disagreement with their methods and techniques. He refused to answer the aforementioned questions because "it would be obnoxious to a truly free citizen to answer the kinds of questions under compulsion that you require."

Schneider brought suit asking that the statute be declared unconstitutional, and requiring that the commandant issue him his papers. Schneider got his papers, but the Court, in a neat bit of judicial juggling, refused to find the statute unconstitutional. Instead, it held that the Congress had the power to prevent sabotage on military vessels by setting procedures to screen out potential saboteurs, when the statute was aimed

37. 50 U.S.C. §191(b).

at actions rather than words and beliefs. Thus, the focus in this case was as Brennan's focus in *Robel*, an administrative rather than legislative action.

Emphasis must be placed on the fact that this opinion did differ from the Brennan opinion. Here the Court was not saying that the administrative body had been delegated too much authority, but rather that the actions they entered into were based on powers not delegated to them. If the Magnuson Act had permitted the president or his agents to eliminate from the Maritime Service persons who had joined, contributed to, or took part in activities of an organization cited as subversive by the Subversive Activities Control Board or the attorney general, the situation would have been analogous to *Robel*.

Brennan's concurring opinion in *Robel* and the *Schneider* opinion are of the most use to public employees. The majority opinion in *Robel*, while exceedingly important to First Amendment doctrine, does not come to grips with the real dangers to public employees from the loyalty-security program—unbridled administrative discretion. Public employees must attempt to stop administrators from asking questions about activities not directly concerned with the performance of the job. Even if the employee would not be subject to dismissal based on his answers, he might suffer other severe consequences, such as loss of promotion or responsibility, because his answers reveal political or social views different from that of his immediate or general supervisors.

The employee faces a trap; since, if he refuses to answer the questions, he could be dismissed for refusal to answer, his main interest is to prevent the asking of the questions. Broad theory, such as found in *Robel*, is not of much use to an employee leary of the dossier being collected on him based in no small part on his answers to official questions.[38]

Since many of these administrative intrusions into the political and social views of public employees is without explicit authority, the holding in *Schneider* is of importance, in that even though it steps back from *Robel* in allowing a loyalty-security program, it also puts some curbs in the power of the agency involved to administer the program. Even the Brennan opinion in *Robel* is somewhat passé, because Congress is more careful about giving administrative bodies such carte blanche authority to formulate standards and procedures for weeding out "subversives" in

38. The test is one of compelling state interest in the disclosure which cannot be broader than the educational interest proposed by the state. See NAACP v. Alabama, ex rel Patterson, 357 U.S. 449 (1957); Gibson v. Florida Legislative Commission, 372 U.S. 539 (1963); Shelton v. Tucker, 364 U.S. 479 (1960); but also see Cole v. Richardson, 405 U.S. 676 (1972), which resulted when a public employee lost her job for refusal to sign an oath.

the public service. Instead, as previously noted, intimidation through the compilation of dossiers without any congressional authority is used. In the future, if public employees and others seek to attack the government's dossier collecting power, *Schneider* may prove to be a very important weapon.[39]

As a result of these decisions, many of the worst abuses of the loyalty-security program will probably not be repeated. Yet the price of the loyalty-security program has been extremely high. Entire departments of government, including the State Department, have been permanently scarred, and an underlying fear of being ensnared in a loyalty probe pervades the entire federal service. By and large, officials, rather than employees, now become extremely uneasy when they see highly qualified officials excluded or dismissed from service because they dared to subscribe to views, often on subjects unrelated to their jobs, which vary from the prevailing orthodoxy. The result is, of course, only to increase the reticence of public employees in asserting those constitutional rights they do possess.

However, the danger from espionage has never been, and will never be, any excuse for loyalty and security programs such as those which followed World War II. Experience has clearly shown that no spy or saboteur could ever have been uncovered through the use of loyalty oaths or administrative screening for beliefs. The revelations of such sources as the Penkovsky Papers show that persons who have been recruited for espionage service are instructed never to engage in any type of controversial speech or association which would bring attention upon them, and that at all times the recruited agent should swear complete and total allegiance to the government and abide by all facets of any loyalty or security program. Even though, as Louis Strauss observed, the stated reason for revoking J. Robert Oppenheimer's security clearance was "a measure taken to safeguard secret information . . . and for no

39. Unfortunately, a great chance to put a judicial limitation on dossier collection was lost when Mr. Justice Rehnquist refused to disqualify himself in Laird v. Tatum, 408 U.S. 1 (1972). In that case a three-judge federal court held that the activities of the U.S. Army Intelligence in its surveillance and collection of intelligence dossiers on civilian political activities constituted a violation of the First Amendment rights of those under surveillance. The Supreme Court by a 5–4 vote reversed the decision, holding that the general surveillance and domestic collection activities of the Army are beyond the scope of federal court jurisdiction and do not present a real case or controversy. The problem of Justice Rehnquist's participation arose because, when he was in the Justice Department, he took an active role in the government's defense of the case and would have been expected to disqualify himself, as had been the tradition. Had he done so, the opinion of the three-judge court would have been affirmed by a 4–4 vote.

other purpose,"[40] the only purpose, in light of the general knowledge of the surveillance and espionage methods of intelligence agencies, was not to protect secret information but rather to enforce a conformity of ideas and beliefs among public employees. While times have changed from the days of the McCarthy era, the danger is by no means over, as the revelations of Watergate so clearly show. What the government can do to its employees it can do to all citizens; thus, everyone has a stake in not subjecting public employees to a loss of rights because of their beliefs and associations.

State and Local Programs

Much of the publicity and controversy concerning the so-called loyalty and security programs which flourished after World War II focused on the federal government and the legislative and administrative programs which applied to federal employees. Nevertheless, public employees on the state and local level were in no way immune from the hysteria which pervaded the times. While nothing on the state or local level has ever quite reached the intensity of the rampages of Senator Joseph McCarthy and his cohorts, the results of the programs on the state and local levels were no less damaging and destructive to individual employees. In fact, in some ways these local programs were more destructive to the individual than those on the federal level. First of all, such programs tended to be fought outside the scope of national publicity; thus, the employee often suffered in silence and anonymity. Second, since the state and local programs, as a matter of law, had much less legitimacy than the basic primacy of the federal program, the thrust of these programs tended to cut across protected constitutional rights, especially First Amendment rights, much more often and with a much greater and more devastating impact than even the worst federal program.

The premise on which the federal loyalty and security programs were based revolved around the desire and fear of the federal government and the Congress to prevent having within the ranks of the federal Civil Service persons who would be beholden to a foreign power, and who would, in the course of their duties, cause irreparable damage to national security through acts of espionage and potential sabotage. Revelations subsequent to World War II about the scope and extent of espionage and subversion programs by the Soviet Union show that this was not merely an idle threat, but that there was and still, in many ways, continues to be a real danger that employees of the federal government

40. Quoted in Stern, *The Oppenheimer Case*, p. 413.

might become actual agents of a foreign government, especially the Soviet Union.

However, if the federal program at least had the pretense of national security and the desire to weed out security risks—risks in the sense of actual commission of criminal acts—no such pretense existed at the state and local level. Unlike the federal government, state and local governments do not engage in any activity which would be of interest to a foreign government. National defense has always been a function solely of the federal government; no state or local government ever will be involved in a national defense program, other than through the National Guard. Likewise, other targets of potential espionage (for instance, information on the national treasury or economic policies) are also functions exclusively of the federal government. This fact has not prevented state governments from attempting to set up programs to weed out security risks, however.

In the case of *Pennsylvania* v. *Nelson*,[41] the state of Pennsylvania indicted the well-known Communist Steve Nelson for sedition—that is, acts detrimental to national security and defense. The Supreme Court held that the entire field of national security had been preempted by the federal government and that the states have no power to enact legislation in that area. The Pennsylvania act was basically a replica of the Smith Act of 1940, and it was on this basis that the Supreme Court held that the Smith Act had to be so governing of law on the question of national security and defense that the Pennsylvania law or any other state law must fall.[42]

41. 350 U.S. 497 (1956).
42. Stat. 670 (1940), now 18 U.S.C. §2385, provides:

> Whoever knowingly or willfully advocates, abets, advises, or teaches the duty, necessity, desirability, or propriety of overthrowing or destroying the government of the United States or the government of any State, Territory, District or Possession thereof, or the government of any political subdivision therein, by force or violence, or by the assassination of any officer of any such government; or
>
> Whoever, with intent to cause the overthrow or destruction of any such government, prints, publishes, edits, issues, circulates, sells, distributes, or publicly displays any written or printed matter advocating, advising, or teaching the duty, necessity, desirability, or propriety of overthrowing or destroying any government in the United States by force or violence, or attempts to do so: or
>
> Whoever organizes or helps or attempts to organize any society, group or assembly of persons who teach, advocate, or encourage the overthrow or destruction of any such government by force or violence; or becomes or is a

While the thrust of the federal loyalty and security programs tends to fall most heavily upon those persons having some connection with the national defense, both members of the military and civilians, the thrust of most state and local programs has fallen and will continue to fall most heavily on persons involved in the educational sectors, both at the secondary and college levels. Teachers invariably have borne the brunt of state and local programs. First of all, teachers make up a very large percentage of the actual total public employee work force at these levels. Remaining public employees tend to fall either within the administrative sphere, at such jobs as low level functionary clerks, or within the authoritarian area, generally members of the police or fire departments. Because of the relationship between the loyalty program and the suppression of speech, the targets of such a program would be those employees most likely to engage in speech-related activities. And, at the height of the loyalty program at the state and local level, these employees would almost invariably be high school and state college teachers.

The real basis of state loyalty programs is to root out ideas rather than espionage agents. Since the function of teachers is to innovate, to challenge existing rules and procedures, they are naturally suspect, especially because at the state and local levels, as well as the national level, innovative thinking and personal beliefs are equated with disloyalty. The act of thinking is suspect, nothing else, and suspicion naturally falls on those persons who "think" for a living.[43]

member of, or affiliates with, any such society, group, or assembly of persons, knowing the purposes thereof—

Shall be fined not more than $20,000 or imprisoned not more than twenty years, or both, and shall be ineligible for employment by the United States or any department or agency thereof, for the five years next following his conviction.

If two or more persons conspire to commit any offense named in this section, each shall be fined not more than $20,000 or imprisoned not more than twenty years or both, and shall be ineligible for employment by the United States or any department or agency thereof, for the five years next following his conviction.

As used in this section, the terms "organizes" and "organize," with respect to any society, group, or assembly of persons, includes the recruiting of new members, the forming of new units, and the regrouping or expansion of existing clubs, classes, and other units of such society, group, or assembly of persons."

See also Hines v. Davidowitz, 312 U.S. 52 (1939).

43. Under the original loyalty-security program during World War II, 2,500,000 persons were investigated, yet only 83 were shown to merit discharge.

An example of how this paranoia operated in state and local programs can be seen by examining what happened in Los Angeles County. Approximately one week after President Truman formulated his Executive Order 9835, the Board of Supervisors of Los Angeles County adopted a loyalty program based on a test oath containing specific disavowals of association and belief. During the war not a single case of disloyalty appeared among the county's 20,001 employees. Yet, with substantially the same employees on the payroll, the county suddenly became concerned with their loyalty only two years after the war. This clearly illustrates that internal tension provides the real motivation for loyalty programs and that this ordinance and many others were adopted as part of a drive for political conformity, one with absolutely nothing to do with security.

State and local loyalty programs were of two types: the "test oath program" and what I like to call the "investigative program," whether handled by legislative or administrative bodies or a combination of both. In many states the two types of programs were integrated into a single program, often as a result of a comprehensive state law. The prototype of such a law was Maryland's Ober Law, named after a Baltimore legislator. The Ober Law had six major provisions: (1) criminal sanctions were provided for sedition (this provision became unconstitutional after the *Nelson* case); (2) a test oath was provided which, in Maryland, applied to candidates for office as well as public employees; (3) a mandate was given to public agencies to institute programs to screen applicants for loyalty; (4) procedures were established for the dismissal of those found to violate the provisions; (5) a special assistant attorney general was appointed to enforce such a program; and, finally, (6) the program was extended to private colleges and schools receiving state aid.[44]

Similar laws (in some cases almost exactly the same as the Ober Law) were adopted for all public employees in twenty-two states. Significantly, seven states (Colorado, Indiana, Michigan, Nevada, New York, North Dakota, and Vermont) adopted exactly the same procedure, but applied it only to teachers. I think that this specific designation of teachers only clearly shows the thrust of, and the primary fears and forces behind, state and local programs.

44. A discussion of the Ober Law can be found in Ralph Brown *Loyalty and Security* (New Haven, Conn.: Yale Univ. Pr., 1958), pp. 97–103. The Ober Law has been the subject of two Supreme Court decisions: Gerende v. Election Board, 341 U.S. 56 (1951), and Whitehall v. Elkins, 389 U.S. 54 (1967).

Investigative Programs

The investigative programs developed after World War II at various state and local levels were, in many ways, replicas of those developed in congressional committees and various agencies of the federal government. While investigative programs on the state and local levels were more limited in scope and fewer existed, they could be as vicious and as devastating as any program on the national level, even if the targets were fewer in number.

One of the most famous bodies was the so-called Tenney Committee, or more precisely, the California Senate Fact Finding Committee on Un-American Activities. Tenney was a state senator from Los Angeles whose activities and general style predated the more famous actions of U.S. Senator Joseph McCarthy. One example of the Tenney Committee's program should suffice as a guide to the entire area.

The Northern California Chapter of the American Civil Liberties Union, a constant and unrelenting foe of the Tenney Committee and other similar groups in the northern California area, found during the course of studying certain depositions taken from some of its cases that the Tenney Committee and the University of California had entered into a truly incredible relationship. According to this information, confirmed by J. R. Combes, the general counsel for the committee, the committee had an agreement with the university by which the committee would clear all prospective employees at the university and pass on to the university derogatory information about present employees. In effect, this gave the Tenney Committee a veto power over all faculty appointments to the University of California. While this arrangement, of course, is no longer in existence, it nonetheless shows the incredible danger that loyalty and security programs, especially on a state level, pose to academic freedom and learning in the United States.

While the Tenney Committee was probably unique in the extent of its influence and the overall damage it committed, a real understanding of the problems can be obtained by examining the actions of a lesser known, yet very representative body, the so-called Cantwell Commission that operated a reign of terror over the University of Washington during the late 1940s. This committee, definitely patterned after the Tenney Committee, was headed by Albert F. Cantwell, a former Deputy Sheriff of the City of Spokane and later a state legislator. An indication of the thrust of Cantwell's mind can be garnered from a statement made by him. When asked his opinion on integration and discrimination against Negroes, he emphatically stated, "if someone insists there is discrimination against Negroes in this country, or that there is any inequality of wealth, then there is every reason to believe that person is a Communist."[45]

While the committee was originally established to investigate the Washington Old Age Pension Union, it soon turned its attention to a much more inviting target, the faculty of the University of Washington. In July of 1948 the committee held open hearings for four days in an armory in Seattle. The subject was the so-called Communist infiltration of the University of Washington. Of the approximately 1,400 faculty members at the university at that time, the committee focused its attention on ten. As a result of such investigation, six members of the faculty had charges brought against them. A newspaper dispatch stated: "University leaders take the position . . . that once the legislature has embarked upon its investigation of campus conditions, the university as a state-supported institution, had no alternative than to submit to investigation and welcome 'findings of facts.' "[46]

While the fact that so many of the university's professors had charges brought against them might not in itself be extraordinary, the Cantwell Committee hearings were so unusual and so much a matter of public concern because of the atmosphere under which they were conducted. The witnesses for the committee were something to behold. One witness was a Seattle private detective who had joined the Communist party so that he might "ferret out Reds in the faculty."[47] When asked about his activities, certain committee officials said they could see nothing wrong with spying on political activities of professors. Another witness was a neighbor of one of the accused faculty members who peeked through a basement window of the professor's house and claimed he saw a picture of Stalin hanging on the wall. Another witness, one of the special breed of professional anti-Communists, made such false accusations against one of the professors that the Seattle District Attorney issued an arrest warrant against him for perjury. However, the committee got him out of the state before the warrant could be served. Great pressure was brought against the district attorney to have him drop the complaint; when he refused, even the university became convinced that the statements against this professor were false. However, this incident was not made a part of official committee records.[48]

---

45. Cited in Carey McWilliams, *Witch Hunt: The Revival of Heresy* (Boston: Little, Brown, 1950), p. 35.
46. Ibid., p. 145.
47. Ibid., p. 166.
48. Ibid., p. 145–46.

The impact of these committees on the individual professors and teachers caught in the net of the investigations for expressing what was considered to be unpopular beliefs or for having unpopular associations was all too real. To the dismissed professor, the fact that he was fired as a result of a small state investigative committee, rather than through the actions of a national subcommittee of Congress, did not matter; the effect was the same, and demoralized many other professors and teachers, consequently forcing them into silence. Fortunately the Army-McCarthy hearings, which had such a sobering effect on Congress, tended to have the same effect on the states.

However, since certain congressional committees, most notably the House Un-American Activities Committee (HUAC), continued to run roughshod over individuals until the early 1960s, the same could only be expected in the states. Indeed, the only reason loyalty committee investigation in the states tended to die out was due to the civil rights movement. State and local governments became so involved in the civil rights struggle that they did not need to look for foreign enemies; they had, to their thinking, the most dangerous one at home. While many of the same people made the same accusations and used the same techniques against the civil rights movement, the civil rights struggle was not a continuation of the loyalty controversy and should not be thought of as such. The loyalty program was unique, and in some ways more controversial. Even today, when racial equality is accepted as the norm, vestiges of the loyalty program remain to poison the atmosphere of the body politic, as witness the exercises of the "Plumbers."

Test Oaths

While the actions of some state legislative investigation committees attracted a certain amount of attention, the vast majority of state and local employees found a difficult and different type of foe to face—the test oaths which were imposed upon them. Test oaths are considerably different in nature and intent than the simple constitutional oaths which most public officials take when they assume office. Test oaths require more than a simple pledge to uphold the Constitution and its laws. They require that the employee swear he is not subversive, that he will not be subversive, and sometimes that he has not been subversive.

The historical antecedents for the loyalty oaths used for public employees go back to the time of the High Commission in the historic Chamber of the Privy Council in England. Starting late in the reign of Queen Elizabeth and continuing up to and through the Long Parliament of 1640, the established powers of England, especially the Church of

England, were locked in mortal combat with the doctrine of Puritanism in no less a manner, and with no less ferocity, than the battle of the American establishment against the suspected forces of Marxism, socialism and, in some cases, liberalism. Indeed, a direct analogy can be drawn between the upheavals and actions of these periods, especially between the 1630s and the period of the deepest part of the cold war, from 1948–55. The High Commission was set up to root out Puritan "heresy" in the clergy, while the Chamber of the Privy Council attempted to stamp out the Puritan press, all Puritan writing, indeed all Puritan ideas. Both the English and the U.S. cold war programs had one thing directly in common: the method through which both attempted to gain their results was the use of the ex officio oath.

The ex officio oath, as it was used in the 1630s, caused the witness to be forced to swear that he would truthfully answer any questions he might be asked. He was not only forced to accuse himself, but was also required to incriminate friends against whom the court had not yet received evidence. The questions asked concerned even private conversations. If a person refused to take the oath, he was committed to prison for contempt of court.

The use of the ex officio oath by Chamber of the Privy Council and the High Commission remained relatively unchallenged until 1638, when John Lilburn forced the issue into the public light; this eventually led to its abolishment. Lilburn was a man of no academic background involved in smuggling Puritan tracts into England from Holland and then having these books and pamphlets delivered to English booksellers and readers. Late in 1637 he was arrested on a London street on an order from the Chamber and charged in a vague indictment with sending "factious and scandalous" books from Holland to England. He flatly denied this accusation, but refused to answer any questions about any other matter. Because of this refusal, no charges were filed against him. Approximately ten days later, Lilburn was taken to the guard chamber office for questioning. He asked why he was being questioned, since no bill of charges had been filed against him. At that point Attorney General Sir John Banks replied that he would examine him first and then charges would be made against him. Lilburn was then asked to take the Star Chamber oath which read: "You shall swear that you shall make true answers to all things that be asked of you; so help you God." Lilburn replied: "Before I swear, I will know to what I must swear." When again brought before the Chamber, this time on February 9, 1638, after having been confined in jail since his arrest, Lilburn was again asked why he had refused to take the Star Chamber oath. His answer to this question still has applicability today:

Most noble lord, I have refused upon this ground, because when I was examined, though I fully answered all things that belonged to me to answer to, I had cleared myself of the thing for which I am imprisoned, which was sending books out of Holland, yet that would not satisfy and give content, other things were put unto me concerning other men, to ensnare me, and to get further matter against me; which, I perceiving, refused, being not bound to answer such things that do not belong unto me. Withal I perceive the oath to me an oath of inquiry; and for the lawlessness of which oath, I have no warrants; and upon these grounds I did and do still refuse the oath.[49]

Lilburn was eventually found guilty and sentenced to prison. However, his stand caused a great national uproar and by 1640 the Puritans had established enough strength to form the so-called Long Parliament. Lilburn presented a petition for his freedom on the day the new parliament first met, and became the first person freed by the Long Parliament of the House of Commons, which soon after wiped out the Star Chamber oath.

In this country, the experiences of Lilburn and others caused a great fear of oaths; indeed a long tradition of judicial repugnance to such oaths was established. After the Civil War certain administrations of former Confederate states attempted to impose oaths of loyalty based upon support of the Union during the war. If the person stated that he was not loyal to the Union before the war, he would be barred from government employment or office; and, if he refused, he would be subject to jail. The Supreme Court, in a series of cases arising from various states, found these oaths unconstitutional because of the constitutional prohibition against ex post facto laws. The Court viewed these oaths as a form of punishment, since the individuals required to take the oaths could not truthfully subscribe to them or, if they did subscribe, would be subject to various types of punishments.[50]

The oaths instituted after World War II resembled the Star Chamber oath more than the oaths imposed on former Confederate supporters. They were concerned with certain "heresies" of belief and association, in that they asked the public employee to swear that he had never been, was not at present, and would never engage in such beliefs and associations. However, these beliefs and associations were described in the broadest, most vague terms, so that a public employee could swear under

---

49. See Chaffee, *The Blessings of Liberty* (Philadelphia: Lippincott, 1956), p. 191, for a discussion of the Lilburn incident. This book is the basis of this discussion of the situation.

50. Cummings v. Missouri, 71 U.S. 277 (1867); Ex Parte Garland, 71 U.S. 333 (1867).

the oath, believing it to apply to a specific type of action or association, and then discover himself subject to disciplinary or sometimes criminal action under statutes prescribing the oaths, because the statute was interpreted in a broader, more general manner.

For example, an oath of the state of Washington, applicable to teachers, stated that an applicant must swear:

> I, ———, solemnly swear that I will support the Constitution and Laws of the United States of America and the State of Washington and will by precept and example promote respect for the flag and institutions of the United States of America and the State of Washington, reverence of law and order and individual allegiance to the Government of the United States.[51]

Other oaths were more specific. In Florida, all public employees had to take an oath that included the language: "I have not and will not lend my aid, support, counsel, or influence to the Communist Party."[52] Finally, an oath from Oklahoma required all public employees, including faculty and staff of the state universities, to swear that they had not in the past five years been a member of the Communist party, of any organization on the attorney general's list, or of any other organization advocating violent overthrow of the government. The crux of the oath was that persons would be disqualified for public employment solely on the basis of organizational membership.[53]

For the first time since the days of the Alien and Sedition Acts political heresies were incorporated into the body politic which, if maintained by persons, especially public employees, either through association or belief, would constitute grounds for disqualification from public benefits, including most especially public employment, and could in certain cases lead to imprisonment. As in the days of the Star Chamber, the required oaths were not simple constitutional oaths which, though broad and nonspecific, at least had never been intended to relate to any particular group, belief, or act. No criminal sanctions are attached to the simple constitutional oaths which public officials must take. Any act of wrongdoing on the part of a public official who takes a simple constitutional oath would simply be considered a violation of the standards of office based on criteria and requirements drafted and enforced independently of any oath.

These test oaths are quite different in their nature and results. First of all, they are not related to performance in office of an employee or

51. Wash. Laws 1931, §103. See Baggett v. Bullett, 377 U.S. 360 (1963).
52. See Gibson v. Florida Legislative Commission, 372 U.S. at 542 (1963).
53. Wieman v. Updegraff 344 U.S. 183 (1952).

official. Of course, some test oaths also contained constitutional oaths within their wording. However, the concern and target of these test oaths were associations and beliefs held by the employee outside of the scope of his employment and which, in many cases, may have been entered into long before the person assumed his employment. Second, unlike the constitutional oaths, the test oaths, even though extremely broad and vague, can be broken down to apply to specific acts, specific associations, and specific beliefs. Third, the oath lends itself to a punitive effect. Unlike simple constitutional oaths, a public employee can be held in violation of these oaths, and thereby subject to either dismissal from employment or denial of employment. Finally, a person merely required to take a simple constitutional oath may be subject to removal from position or office, but the acts leading to such removal would be measured according to the fine standards of propriety or legality having absolutely no relationship to a person's belief, association, or opinion. Under the test oaths, however, punitive action may be based on matters of belief and association which not only are not criminal in nature, but may actually be protected by the First Amendment to the Constitution.

Any public employee engaging in espionage or subversive activities on behalf of a foreign government or directly advocating specific violent actions obviously can be subject to prosecution for such acts. However, statutes had been on the books making such acts criminal before any test oaths were devised, and any person who committed these acts could be punished for violation of a specific statute, not punished for violation of the test oath. The test oath makes punishable beliefs, association, and acts below the level of criminal activity. Because of this, test oaths pose an extraordinary threat to the constitutional rights not only of public employees, but of all citizens. The paranoia which led to the enactment of test oath statutes had the effect of causing an abrogation of the rights of all citizens.

Judicial Reactions

As with the judicial reaction to the federal loyalty-security program, the first cases before the United States Supreme Court regarding state and local loyalty oaths found the Supreme Court agreeing with the government as to the validity and necessity of such oaths. Significantly, these cases came before the Court in the darkest days of the cold war and the Vinson court found, as with the trials of Communist leaders in the *Dennis* case and other similar matters from this period, that these loyalty oaths were constitutional.[54]

54. Dennis v. United States, 341 U.S. 494 (1951). See also Yates v. United States, 354 U.S. 298 (1957).

In *Garner* v. *Board of Public Works of Los Angeles*,[55] the issue before the Court was a loyalty oath administered to all Los Angeles public employees. Basically, the oath proscribed affiliations of the employee for five years prior to taking the oath with any organization which would "devise, advocate or teach" overthrow of the government. A majority of the Supreme Court upheld this oath as a reasonable regulation to establish employment qualifications of loyalty to the states and the United States government. The Court stated that such an oath was "reasonably designed to protect the integrity and competency of the service." The Court did hold that such an oath should not affect those that did not know about the nature of the organization or who had severed ties with these organizations after the character of the organization became apparent. The majority opinion decided that the oath was not a bill of attainder; the First Amendment was never discussed. Justices Black and Douglas dissented on the grounds that the oath was a bill of attainder and thus unconstitutional. Justice Frankfurter, also in dissent, allowed the states could inquire about Communist affiliations, but felt that the oath was invalid because of vagueness of language.

In his dissent, Justice Frankfurter pointed out the very real First Amendment problems that this particular oath and similar oaths have in terms of their deterrent or chilling effect on the First Amendment rights of employees, previewing the line of thinking later taken by the Supreme Court with respect to all major First Amendment cases. Interestingly, when the doctrine did receive a judicial majority some nine years later, Justice Frankfurter dissented from the views of the Court which, in many ways, was based on his own earlier dissenting opinion. He stated, in *Garner*,

> Not only does the oath make an irrational demand, it is bound to operate as a real deterrent to people contemplating even innocent associations. How can anyone be sure that an organization with which he affiliates will not at some time in the future be found by a State or National official to advocate overthrow of government by "unlawful means"? All but the hardiest may well hesitate to join organizations if they know that by such a proscription they will be permanently disqualified from public employment. These are considerations that cut deep into the traditions of our people.[56]

The chilling effect doctrine Justice Frankfurter first proposed in his dissent in *Garner* holds, in effect, that law, whether it be a statute, ordinance, decree, or administrative action, may be held unconstitutional

55. 341 U.S. 716 (1951).
56. 341 U.S. at 727–28.

(in violation of the First Amendment) when it causes people to refrain from asserting their First Amendment rights due to their uncertainty as to whether or not this assertion would be in violation of the particular law.

The question of degrees of association and knowledge of the activities of the organizations being proscribed was a matter which had previously troubled the Court. Prior to *Garner*, in the case of *Gerende* v. *Board of Supervisors of Elections in Baltimore*, the Court upheld the constitutionality of a provision of the Maryland Ober Law (discussed previously) which provided that, in order to obtain a place on a ballot, the candidate for public office must take an oath that he was not a "subversive person" within the meaning of the statute.[57] The Supreme Court affirmed an opinion of the Supreme Court of Maryland which stated that:

> A candidate need only make oath that he is not a person who is engaged in one way or another in the attempt to overthrow the government by *force and violence*, and that he is not knowingly a member of an organization engaged in such an attempt.[58]

The next major case in the area was *Adler* v. *Board of Education*.[59] At issue in *Adler* were Section 12–a of the Civil Service Law of New York and the 1949 amendments to the education law (known as the Fineberg Law), passed to implement the provisions of 12–a. Section 12–a made a person ineligible for any kind of government service if he "advocates, advises, or teaches" forceful overthrow of the government or joins an organization that did the same. The Fineberg Law required the Board of Regents to make up a list (after notice of hearing) or organizations considered subversive under 12–a. If a person was a member of an organization on that list, his membership was to be considered "prima facie evidence of disqualification" for employment or retention in the school system.

This legislative scheme was upheld by the Supreme Court on virtually the same grounds as *Garner*, except that, in finding for the constitutionality of this statute, the Court also expounded the idea that public employment is taken according to the terms presented by the government, almost an affirmation of the old Holmes doctrine. The majority view, written by Justice Minton, was that an individual does not lose his right to freedom of speech if he loses his job. That is, if a person chooses to

---

57. 341 U.S. 56 (1951).
58. Gerende v. Board of Supervisors of Elections in Baltimore, 341 U.S. at 60.
59. 342 U.S. 485 (1952).

accept employment which involves a limitation on associational and similar types of activities, he does not necessarily give up his right to such activities. The law simply means that in order to pursue these activities further, a person might be obligated to give up his public employment. Since this situation is reasonable in terms of the states' right to determine conditions of employment, the individual is not deprived of rights when forced to make a choice between membership and employment.

The dissents of Justices Black and Douglas raised broad constitutional issues. Justice Black talked in terms of First Amendment freedom of speech which would be violated if public officials had the power "to select the ideas people can think about, censor the public views they can express, or choose the persons or groups people can associate with." Justice Douglas held the view that the Fineberg Law violated the principle of guilt by association, because a teacher could be disqualified from membership in an organization found to be subversive in a proceeding to which the teacher was not a party.

The *Adler* case marks the high-water mark of Supreme Court sanction of governmental loyalty and security programs. While, in some later cases, the Supreme Court indeed upheld certain aspects of state loyalty and security programs, nonetheless, the Court never again followed the sweeping language of *Adler*, which strongly implied that state and local employees must be willing to subject themselves to any and all loyalty and security programs simply because they were employees of the state, and that the state, because it had the right to set all conditions, might in fact subject employees to any and all types of potentially unconstitutional conditions as an aspect of their employment.

One year after the *Adler* case, the Supreme Court took a long step away from the rigid doctrine of *Adler* in the case of *Wieman* v. *Updegraff*.[60] This case is of significance less because of the actual decision than because it was the first case in which the Supreme Court found in favor of public employees asserting that they should maintain certain of their constitutional rights despite the fact that they were employed by an agency of the government. At issue in *Wieman* was the constitutionality of an Oklahoma loyalty oath which required (again, in almost the same language as many other states) that every state employee, including faculty members of state universities, swear that he had not during the past five years been a member of the Communist party or any organization of the attorney general's list of any organization advocating violent overthrow of the government. Mere membership without knowl-

60. 344 U.S. 183 (1952).

edge of, and approval of, the legal activities of the organization was sufficient to deny public employment. The opinion, written by Mr. Justice Clark, found a violation of due process in the Oklahoma statute; of significance was that the Court based its opinion in large part on the effect on a public employee of a finding of disloyalty. Because the finding of disloyalty had such a drastic impact, the public employee has to be constitutionally protected from a program which casts a stain of disloyalty in an indiscriminate and arbitrary manner. Justice Clark held, in what has become classic language:

> But membership may be innocent. A state servant may have joined a proscribed organization unaware of its activities or purposes. . . . There can be no dispute about the consequences visited upon a person excluded from public employment on disloyalty grounds. In the view of the community, the stain is a deep one; indeed, it has become a badge of infamy. Especially is this so in time of cold war and hot emotions when "each man begins to eye his neighbor as a possible enemy." Yet, under the Oklahoma Act, the fact of association alone determines disloyalty and disqualification; it matters not whether association existed innocently or knowingly. To thus inhibit individual freedom of movement is to stifle the flow of democratic expression and controversy at one of its chief sources.[61]

The strength and eloquence of this language, especially the phrase "badge of infamy," was a critical factor in the case's impact. By focusing on the impact on the employee of the oaths and a finding of "disloyalty," rather than an abstract discussion of due process, the controversy over loyalty oaths took on a new dimension. Indeed, the excesses of the early Eisenhower years made Clark a relevant prophet and deepened judicial distrust of these laws.

Following the *Wieman* case, the Court accepted several cases in the area of law which concerned the rights of public employees to take the Fifth Amendment before various investigative committees. While the results of these decisions were not totally satisfactory from the public employee's point of view, nonetheless, the method of analysis and basic decisions at least showed that the Court had come a long way from its doctrine and disposition in *Adler* and was beginning to weigh the constitutional rights of public employees as a factor in determining the validity of government loyalty and security programs.

61. 344 U.S. at 190–91.

The first case in this area which won a major victory for public employees was *Slochower* v. *Board of Higher Education*.[62] The issue in *Slochower* was the constitutionality of a New York City ordinance which provided that if an employee of the city utilized the privilege against self-incrimination to avoid answering a question relating to his official conduct, he would be dismissed. Slochower invoked the Fifth Amendment before a Senate committee in response to questions concerning his possible membership in the Communist party; he was summarily dismissed. The Supreme Court ordered Slochower's reinstatement because the nature of the questions had nothing to do with the appellant's official duties and his performance of these duties, holding that to impute a sinister motive to the invoking of a constitutional right was totally improper; and further, the local government had no interest in the result of the congressional hearing, which did not concern local affairs.

Following *Slochower*, the Court was faced with two cases which concerned the question of whether a public employee was protected when taking the Fifth Amendment when the question of his competency to serve as a public employee has been raised. In *Beilan* v. *Board of Education*,[63] a public schoolteacher in Philadelphia took the Fifth Amendment in answer to questions concerning Communist associations, first before his superintendent of schools and later before the House Un-American Activities Committee. On the basis of his refusal to answer his supervisor's questions he was dismissed on the grounds of incompetency.

Similarly, in *Lerner* v. *Casey*,[64] a subway conductor in New York City was dismissed when he refused to tell the city commissioner of investigation whether he was a member of the Communist party. His dismissal was based on a charge of being a person of doubtful trust and reliability.

This time, by five to four decisions in each case, the Supreme Court affirmed the dismissals. Its holding was based on the grounds that the employees had not really been discharged for invoking the Fifth Amendment. Rather, their dismissals were based upon questions of incompetency and unreliability, which the government is not prevented from using as a basis of dismissal. Justices Black and Douglas, in dissent, based their opinions on the theory that governments can only punish actions, not words, and that the real issue in these cases was not whether a public employee can be punished for taking the Fifth Amendment, but rather whether or not the questions posed to them were constitutionally permissible. They said that the proper way of handling these cases is to look at the nature of the job to determine whether or not the

62. 350 U.S. 551 (1956).
63. 357 U.S. 399 (1958).
64. 357 U.S. 468 (1958).

questions have any relevance as to the ability of a person performing the job for which he was hired.

Justices Warren and Brennan, while also in dissent, felt that the real basis of the case was somewhat different. Justice Brennan felt that in each case the use of such terms as incompetency really served as a mask for the employees having invoked the Fifth Amendment, which could not be the basis of dismissal under *Slochower*. Justice Brennan also stressed the fact that in each case the basis of dismissal was disloyalty and that in neither case was there evidence to support such a finding. Chief Justice Warren agreed with Mr. Justice Brennan, also expressing the applicability of *Slochower* to each case.[65]

While the Supreme Court discussed, in later decisions, the matter of the right of a public employee to invoke the Fifth Amendment with respect to official misconduct, the holdings in *Beilan* and *Lerner* still technically remain the law and the Supreme Court has not yet officially overruled these cases. However, in many ways these cases have become moot, because the Supreme Court has taken the lines of attack used by Justices Black and Douglas, and instead of focusing on the effect on the public employee as such, has focused on the constitutional validity of the questions asked, that is, the subjects of inquiry, albeit by investigation or oath. As a result, state and local governments have been given so little area on which to base loyalty and security programs as to render them virtually obsolete. Instead of testing oaths and administrative practices on due process grounds (which implies that the practices are correct and only the impact unconstitutional), the Court began to apply First Amendment standards to these oaths and investigations; as a result, public employees all over the country were relieved of burdens resulting from oaths and investigations in a way no due process analysis could ever have accomplished.

The major breakthrough came in 1960, soon after the *Beilan* and *Lerner* cases, in a case which ironically had nothing to do with loyalty and security programs as such. This case was *Shelton* v. *Tucker*,[66] and the issue involved the constitutionality of an Arkansas statute which required all teachers to disclose all organizations to which they had belonged within the past five years as a condition of employment. Unlike loyalty

---

65. The problem of the alternate grounds for dismissal based on incompetency on insubordination is a thread which runs through the entire area of public employee law. Invariably, when a public employer is brought to court by a public employee who claims he has been dismissed for engaging in protected First Amendment activities, the employer will make the claim of incompetency or insubordination and often succeed. See Hodgin v. Noland, 435 F.2d 859 (1970).

66. 364 U.S. 479 (1960).

oath cases, in which specific illegal organizations were involved, this statute was open ended, and the teachers had to disclose all organizational ties. What made this case and this statute different from the other statutes previously discussed was that the real purpose of the statute was not to find members of the Communist party or Communist front organizations, but to find members of the National Association for the Advancement of Colored People (NAACP). While the fact that a state would go to elaborate lengths to discover NAACP members seems incredible today, nonetheless, in the late 1950s in Arkansas this was a matter of intense controversy. In this period the Little Rock controversy burst forth as a matter of national and international importance, and the NAACP was at the forefront, indeed was the moving force in the attempt to integrate the schools of Little Rock. This statute was passed as a reaction to the Little Rock incident in the hope that forced disclosure of organizational ties of public schoolteachers would cripple the NAACP. This was not a farfetched idea, because at that time the heart and strength of the NAACP was found among teachers. If teachers were forced to disclose their organizational activities, they could be subjected to intense pressure and harrassment, thus severely crippling the civil rights movement.

The Supreme Court held that, even though a state may require a teacher to list professional organizations to which he belongs as a means of evaluating professional ability, it could not constitutionally require teachers to disclose all the organizations to which they belonged.

The significance of the *Shelton* case cannot be underestimated. Even though the language of the majority opinion assumes the legitimacy of the state loyalty and security programs as such, nonetheless, the grounds on which this particular statute was declared unconstitutional foretold the doom of other loyalty oaths and administrative programs of a more traditional variety. Instead of focusing strictly on the employee in a due process form of analysis, the opinion focused on the statute itself in determining whether or not the statute in all its ramifications and all its terms constituted a legitimate exercise of state power. What the Court found was that even though the state indeed has a legitimate interest in seeing that it employs competent teachers, this particular statute, with all of its facets of disclosure provisions, was much too overbroad for any legitimate state need. The Court then declared the entire statute unconstitutional, even though certain regulations were incorporated in the statute over which the state had a legitimate interest.

The Court then took the matter one step farther, and held that if a state could have accomplished its legitimate means through use of less drastic methods, the Court would hold such statutes unconstitutional where they impinged upon First Amendment rights, despite the presence of a legitimate state interest in terms of the statute.

Shelton v. *Tucker* is the wellspring from which not only public employees but indeed most groups within American society gained a measure of First Amendment rights. The introduction in this case of the overbreadth and "less drastic means" test had the effect, in one single swoop, of cutting away many decades of doctrines which had been deadweight in the assertion of First Amendment rights.

That the doctrine of *Shelton* v. *Tucker* indeed represented a radical break from the past was borne out by the next loyalty-security cases to come before the Court.[67] *Cramp* v. *Board of Public Instruction* questioned the validity of a Florida statute requiring all state employees to take an oath which included this language: "I have not and will not lend my aid, support, advice, counsel or influence to the Communist Party." This statute was unanimously declared unconstitutional on the grounds that it was void for vagueness, in that the language of the statute was not subject to general or common understanding so as to enable a person to know whether or not his acts fell within the context and terms of the statute.[68] The void for vagueness doctrine was an old technique of judicial interpretation which came into prominence in a series of cases based on statutes in the late 1920s and 1930s designed to crush the criminal syndicates.[69] However, in the *Cramp* case it was given an added First Amendment dimension, in that a statute could now be considered vague in a constitutional sense if its language was such that a person was deterred from engaging in legitimate First Amendment activities if he felt that such activity could conceivably be considered a violation of a criminal statute.

The twin strands of overbreadth and the vagueness theory were worked together by the Court in the case of *Baggett* v. *Bullitt*.[70] At issue in *Baggett* v. *Bullitt* was the constitutionality of two loyalty oaths from

67. Shelton v. Tucker was only one of many cases in which southern states attempted to curb the NAACP. The results of this litigation were major advances in First Amendment law going far beyond race relations. See NAACP v. Alabama ex rel Patterson, 357 U.S. 449 (1958); Bates v. City of Little Rock, 361 U.S. 516 (1960); Louisiana ex rel Gremillion v. NAACP 366 U.S. 293 (1961); NAACP v. Alabama ex rel Flowers, 377 U.S. 288 (1964); Gibson v. Florida Legislative Investigating Committee, 372 U.S. 539 (1963).

68. 368 U.S. 278 (1961).

69. Lanzetta v. New Jersey, 306 U.S. 451 (1939); this statute, making it a crime to be a "gangster," was declared unconstitutionally vague. See also Connally v. General Construction Company, 269 U.S. 385 (1926); Winters v. New York, 333 U.S. 507 (1947).

70. 377 U.S. 360 (1964).

the state of Washington. The first, which applied only to teachers, required them to swear as follows:

> I solemnly swear (or affirm) that I will support the Constitution and laws of the United States of America and the State of Washington and will by precept and example promote respect for the flag and the institutions of the United States of America and the State of Washington, reverence for law and order and undivided allegiance to the Government of the United States.[71]

The second oath, which applied to all state employees, provided generally that:

> [No] subversive person, as defined in this act, shall be eligible for employment in, or appointment to any office, or any position of trust or project in the government, or in the administration of the business of this state, or any county, municipality or other political subdivision of this state.[72]

The statute itself defined a subversive person as follows:

> "Subversive person" means any person who commits, attempts to commit, or aids in the commission or advocates, abets, advises, or teaches by any means to commit, attempt to commit, or aid in the commission of any act intended to overthrow, destroy or alter; or to assist in the overthrow, destruction or alteration of the constitutional form of the government of the United States or of the State of Washington, or any political subdivision of either of them by revolution, force or violence; or who with the knowledge that the organization is an organization as described in subsections (2) and (3) hereof, becomes or remains a member of a subversive organization or a foreign subversive organization.[73]

The Supreme Court, with only two justices dissenting, declared both the oath and statute to be unconstitutional on the grounds of vagueness. The sheer scope and extent of the language in the coverage of the oath and statute shows without need for any further delineation why the statute would be considered vague in a constitutional sense. However, the doctrine of the Court went even further, in that a major portion of the basis of its finding that the statute was vague was based on the Court's fear that by the very terms of the statute certain protected constitutional rights would be violated.

71. Wash. Laws 1931, §103.
72. Wash. Rev. Code §9.81.060.
73. Wash. Rev. Code §9.81.010.

This decision was very significant for public employees because a testing of oaths such as these in light of First Amendment rights clearly implied that public employees have First Amendment rights despite their public employment. If the Court is protecting other employees from having their First Amendment rights impugned by unconstitutional loyalty oaths, would not the same constitutional rights be held valid in different contexts?

Following *Baggett* v. *Bullitt*, the Supreme Court, in a series of decisions, virtually wiped out most state loyalty-security programs which went beyond simple oaths or investigations for competency. In *Elfbrandt* v. *Russell* the Court, by a five to four vote, declared unconstitutional a provision of an Arizona statute which stated that any employee of the state of Arizona who takes a simple oath of allegiance would be guilty of perjury if, at the time he took the oath or while employed by the government, he "knowingly and willfully" became or remained a member of the Communist party or any other subversive organization, if he knew the organization advocated the "overthrow by force or violence of the government."[74]

Justice Douglas, writing for the majority, focused on two particular aspects of this statute: first, that the membership provision was not limited to a specific intent to further the unlawful aims of the organization; and, second, that the lack of the specific intents provisions in effect constituted a conclusive assumption that the members share in the unlawful aims of the organization.

The minority opinion, written by Mr. Justice White (who had written the majority opinion in *Baggett* v. *Bullitt*), held that this statute was a simple perjury statute punishing false swearing with the loyalty provisions of the statute based upon the prior hearing of the Court. The minority felt that a state is entitled to condition public employment upon its employees abstaining from knowing membership in the Communist party and other organizations which advocate the violent overthrow of the government employer. It was Mr. Justice White's opinion that the state is constitutionally authorized to inquire into such affiliations and that the state may discharge those who refuse to affirm or deny them.[75]

The effect of the *Elfbrandt* decision was really to eliminate the test oath as a valid state procedure. While never stating this directly, by requiring specific intent and possibly even acts of participation in the un-

---

74. 384 U.S. 11 (1966).

75. 384 U.S. 19 (1966). The view of Mr. Justice White has recently been adopted by the Supreme Court in Cole v. Richardson, which will be discussed later in the chapter.

lawful activities of an organization, the Supreme Court was in fact saying that the state could only include as the basis of a test oath membership acts which would be illegal anyway. The simple constitutional oath requires every state employee to uphold the laws and Constitution of the United States and/or the state in which he is employed. The *Elfbrandt* decision left little or no room for additional criteria to be imposed by test oaths.

The *Baggett* and *Elfbrandt* decisions held that states could not require employees to take oaths that would require more than the swearing to noncommission of acts considered criminal in any case. The next question involves the determination of which specific acts (in the context of the loyalty and security program) would be considered criminal, and to what degree. To be even more exact, to what degree did present state loyalty programs, those limiting associational activities of public employees, meet the test which required that organizational activities of public employees would only be subject to state action *if* they had specific intent and possibly involved active participation in the furtherance of illegal activities.

With these new constitutional requirements, clearly the elaborate New York State provision upheld in the *Adler* case was now subject to a brand new and more intensive review. Thus, in the case of *Keyishian* v. *Board of Regents*, the Court was again faced with the constitutionality of the New York state law.[76] All the provisions in *Adler* still existed, but in addition the board of regents, based on the *Adler* decision, also held that membership in the Communist party constituted prima facie evidence of disqualification.

This time, the Court ruled in a five to four decision that many of the provisions of the New York state scheme were unconstitutional on the grounds of vagueness and overbreadth. However, and of even greater importance to public employees, the Court in the *Keyishian* case finally dealt with the issue present in the majority opinion in *Adler* and eluded to in the minority opinion in *Elfbrandt*: Do public employees, as a matter of doctrine, take their employment under any conditions which are presented by the employing agency? This is a key issue; until *Keyishian*, all other language in cases coming under loyalty oath provisions might, in fact, be limited exclusively to questions of the constitutionality of state legislative schemes, be they by oath or regulation. This was a legitimate question, because a reading of the cases from *Shelton* forward could lead an observer to believe that the Court was not so much revoking the old doctrine of *McAuliffe* v. *Mayor of New Bedford* as pronounc-

76. 385 U.S. 589 (1967).

ing strict constitutional steps for legislative drafting. Under this theory, if the legislature chose to enact a comprehensive legislative scheme, it must do so within the requirements that it must draft statutes neither overbroad or vague, but the least drastic means of accomplishing their goals. However, those cases left undecided the issue of whether or not, within the limits of constitutional draftsmanship, the state might still, as a matter of doctrine, proscribe the exercise of constitutional rights of its employees as a condition of employment.

What *Keyishian* said, in most emphatic and unequivocable terms, was that the line of cases from *Shelton* onward was not limited to questions of draftmanship, but was focused on the substance of rights of employees, and that state actions could be proscribed as to those rights, not merely as to the form of legislation. The Court stated:

> However, the Court of Appeals for the Second Circuit correctly said in an earlier stage of this case, ". . . the theory that public employment which may be denied altogether may be subject to any conditions regardless of how unreasonable, has been uniformly rejected" [cite omitted]. Indeed, that theory was expressly rejected in a series of cases following Adler. The Court said, in *Sherbert* v. *Verner*, that: "It is too late in the day to doubt that the liberties of religion and expression may be infringed by a denial of or placing of conditions upon a benefit or privilege."[77]

Thus, the use of the overbreadth and void vagueness doctrines was significant, enabling the Court to attack more involved and detailed state loyalty and security programs. In *Keyishian* the Court accepted the theory of unconstitutional conditions and held that this theory was not only the basis of this particular case, but would be the basis of decisions in other cases concerning loyalty and security oaths. Indeed, this decision was even more significant in other contexts, because loyalty and security programs at least involve a situation in which the state is attempting to prohibit employment, or prohibit employees from engaging in activities at least arguably illegal. But the application of *Keyishian* to all public employees seeking to assert constitutional rights was to lead to some important decisions in other areas.

The *Keyishian* decision represented the high point of the Supreme Court's limitation on the imposition of loyalty oaths on public employees. The passing of the Warren court and the commencement of the Burger court, with its more conservative outlook, indicated that changes would occur in Supreme Court holdings on loyalty oaths, especially since

77. 385 U.S. at 606 (1967).

Keyishian, decided at the height of the Warren court, was only a five to four decision.

The first break in the string of cases which had held against loyalty oaths since 1960 occurred in a series of cases which did not directly concern public employees, but rather concerned a related field: admission to the bar. In two of the cases, *Baird* v. *State Bar*[78] and *In re Stolar,*[79] the Supreme Court ruled, using the standard line of decisions from *Shelton* v. *Tucker* onward, that bar applicants could not be denied admission to the bar for refusing to supply lists of all organizations to which they belonged. In these cases the applicants supplied the bar committees with all the personal references required and all personal data, but refused to state in writing whether they had ever been members of the Communist party or of any other organization which advocated the forceful overthrow of the government. Stolar also refused to supply in writing the names and addresses of all organizations to which he belonged. On the basis of these denials both were denied admission to the bar, even though they had passed their respective bar examinations.

Writing for the majority, the late Justice Black held that the state has no compelling interest in requiring disclosure of memberships except for the probing of personal beliefs and protected associational ties. He held that no relationship existed between this information and the ability to practice law and the applicants fitness to practice law. As for the Ohio State Bar's request that Stolar supply all associational memberships, this was held by Justice Black to be a straight *Shelton* v. *Tucker* situation.

In dissent, Justice Blackmun conceded that *Shelton* v. *Tucker* applied, at least so far as Stolar was concerned, but held that, on the basis of an older case, *Konigsberg* v. *State Bar,*[80] which had given state bar committees almost unlimited powers over their applicants, the right to ask these questions was to protect the bar from membership of individuals who professed an interest in the forceful overthrow of the government.

However, these decisions were, like *Keyishian* several years before, five to four decisions. The third case decided by the Supreme Court that day, *Law Students Civil Rights Council* v. *Wadmond,*[81] the Court, also by a five to four decision, upheld the validity of a loyalty oath, legislative and regulatory scheme. This marked the first time since the *Lerner* and *Beilan* cases of 1958 that the loyalty oath provisions of federal and state governments had been upheld by the Supreme Court.

78. 401 U.S. 1 (1971).
79. 401 U.S. 23 (1971).
80. 366 U.S. 36 (1961). See also Konigsberg v. State Bar, 353 U.S. 252 (1957), first hearing of same case sent back to state court for factual inquiry.
81. 401 U.S. 154 (1971).

In the *Wadmond* case, various individual law students and bar applicants, none of whom had actually been denied. admission to the bar, sought a declaratory judgment and injunctive relief, alleging that New York Bar admissions procedures chilled students' First Amendment rights.

The procedure complained of was not very different than that found in many other states. It required affidavits of two reputable persons, one of whom must be a lawyer, plus an application form to be completed, plus a personal interview. Finally the applicants would take an oath that he would support the federal and state Constitutions. The real issue concerned certain items in the questionnaires which were claimed to be vague, overbroad, and to impinge on the applicant's privacy so as to be unconstitutional. The lower courts indeed found some of these questions unconstitutional, but between the time of their ruling and the Supreme Court ruling, the state had changed certain questions so that, when the case came before the Supreme Court, it found it to be of constitutional validity. In fact, the Court found the entire admissions scheme to be constitutionally correct and in addition found that a question about knowing memberships in organizations that advocated violent overthrow of the government was "precisely tailored to conform to the relevant decisions of this court." It finally stated that it could not see how a carefully tailored and administered system like New York's need result in "a chilling effect on the exercise of constitutional freedom."[82]

In dissent, Justices Black and Douglas argued that, on its face, the New York procedure required applicants to prove their loyalty and belief to the U.S. form of government, which had been held unconstitutional in a prior case. In a separate dissent, Justices Brennan and Marshall argued that, even assuming good faith on the part of New York in administering the provisions, the procedures permit overreaching into an area of political belief which, looked at as a whole, would impermissably chill applicants' First Amendment rights.

While *Wadmond* was not in itself a very extensive change in prior law, in that the entire Court was unanimous in recognizing the validity of the general admissions procedure, and the decision was upheld basically because of its narrowness, nonetheless, the significance of the case was that the Supreme Court would now take a much different look at loyalty oaths without the assumption of invalidity which was the basis of cases coming down during the 1960s. In effect, in *Wadmond* the Court introduced into the whole area of loyalty oaths a balancing test, instead of the compelling interest test which had been the previous basis of the law. The compelling state interest test was a presumption in favor of the

82. 401 U.S. at 167 (1971).

speech, in that the speech is considered to be valid unless a compelling state interest could be shown to allow the limitation; thus the burden is on the state. A balancing test is exactly as defined, with the difference being that under such a test the state's interest is presumed to be higher than in the compelling state interest test.

One side of the balance would feature the state's interest in setting up procedures for weeding out people from government benefits who might constitute so-called security risks, while the other side would feature the right of the applicant to First Amendment rights. Obviously, a balancing test affords less protection to a public employee than a compelling state interest test, and, for that reason, without looking at the actual terms of *Wadmond*, this decision represents a turning of the corner which would lead (and indeed has led) to the upholding of state loyalty oaths on grounds which would not have been followed earlier.

Another indication of the Supreme Court's trend in its thinking on the loyalty oath issue came later on in the 1970 term in the case of *Connell* v. *Higginbotham*,[83] which concerned a Florida loyalty oath. In this decision the Supreme Court upheld a portion of a loyalty oath and declared unconstitutional another portion of this same oath. While the result would have been the same under the Warren court, the thinking of the Supreme Court showed a definite shift against the public employee. The part of the oath upheld was the affirmative oath, in which a person swears support of the Constitution and that he does not believe in the overthrow of the government by force or violence. The second part of the oath stated that an unwillingness to take the oath constituted conclusive proof of the proscribed belief; this section was declared unconstitutional on rather narrow due process grounds based upon the unconstitutionality of the absolute presumption of guilt, rather than on a First Amendment ground based on the impact of the presumption of the oath in chilling speech.

This decision falls into a very disquieting pattern, shown by the Burger court, of using procedural due process as a substitute for the granting of substantive constitutional rights. Even more alarming is the fact that when the procedural due process has a substantive constitutional impact, as in the case of dismissal of public employees, the Burger court has refused to even grant procedural due process. Thus, that the Burger court would begin to emasculate the law protecting public employees from loyalty oaths and programs which impinge upon their protected constitutional rights should come as no surprise.

83. 403 U.S. 207 (1971).

In April 1972, the trend away from the position of the Warren court reached its highest point yet in the case of *Cole* v. *Richardson*.[84] In this case the Court upheld a Massachusetts loyalty oath which provided that the employee "uphold and defend" the Constitutions of the United States and Massachusetts and "oppose" the overthrow of the "government of the United States of America or of the Commonwealth by force, violence, or by any illegal or unconstitutional method."

In upholding the oath, the Court ruled that the "uphold and defend" and "oppose" provisions were really stating the same thing, since the second clause did not require any specific action on the part of the employee.

A concurring opinion of Justices Stewart and White held that since all the members of the Court, including the dissenters, agreed that the first clause was neither vague nor overbroad, then neither was the word "oppose" vague or overbroad.

The dissent argued that the word "oppose" was not a mere redundancy, but rather, in the context of the oath, meant that the oath-taker must now oppose that which he would have a right to advocate, certainly in the abstract. In addition, since the oath went beyond opposing overthrow by force or violence and into the area of unconstitutional or illegal means, it creates a very special problem, since obviously unconstitutional or illegal acts, used in attempting to overthrow the government, could exist which would not be criminal per se, and thus protected at the point of advocacy.

Again, like *Connell*, the most serious aspect of *Cole* v. *Richardson* is not the holding, but the method of analysis. While the Massachusetts oath is in no way as oppressive as those of the McCarthy period, nonetheless the Court's method of analyzing the issue shows a singular lack of sensitivity to the finer points of First Amendment law. What scares so many people is the fear that with the Supreme Court beginning to uphold loyalty oaths, states will now become bold enough to begin passing more restrictive loyalty oaths and programs, with at least some chance that they will be upheld, especially if new, more conservative judges are appointed as the remaining liberal judges leave the Court.

While this is all speculative now, a more pessimistic outlook is inevitable over whether public employees will continue to be subjected to the indignity of loyalty oaths and programs other than the simple affirmative pledge to uphold the Constitution and laws of the United States and the states in which they are employed.

84. 405 U.S. 676 (1972).

Chapter 6

Procedural Due Process Rights

Much of this book has been concerned with the expansion of the rights of public employees over the years, to a point where public employees now enjoy a full panoply of protective constitutional rights heretofore denied them. Unfortunately, however, in one area this trend has recently been stopped, with the result that many of the other protective constitutional rights of public employees are now in jeopardy. This area is that of the procedural due process rights of public employees.

What exactly is the concept of procedural due process of law? Due process of law is not easily defined. Indeed, it is probably better so, as it then would be subject to rigidity. Probably the best explanation of due process comes from Justice Frankfurter in his concurring opinion in the case of *Joint Anti-Fascist Refugee Committee* v. *McGrath*,[1] in which he wrote:

> Fairness of procedure is due process in the primary. . . . But due process, unlike some legal rules, is not a technical conception with a fixed content unrelated to time, place and circumstances. Expressing as it does in its ultimate analysis respect enforced by law for that feeling of fair treatment which has been evolved through centuries of Anglo-American constitutional history and civilization, due process cannot be imprisoned within the treacherous limits of any formula.

1. 341 U.S. 123 (1950).

> Representing a profound attitude of fairness between man and man, and more particularly between the individual and government, due process is compounded of history, reason, the past course of decisions, and stout confidence in the strength of the democratic faith with which we profess. Due process is not a mechanical instrument. It is not a yardstick. It is a process. It is a delicate process of adjustment inescapably involving the exercise of judgment by those whom the Constitution entrusted with the unfolding of the process.[2]

Thus fairness is the keynote to due process, fairness derived from the concept that whenever the government acts, it must act in such a way as to be even-handed with all persons subject to its actions, and not in a way that would be classified as either arbitrary or capricious.

While the form of due process has many different applications, especially in the area of criminal law, in the context of public employee relations the idea of due process refers to that method by which the government acts when it either terminates employment of a public employee or terminates some other employment-related benefits, such as tenure.

In the context of public employment law, due process of law, as applied to the termination of employment-related benefits, takes many forms. Full due process of law means, however, that the following requirements, in whole or in part, must be met by a governmental body before it can terminate the employment-related benefits. They are:

1. The employee should be entitled to notice in writing of his termination.
2. Such a statement must give the reasons for the termination.
3. Following receipt of such statement a reasonable time must be allowed for the employee to respond.
4. The employee is to be given a hearing at which time he may be given the right to present evidence in his behalf. Such a hearing should be afforded before the effective date of the action.
5. At such hearing he will be allowed to be represented by counsel.
6. At such hearing evidence shall be presented against him by his accusers.
7. The employer and/or his counsel will be permitted to cross-examine witnesses against him.
8. The employee shall be entitled to an appeal to a higher authority from any adverse decision.

Very few courts have ever held that all eight of these provisions are constitutionally required, though various governmental bodies have regula-

2. 341 U.S. at 167.

tions requiring that a public employee is entitled to all those requirements before he may be dismissed, or at least soon after dismissal.[3]
Nevertheless, a public employee does not need each and every one of
those provisions to be guaranteed due process of law, because some are
more important than others; if he is guaranteed these provisions, his
rights will be ultimately be protected.

Without getting into the question of who is entitled to procedural due
process of law at this time, every court has held that the most important
provisions are numbers 1 and 2, namely that the person is given notice
in writing of his dismissal or termination of whatever benefits in question, and the reasons upon which this dismissal was based. Obviously
these are the most important types of procedural due process rights because, unless the person knows that he is being fired and the exact reasons for his dismissal or removal of benefits, all the other rights pale in
importance and become meaningless procedural shells.

Although the provisions of 1 and 2 are often used synonymously, they
nevertheless have distinct importance. The question of the right of specification of reasons for governmental action is legally quite different from
the question of when the employee should be entitled to be given this
notice and specification of charges.

The question of specification of charges is probably the most important
of all the rights to procedural due process, because requiring the government to set down in writing the reasons for its actions sets off a whole
series of correlated legal situations. First of all, experience has shown
that when the government is required to specify why it acts, it is less
likely to act.

Governments, like many other institutions, find it easier to act by fiat,
using arbitrary means, rather than give detailed explanations of its
actions. This is equally true when dealing with personnel matters. Most
cases involving a public employee which have gone to court have been
after the public employee has been fired without notice and without
reasons. Indeed, when public employees have prevailed in court, ironically it has been in those situations in which the government has given
a reason for dismissal, and that the reason specified turns out to be unconstitutional.[4] Thus, governmental employers understandably prefer
not to give more than a broad general statement of reasons.

3. The lower court opinions in Roth v. Board of Regents, 310 F.2d 972 (W.D.
Wisc. 1970) and 446 F.2d 806 (7th Cir. 1971) would have afforded that form of
due process. The subsequent reversal was on the issue of entitlement to due process.
4. This was true in *Pickering* and partially true in the most recent case, Mt.
Healthy School District v. Doyle.

The most prominent case bearing out this point was the *Pickering* case discussed extensively in previous parts of this book. Here the government specified that Pickering was being fired because of his letter to the paper, and this reason was held to be unconstitutional. If Pickering had not been entitled to an explanation as to why he was being dismissed, he might not have prevailed, especially since a factual connection between an action and the reason given for the action is always more difficult to provide than a challenge of the legal efficacy of the action. Furthermore, it is infinitely more expensive. In *Pickering*, the real reason was specified by the employer, and only minimal evidence was needed, with the points in issue clearly delineated. When no reason is given, a case must be made using numerous witnesses to support strands of circumstantial evidence. This produces large and expensive transcripts both in pretrial disposition and at trial; and if an appeal is made this evidence must be made part of an appendix which is much larger than the brief but costs as much per page to print.

Of course, if the employee prevails he will win costs of court (in most jurisdictions), but if he loses he is not only out of a job, but heavily in debt. Thus the issue of procedural due process of law not only has legal ramifications, but practical ones as well.

Even when the government specifies a wrong or misleading reason for dismissal, the employee at least has something to work with and base later court challenges to his loss of benefit. A prominent case proving this point was the case of Ernest Fitzgerald, the cost analyst for the Department of Defense fired when he gave his testimony before Congress concerning cost overruns in a defense project. The government said that it simply had eliminated his job for reasons of economy and costs. By attacking the particular grounds specified for losing his job, Fitzgerald was able to show that this was a completely erroneous reason and, using analogies to other governmental projects and similar types of evidence, he was able to show that this was also a complete fabrication for the real reason he was fired; the only reason he could have been fired was because of his testimony. Thus even a governmental lie can be in the interest of the employee, as long as that lie is in writing, part of the record, something concrete that can be proven or disproven.

The most difficult situation for the public employee is one in which he is fired or loses his benefits without any reasons being given. The hardest thing in the world to do is to prove a negative, and, in the context of public employment law, this axiom makes the use of the courts to rectify an illegal dismissal a most difficult task. Without any official government reason for its action, the public employee has the difficult task of showing that the action of the government was for unconstitutional reasons; this is also, of course, much more expensive. Two cases, one successful, one unsuccessful, may illustrate this point in somewhat greater detail.

In the case of *Lucia* v. *Duggan*,[5] a teacher (Lucia) was fired because he refused to shave his beard. He was ordered reinstated because he was not afforded due process of law during dismissal proceedings. Lucia had been hired to teach in a high school in Massachusetts in 1966 and his contract was renewed twice. He began to grow a beard during 1968; when he returned from the winter break he had a fully grown beard. A formal letter was written to the plaintiff at the instigation of the school board to that effect. The plaintiff then had a meeting with the superintendent, who told him to shave his beard. As a result of some words with the superintendent, he was suspended for seven days. While the defendant scheduled a special meeting to discuss Lucia, he did not notify Lucia about the meeting. Lucia found out about it and asked first that a formal set of charges be made against him so that he might defend himself, and second, that the meeting be postponed so that he could secure counsel. Both requests were refused. At the meeting all that was said about Lucia was "Mr. Lucia knows what the charges are." The board then met in an executive session and voted to dismiss the plaintiff.

After dismissal, the plaintiff filed suit in federal court, in which he charged that he was denied due process of law upon being fired without any reason given for the firing. The court upheld him on this position. In its decision, the court gave one of the most complete statements of what due process of law means in practice:

> Two substantial deficiencies were present in the procedure followed in suspending and dismissing the plaintiff. First, the plaintiff was not told what the charges against him were, and that his refusal to remove his beard would result in his dismissal. The plaintiff was forced to guess as to the charges against him and as to what action, if any, the school committee might take. . . . The second deficiency involved the form of the decision-making process of the school committee. Prior to plaintiff's dismissal, there was no written or announced policy of the school committee that male teachers should not wear beards in their classrooms. The proceeding against the plaintiff were therefore of a dual nature involving, first a rule-making or legislative type function to determine whether the wearing of the beard without reasonable explanation, should be the grounds for dismissal of a teacher, and secondly, the judicial type function to determine whether the plaintiff was wearing a beard without a reasonable explanation and whether dismissal was a suitable sanction. The indiscriminate merging of these

5. 303 F. Supp. 112 (D.C. Mass. 1969).

two functions served to cloud the question at issue, and to shield the board's determination from public view. The plaintiff, in effect, lost any right to present evidence in the judicial type proceeding and the community as a whole lost any right to participate in a meaningful way in legislative type rule-making proceedings.[6]

In this case, Lucia was fortunate because the series of events, including an easily proven warning to Lucia that he should not grow his beard, made it clear that the firing could only be for that particular reason and no other. Had the school board been somewhat more sophisticated and not made its objections to his beard so obvious, they might well have been able to make the firing stick because of Lucia's inability to prove the particular reason for firing, especially if the court held he was not entitled to any form of procedural due process.

An example of how that latter situation might well prevail occurred in the case of *Hodgin* v. *Noland*,[7] discussed in chapter 3. The *Hodgin* case, while not unique in its facts in terms of an arbitrary dismissal, would never have occurred as it did if a rule had required that all public employees must be given notice of, and reasons for, dismissal at the time of dismissal. While the Supreme Court has extended these rights of procedural due process to those persons having what the Court called substantive rights of independent origin, such as tenured teachers, only a limited number of employees are so protected.

The lack of a firm rule requiring specification of charges protects the government in those very instances when it seeks to fire a person for an unconstitutional reason. Instead, the government should be required to give a reason for its actions, whether the right reason or not, since the chances of the employee succeeding in a later court action will become that much better if the employer has a specified cause.

When due process, either by statute or judicial decision, is required, before a person can be dismissed from public employment, in all such instances a specification of charges must be given. However, even though a specification of charges is required, when these charges are given is also of primary concern; that is, before or after the firing takes place. This, as a matter of practicality, can make a great deal of difference. If notice is given before dismissal, all the other forms of procedural due process previously mentioned become matters very useful to the employee, and which he would obviously desire to see implemented in full. However, if notice is given after dismissal, all requirements, including hearings in addition to specification of grounds, simply become an im-

6. 303 F. Supp. at 118.
7. 435 F.2d 859 (4th Cir. 1970).

pediment to the employee in his attempt to seek eventual vindication from the courts. Indeed, no matter how extensive the procedural guarantees are for hearing and appeal after termination, the employee will suffer irreparable injury if his procedural rights only extend to presenting evidence to reverse his dismissal or termination, rather than the right to present evidence to prevent the termination or dismissal.

This timing factor is thus more than a procedural nicety; it is the most crucial factor, because if the government is allowed to act before providing the required notice, the employee will have lost his substantive rights before he gets a chance to redeem or defend himself. Just as an accused criminal defendant is allowed to lead a normal life on bail, except in unusual cases while charges against him are pending, so too should a government employee maintain his rights of employment until the government shows it has just cause for dismissal.

The Supreme Court does not have a distinctive ruling on the question of whether a public employee is constitutionally entitled to procedural due process before dismissal. The Court has, in certain related cases, held that due process rights must be given before the action rather than afterwards. In the case of *Goldberg* v. *Kelly*,[8] the Court found unconstitutional a termination of welfare benefits without a prior evidentiary hearing as to the merits of the termination, even though an elaborate posttermination appeal procedure was available. The Court based its opinion on the fact that in consequence of termination, the welfare recipient was totally destitute, and that any cost to the government would be insignificant in comparison to the impact of benefit termination on the recipient.

However, in the case of *Arnett* v. *Kennedy*,[9] this issue of when procedural due process should be afforded arose indirectly. Arnett was a protected Civil Service employee. Under federal law, the discharge provisions require that a covered employee be given thirty days notice of pending charges. The employee may file written answers with affidavits and has a right to appear before the employer and be given a written statement of decision. After discharge or other punishment, the employee is entitled to a full evidentiary hearing either in his agency or at the

---

8. 397 U.S. 254 (1970). Due process was also extended in Fuentes v. Shevin, 407 U.S. 67 (1972), as to repossession of personal property; Bell v. Burson, 402 U.S. 535 (1971), drivers license revocation. However, even before *Roth* and *Perry*, government employment was always different for cafeteria workers. Local 873 v. McElroy, 367 U.S. 886 (1961); Green v. McElroy, 360 U.S. 574 (1959).

9. 416 U.S. 134 (1974).

Civil Service Commission. If the employee wins he is entitled to reinstation with back pay.[10]

Arnett was discharged for making false statements against his superior, charging him with bribery. He chose to go into federal court instead of using administrative procedure. The case eventually reached the Supreme Court which, in a major opinion, held that his rights were not violated.

Arnett was discussed in a previous chapter in the context of the standard of discharge. The theory behind the decision will be discussed later in this chapter. However, a very important aspect of this case, theory not withstanding, is the Court's holding regarding those employees entitled to due process in conjunction with any job action, that such due process does not include the right to an evidentiary hearing *before* dismissal. In upholding the federal procedure, the Court apparently indicated that this procedure would be the minimum procedure permissable for the dismissal of a government employee at all levels of government, when the employee is entitled to procedural due process. The dissenting justices, Brennan, Douglas, and Marshall, would have required a pre-termination evidentiary hearing as an element of procedural due process. They cite especially the requirement for such a hearing as to removal of welfare benefits or revocation of parole.

On this issue I think the dissenting justices miss the main point; the real problem facing the public employee is not *when* the hearing takes place, but *who* is to conduct the hearing.

By definition, pretermination hearings are to be conducted by the employing agency; thus they are almost an exercise in futility. If the employer is to be convinced of an injustice prior to termination, an informal notice and affidavit system would be equally adequate because, if a written response plus an informal hearing are to be presented to a truly impartial party, these methods would be sufficient to cause further pretermination fact finding in the presence of a real injustice. If the hearing party is not impartial, no amount of procedure would make a difference.

Likewise, in posttermination hearings the employee's interest is served by limiting the procedural requirements. What the employee needs is *one* evidentiary hearing, before an impartial reviewer, with this hearing having finality. The hearing should be transcribed with both the employer and the employee represented by counsel.

---

10. 5 U.S.C. §7501 (1970). 5 CFR §754.102–4. (The Civil Service Regulations issued pursuant to the statute.)

Such a hearing is of great value to the employee who may have a substantive constitutional claim. First, it enables him to draw out the employer's positions and subject them to cross-examination. Second, it can serve as a deposition, with the employee having to pay the cost. While such a transcript could not be submitted as evidence without the written agreement of both parties, an attorney in examining or cross-examining a witness could use any statements made at such a hearing with good effect. Finally, it could alert government lawyers to a real weakness in their case and easily facilitate settlement. A final refinement would be the requirement of a quick decision, such as within ten days of the hearing, with only a perfunctory review by a higher authority based on the transcript.

The employee should recognize that a much better system is not possible. Under any system, a dismissal will be extremely harmful and, if it is for the assertion of a constitutional right, doubly so.

Under any system of procedural due process some type of posttermination procedure is necessary and since the Supreme Court requires that all administrative remedies be exhausted before going into court (Arnett was allowed to maintain his suit without exhausting remedies, so the Court could use this case to reaffirm the exhaustion rule). Thus, no quick method of getting into court exists, nor should one. Matters like this are terribly complicated and are not subject, except in rare instances, to summary procedures. Any lawyer handling such a case needs some kind of "discovery." And if the employer pays for the transcript, rather than the employee, so much the better; transcripts in government employment cases are often voluminous, since issues leading to dismissal are often long in developing.

No easy way to handle a dismissal is possible. I usually tell my clients to if possible get a job, any job, while fighting their case. The employee loses no rights in court by getting a new job, other than his salary is offset against an award of back pay. Likewise, an unemployed client is often a very difficult client, one more likely to make a serious mistake on the stand than one with a financial cushion.

Thus, procedural due process needs, first, that notice of charges be given; and second, that before termination the employee have access to someone with the power to prevent, if convinced of the injustice of the situation. If this cannot happen subsequent to termination, the employee should be given one full evidentiary hearing before a supposedly impartial person, with the hearing having finality and a requirement of quick decision. This would make the best of a bad situation.

Who Is Entitled to Due Process?

While the previous discussion about the nature of due process and elements thereof is, of course, important, nevertheless it becomes rather irrelevant unless most or all public employees become entitled to some degree of due process.

While many public employees in the United States are entitled to some form of procedural due process before or after any job action can be taken against them as an aspect of the employment relationship, a large number of public employees all over the country do not have rights of procedural due process guaranteed to them as part of the employment relationship or regulation. And the largest number of these public employees are, unfortunately, the very employees most likely to be subject to some kind of job action. This is especially true of teachers on the college, secondary, and elementary levels, and such employees as librarians, and social workers. These employees are often engaged in the most controversial work of all public employees and are usually expected to, or feel compelled to, speak out on the record with respect to the vital issues they confront in their jobs. A certain number of these employees are, of course, protected by the tenure system. Tenure, unlike other kinds of job security and most other aspects of public employment, is difficult to come by, and public employees seeking tenure are more vulnerable to unconstitutional action in a case against them than most other public employees.

In this context a great amount of litigation has developed over the last few years whereby teachers and others dismissed for what they considered to be reasons pertaining to their exercise of protected constitutional rights have gone to court to try to get judicial decisions requiring that procedural due process be afforded any teacher prior to dismissal. Such procedural due process would be of the type discussed previously and would be constitutionally guaranteed. They believed that if these requirements for procedural due process were instituted, they would be much less likely to be subject to arbitrary dismissal or nonrenewal of contract.[11]

Such cases were tried throughout the country, and finally reached a head when the Supreme Court decided the cases *Board of Regents* v.

11. The present standard of prudent due process was developed in the case of Cafeteria Workers v. McElroy, 367 U.S. 886 (1960), which set up a balancing test of rational relationship to a governmental interest opposed to the employees' interest in not being subject to arbitrary dismissals, especially in view of the value impact on

Roth[12] and *Perry* v. *Sindermann*.[13] In those cases the Supreme Court held that public employees do not have rights of procedural due process in the context of dismissal unless they are tenured or have an expectation of employment equivalent to tenure, or if procedural due process is given by state law or contract.

The *Roth* case concerned David Roth, an assistant professor on a one-year contract without tenure at a state university in Wisconsin. About five months before the end of his contract he was told by the university president that his contract would not be renewed. No reasons were given to him for the nonrenewal. Roth sued in federal court, alleging that the decision not to rehire him violated his rights under the First and Fourteenth Amendments, in that his nonretention was related to his political activities and speeches; he further claimed that, whatever the reasons, he was entitled to be notified of them by the school before he could be dismissed. The district court agreed with Roth and ordered the university to provide him with reasons and a hearing.

In handing down his opinion, Judge Doyle emphasized the impact on the professor of a dismissal or nonretention, namely the difficulty he would have to find another job once he has been so dismissed.[14] According to Judge Doyle this, coupled with the potential for violation of the teacher's First Amendment rights, makes it absolutely imperative that certain forms of due process must be afforded a teacher no matter what his contract status before dismissal. To Judge Doyle the procedure would be two-fold: (1) a statement of the reason why the university intends not to retain him be furnished upon his request; and (2) notice of a hearing, at which time he may respond to the stated reasons provided upon his request; or at such a hearing the professor must have a reasonable opportunity to submit evidence relevant to the stated reasons. The burden of going forward and the burden of proof rests with the professor. Only if he can reasonably show that the stated reasons are wholly inappropriate as a basis for the decision, or that they are wholly without basis and fact, would the university administration be obliged to show that the stated reasons are not inappropriate but have basis in fact.

The *Roth* case was later upheld on appeal by the United States Court of Appeals for the Seventh Circuit.[15] The opinion of the circuit court,

---

the employee of the dismissal. It was the later aspect which convinced Judge Flogle who tried Roth v. Board of Regents, 310 F. Supp. 972 (W.D. Wisc. 1970) at the district court level to apply that test and lean heavily to the dismissed employee.

12. 408 U.S. 564 (1972).
13. 408 U.S. 593 (1972).
14. Roth v. Board of Regents 310 F. Supp. at 983–84.
15. 446 F.2d 806 (1971).

while not as extensive as that of the district court, emphasized two main situations in which procedural due process must be given to the employee: first, when the government action can jeopardize the right to follow a chosen trade or profession. The circuit court reasoned that the higher the level of the job and the more it involves professional licensing and such, the more the person could be harmed by the dismissal, and therefore the greater need for procedural due process.

Second, the circuit court emphasized that this nonretention came at a period of turmoil on the campus, and an arguable case could be made that this dismissal could have been related to certain statements made by Roth which, if true, would be a violation of his First Amendment rights. Thus, to prevent such a situation, a minimum level of procedural due process would be required. Unfortunately, when the case came to the Supreme Court, it was reversed at a great loss to public employees.

The second case, *Sindermann* v. *Perry*, concerned the dismissal of a teacher at a community college in Texas. Sindermann had been employed in this state college system for ten years, the last four years at the school in question under a succession of one-year contracts. However, a controversy arose between the school and Sindermann following his election as president of the Texas Junior College Teachers Association. As president he was required on several occasions to testify before committees of the Texas legislature and became involved in public disagreement with the college's board of regents. As a result, he was not given a new contract. The board of regents issued a press release setting forth allegations of subordination, but made no official statement to Sindermann of the reasons for the nonrenewal of his contract. He brought suit in federal district court, but lost because this court held that, since there was no tenure system, he had no right of contract.

The Court of Appeals for the Fifth Circuit reversed that case, holding that no matter what his tenure rights, nonrenewal of contract would be in violation of the petitioner's First and Fourteenth Amendment rights if the dismissal were based on his exercise to protect his free speech.[16]

Second, the court held that despite Sindermann's lack of tenure, the failure to afford him procedural due process would violate his constitutional rights if he could show he had an "expectancy" of reemployment. The state appealed the case to the United States Supreme Court, and even though Sindermann there won his case for reinstatement, the grounds on which he did so were unfortunately so narrow as to afford small surcease to a large number of teachers and other public employees dismissed or nonretained without reason.

16. 430 F.2d 939 (CA5 1970).

In *Roth*, the Supreme Court laid down a two-pronged test to determine whether or not a public employee is entitled to procedural due process prior to or subsequent to termination. Under the terms of this test a court must (1) look not to the "weight" but to the *nature* of the interest, and (2) see if the interest is within the Fourteenth Amendment's protection of liberty and property.

By "weight," the Court is considering the possible harm that the employee might suffer by arbitrary governmental action. By "nature," the Court is considering the general class of entitlement, regardless of harm. While the terms "weight" and "nature of interest" are somewhat obscure and subject to interchangeable use depending upon the view of the issue in question, Mr. Justice Stewart, writing for the majority, is of the opinion that when looking into the context of dismissal, an employee is not necessarily guaranteed procedural due process even if the harm of the dismissal, when weighted against the cost of the state in the affording of due process, comes out strongly on the side of the employee. Rather, he stated that no matter what the harm may be, procedural due process may accrue to the employee only if the employee has an entitlement to his job or if the dismissal violates the Fourteenth Amendment concept of "liberty," as applied in the context of public employment.

According to Justice Stewart, the concept of "liberty" under the Fourteenth Amendment connotes "not merely freedom from bodily restraint but also the right of the individual to contract, to engage in any of the common occupations of life, to acquire useful knowledge, to marry, establish a home and bring up children, to worship God according to the dictates of his own conscience, and generally to enjoy those privileges long recognized . . . as essential to the orderly pursuit of happiness by free men."[17]

In so defining liberty, Justice Stewart stated that circumstances might occur under which the refusal of the state to employ a person might violate this concept of liberty, but not in this particular case. Justice Stewart held that the college, in dismissing Roth, did not make any allegations against him which would harm his standing in the community and thus entitle him to procedural due process. The Court did concede that, had such statements been made, the case might have had a different conclusion.

Likewise, the Court held that the mere fact of nonemployment did not impose on Roth any stigma or disability which would foreclose his chances for reemployment at some other school. Justice Stewart's position

17. 408 U.S. 569–71. By citing specific examples of liberty, which Steward would have us believe develop unrelated to any governmental activity, he is setting the stage for his theory of entitlements.

was to differentiate between nonretention and outright dismissal. This reason causes this case to be a rather narrow view of the concept of liberty; in reality it is blind to the personal effects of a teacher's non-retention. True, nonretention has absolutely no stigma in certain situations, such as that involving teaching assistants in large universities, in which a large yearly turnover of employment is expected. However, when the teacher is considered part of the faculty and is in such a position that he could eventually be eligible for promotion and tenure, the mere fact of nonretention, especially in the first or second year of teaching, is automatically considered to be as a result of incompetence or worse.

Interestingly, the district court in *Roth* made a very important factual finding concerning teacher retention at this particular university. According to the court, of the 441 nontenured teachers at the university, only 4 did not have their contracts renewed.[18] Thus, from a strictly factual standpoint, the nonrenewal was the extraordinary event. As Van Alstyne states,

> the very fact that non-renewal may be *known* to be a rare event in the practices of the particular institution makes the fact of non-renewal in a given case a much more severe judgment than otherwise and one which is correspondingly more likely to affect a teacher's opportunities elsewhere as well.[19]

Unfortunately, in its attempt to establish a general precedent, the Court chose to ignore major facts which tend to show the connection between procedural due process and First Amendments rights. At the very least it could have introduced a limitation of its strict rule based on factual findings of practice at an institution. This could be found, just as any other fact. If history shows great turnover, no stigma would attach to dismissal or nonretention. On the other hand, when an institution has a history of stable employment relations, nonretention would be rare and have more of an impact on the employee. Likewise, the rarer the event the less onerous the burden on the institution punishing the procedural due process.

Ironically, if Justice Stewart had actually accepted the nature of the interest test as he said he did, it would be absolutely irrelevant whether or not there was in fact harm to the standing and reputation of the teacher. If only status was involved, any nontenured teacher could be denied procedural due process according to Judge Stewart's opinion. However, Justice Stewart discussed in great detail why this would not,

18. 310 F. Supp. at 973.
19. Van Alystne, *The Constitutional Rights of Teachers and Professionals*, 1970 DUKE L. J. 871.

as a matter of fact, harm teachers. In trying to explain something unnecessarily, he was really saying that the weight of the interest was also
involved, but that the teacher's weight was not as strong as the institution's. This may be so, although I think the opposite is true; but, nevertheless, if Justice Stewart and the Court wanted to go through a discussion of the weight of interest involved, they should have discussed it
that way, and not tried to hide it.

The second part of the test proposed by Justice Stewart is that the
interests at stake need not only be within the protection of the Fourteenth Amendment concept of liberty, but also the concept of property
under the Fourteenth Amendment. According to Justice Stewart, "The
Fourteenth Amendment procedural protection of property is a safeguard
of the security of interest that a person has already acquired in specific
benefits."[20] In defining this concept, he examines the different forms these
benefits may take in the area of acquired benefits. Thus, he says that a
person receiving welfare has an interest in a continued receipt of those
benefits, and that this continued receipt is guaranteed by procedural due
process; likewise, in the area of public employment, a college professor
holding his job under tenure has an interest in seeing that his tenured
employment is not ended without his being afforded procedural due
process. According to Justice Stewart, "to have a property interest in the
benefit a person clearly must have more than an abstract need for it. He
must have more than a unilateral expectation of it. *He must instead have
a legitimate claim of entitlement to it.*"[21]

Taking this idea one step further, he believes that property interests
are not created by the Constitution, but rather are created from an independent source, such as state law. Thus, in this context, welfare benefits or tenure would be a property interest requiring procedural due
process, strictly because state law protects welfare recipients or guarantees tenure; in the absence of such statutory terms no other source
exists from which the property interest, which would give rights to procedural due process, would flow.

Looking at the *Roth* case, the Court held that the terms of his employment were entirely derived from state law and that, since he was a nontenured professor on a one-year contract which would have expired at
the end of the year, and since no provision was indicated for automatic
renewal, Roth had no property interest in his job and therefore could
have no entitlement to procedural due process.

On the question of the property interest residing in a government bene-

20. 408 U.S. at 575.
21. 408 U.S. at 577 (emphasis added).

fit, I think that the Court has taken an entirely too narrow and misleading approach to the definition of what constitutes a government benefit. Unlike private rights, which develop entirely through contract and have no greater validity or scope than that provided for in the contract which created the right, government benefits are of an entirely different nature. While no constitutional rights compel the government to do something, and indeed the government can conceivably abolish in total any act it has originally created, nevertheless the fact that it might have absolute power not to establish or to totally disestablish a benefit does not mean that it also has power to make any and all conditions on the receipt of that benefit or to subject the receipt of benefits upon the giving up of another right. Likewise, when the government acts, it must act in accordance with due processes of law, and no matter what the reason for establishing the benefit and no matter whether or not it was wise or unwise, once the benefit or the policy exists, it must be dispensed on an evenhanded basis. Thus, the concept of unconstitutional conditions and due process of law makes the relationship between the government and the beneficiary of a government program much different than a similar private contractual relationship, even in the absence of a "property" right to employment.[22]

In short, these constitutional provisions give every citizen with a government benefit a vested interest in its continuation, and this vested interest can only be ended according to constitutional provisions. While a professor at any private university is employed solely on the terms of his contract, whether that contract calls for one-year appointment or lifetime tenure, his employment is no greater or lesser than the contract. However, a state university is a state agency no less than a police department, welfare department, or any other government agency, and just as the welfare department cannot terminate a benefit without due process of law, the state university should also not be able to do so.

This does not mean that the imposition of rights of procedural due process would make it impossible for a state college to dismiss its employees, as often stated by those opposing due processes of law. Quite the contrary; the requirement of due processes of law prior to or subsequent to termination has absolutely nothing to do with the substantive basis of the termination. Previous parts of the book have discussed the two different sides of the substantive question of termination. One part illustrated that the concept of cause has varying legal significance, depending upon the lack of evidence presented against the public em-

22. Reich, *The New Property*, 73 YALE L. J. 733 (1964); comment, Entitlement: Enjoyment and the Due Process Law, 1974 DUKE L. J. 89, 110–11.

ployee. Second, the limitations that the First Amendment imposes upon the grounds of dismissal of public employees have been pointed out. Likewise, in the context of certain types of public employment such as teaching, police work, or even the military, the specific requirements of the agency may very well allow employers greater or lesser leeway in handling their personnel than allowed in agencies having less sensitive or less skilled employment. Again, all this is a matter of substantive grounds for dismissal and has absolutely nothing to do with the idea that the public employee, because he is a public employee, is entitled to rights of procedural due process before he is dismissed.

The impact of the *Roth* opinion on public employees can be seen in the companion case of *Sindermann* v. *Perry*, which graphically shows how this case limited protection for public employees. In *Sindermann*, the Court upheld the lower court finding that Sindermann was fired in violation of his constitutional rights to procedural due processes. However, while this would seem to be a victory for public employees, it was unfortunately quite the contrary. The Court held that Sindermann was entitled to procedural due process because, although the junior college in which he was teaching had no tenure system, the fact that he had been employed at that particular college and in the general Texas community college system for a number of years gave him a property right equivalent to tenure; thus he was at least entitled to a hearing in which he could be informed of the grounds for his nonretention and an opportunity to challenge for insufficiency.

One of the many problems with the *Sindermann* case is that the Court's discussion of the tenure concept was probably irrelevant to the decision, or at least was elevated to an unnecessary high level. Correctly stated, the facts of the case could have proven that Sindermann was fired for assertion of protected constitutional rights. Thus, the issue of tenure was probably unnecessary, other than mentioning it in passing as related to *Roth*.[23] Since vindications of First Amendment rights are not dependent on contractual limitations, and since Sindermann's employers were not asserting their rights to fire him for reasons other than the fact that he technically did not have tenure, the Court raised the right to re-employment issue, while at the same time specifically stating that no limitations are placed on First Amendment rights of employees. Nevertheless, the First Amendment rights which the employers had so generously accorded the employees were taken away.

23. But in the most recent case, Mt. Healthy School District v. Doyle, 429 U.S. 274 (1977), Justice Rehnquist made great importance of the fact that tenure confers powerful benefits on its recipients.

First Amendment rights are a higher degree of rights than procedural due process, because all procedural due process can offer the employee is a reason, whereas vindication of the First Amendment rights offers him a job. Since the lower federal courts had found a violation of constitutional rights, or at least strong factual issue of such a violation, and since the state was appealing the case on the basis of contractual status, the Supreme Court should have avoided indicating that contractual status may have a higher status than constitutional rights by sending the case back to the lower court on the factual issue of the denial of First Amendment rights; or, better yet, simply not accepted this case, since the court of appeal's decision would have given Sindermann due process, plus a trial on the constitutional issue.

In addition, taking the argument strictly within its own terms of tenure or right of expectation of employment, I strongly disagree with the Court's approach to the concept of tenure. The *Sindermann* case especially raises the problem of attempting to give due process to certain public employees who do not fall under a strict tenure system based on their expectation of reemployment; yet this expectation is couched in terms of length of employment, rather than the certainty of reemployment.

First of all, the Court is apparently looking upon academic tenure as strictly a contractual matter, in which a teacher judged to meet certain standards by his colleagues is guaranteed the equivalent of a lifetime job. The Court then apparently applies this to situations of common public employment in which an employee, once past the probationary period, is entitled to be considered a full-time public employee. However, two immediate distinctions come to mind which bear some discussion. Tenure is not like other kinds of job probationary periods; tenure is a special type of situation wrapped up in the entire "common law" of academic life, with its concepts of "academic freedom".[24] Second, if in

---

24. Justice Douglas, dissenting in both cases, specifically made reference to academic freedom, quoting Professor Will Herberg as to academic freedom:

> It is sometimes conceived as a basic constitutional right guaranteed and protected under the First Amendment.
>
> But, of course, this is not the case. Whereas a man's right to speak out on this or that may be guaranteed and protected, he can have no imaginable human or constitutional right to remain a member of a university faculty. Clearly, the right of academic freedom is an acquired one, yet an acquired right of such value to society that in the mind of many it has verged upon the constitution. [*Washington Evening Star*, January 23, 1972.]

However Herberg, as Douglas so correctly pointed out, underrates the constitutional basis of academic freedom. Sweezy v. New Hampshire, 354 U.S. 234 (1957); Keyishian v. Board of Regents, 385 U.S. 583 (1967).

fact the Court is correct in analogizing tenure to probationary periods in other jobs, does the Court mean that if a person has passed his probationary period he is then entitled to due process prior to dismissal despite the shortness of this period? Will this be true, even if the probationary period is a short one, say, several months? Judging from the tone of the *Roth* case, the answer would obviously be negative; but if the logic of the *Sindermann* case is accepted, a severe contradiction in the Court's decision is apparent, one not so easily dismissed.

Unlike other types of job security, tenure is, in fact, a peer group approval process. Tenure is given by faculty members to other faculty members. It is not given at the first instance by university or college administrators to individual faculty members. True, often the administration in a given school plays a part in or ultimately claims the final decisions in a tenure situation. However, when such a situation exists, it violates the spirit of tenure. And, no matter how tenure may be guaranteed, whether by law, contract, moral commitment under academic code, or simple courtesy, it is a product of long attempts by the academic profession to preserve its freedom, not simply an administrative convenience to help personnel policies, as is the case in other public employment.[25]

Because of the special nature of academic life and its close interconnections with First Amendment rights or the equivalent of such in the context of a private university, the Court, if true to its opinion that the nature, rather than the weight, of the interest applies, should have taken into account the fact that once a teacher has a job which puts him on a rung leading to possible tenure, he then has a special interest in the job. This would require that before the teacher is dismissed or nonretained, he should at least be afforded procedural due process.

A recognized fact of academic life acknowledges that the decision to grant or not to grant tenure is based on factors quite different from those which go into a dismissal or nonrenewal of a nonacademic employee. Many subjective factors are included, such as the department chairman's attitude to the ideas expressed by junior faculty members aspiring to tenure, or questions of whether a teacher has published in a sufficiently prestigious journal. Thus, nongranting of tenure generally has no derogatory connotations to other potential employers. Indeed, when dealing with major universities, a person qualified enough to be hired to the faculty as an assistant professor and kept on for a period of

---

25. See Albaum v. Carey, 283 F. Supp. 3 (S.D. N.Y. 1968); Thaw v. Board of Public Instruction of Dade County, 432 F.2d 98 (5th Cir. 1970).

six years pending the decision on tenure, is assumed a qualified teacher. James Schlesinger never received tenure at the University of Virginia, and it took Henry Kissinger ten years to receive tenure at Harvard.

However, the focus on tenure is quite unfortunate, since the majority of persons employed as teachers in public institutions are employed at institutions that do not grant tenure, especially the junior colleges, as was the case in *Sindermann*, or public schools; and, in many of the major public universities, tenure has been abolished. Second, because those institutions which grant tenure require a six-year period before tenure is granted, while those which do not have a much shorter probationary period, if any at all, the focus on tenure leads to the contradiction previously mentioned.

Even assuming that the Court had attempted to give public employees certain rights of procedural due process, which would not logically flow from its concepts of liberty and property as expressed in *Roth*, the expectation of reemployment test really does not help the employee. First of all, in those institutions granting tenure, six years are provided before a decision is reached and, in fact, the grounds for denying or not denying tenure are not necessarily the same as those for dismissing or nonretaining a teacher. Indeed, the dismissal or nonretention of a teacher at a tenured institution, at a time before the tenure decision is made, is such a clear allegation of misconduct or incompetence that the teacher could be damaged for life unless given a chance to challenge the allegations.

As for nontenured institutions, teachers in such schools nonretained or dismissed are often harmed less than their counterparts in tenured institutions, yet are given more protection theoretically by this case. In attempting to strike a balance between conceptual ideas of no property right or basic liberty in a job and a desire to somehow protect the teachers, the Supreme Court has, in effect, destroyed the procedural due process rights of those teachers who need them the most, while at the same time diminishing the First Amendment rights of all teachers.

These two decisions are most unfortunate for public employees, especially teachers, in that they take away the special constitutional protection developing as a public employee equivalent to collective bargaining rights in the private sector.

Mr. Justice Douglas, in dissenting in *Sindermann*, clearly understood that in teaching, unlike other areas, First Amendment ideas are often involved in a decision for dismissal, nonretention, or even nongranting of tenure, and that, because of this, teachers may need special protection to prevent retaliation for the expression of ideas. This can only be accomplished by requiring public school employers to give both their reasons and an opportunity for a hearing before dismissing or nonretaining a teacher.

Justice Douglas listed a series of cases in which the Court found that where such important interests of the citizen were implicated, it could not act against a citizen without due process of law, both procedurally or substantively.[26] His position was that in all of these situations (and others) the Court had found that the weight of the interest, in terms of loss to the individual and the denial of governmental benefits, was sufficient to justify the granting of procedural due process in connection with any action to withdraw such benefit or interest.

In analyzing the consequences of nonrenewal or dismissal to a teacher, Justice Douglas found that "nonrenewal of a teacher's contract is tantamount in effect to a dismissal and the consequences can be enormous. Nonrenewal can be a blemish that turns into a permanent scar and effectively limits any chance the teacher has of being rehired as a teacher at least in the state."[27] Likewise, a teacher's firing may also have First Amendment consequences, thus creating a double impact from the nonrenewal or dismissal. The effect of such action on nonteachers will vary only in degree, not in kind.

Douglas here is indicating that the requirement for the affording of procedural due process is a means to vindicate rights without the necessity of resorting to a lawsuit in every instance. The individual teacher may well be at fault and the school may have justifiable reasons for taking action. In such a case, the granting of reasons, rather than burdening the system (as many school administrators would do) has the effect of limiting court actions, since a teacher faced with what he knows to be legitimate reasons for the action may not wish to have those reasons made public; thus the teacher would accept dismissal without filing suit. But, if the reasons are invalid or not serious enough to justify a dismissal or nonretention in the absence of other valid reasons, the requirement for the specification of charges forces the school to go on record at the time of the dismissal and list its reasons, preventing a conjuring up of reasons in answer to a lawsuit, as in the *Hodgin* case. Thus, the affording of procedural due process would benefit all parties.

26. Slochower v. Board of Higher Education, 350 U.S. 551 (1956), disbarment of lawyers; Bell v. Burson, 402 U.S. 535 (1976) drivers licenses; Sherbert v. Verner, 374 U.S. 398 (1963), denial of unemployment compensation for religious reason; Speiser v. Randall, 357 U.S. 513 (1957), conditioning of tax exemption and giving up Fourteenth Amendment rights; Goldberg v. Kelly, 397 U.S. 254 (1970), due process before termination of welfare rights.
27. 408 U.S. at 587.

Since the *Roth* and *Sindermann* cases, two Supreme Court cases have discussed procedure. The first was the case of *Arnett* v. *Kennedy*,[28] discussed in the context of dismissal for cause. In that case, the federal statute, the Lloyd-La Follette Act, provided that federal Civil Service employees covered by such an act would be given full rights of procedural due process, including notice of charges, opportunity to file answers, right to appear before union examiners, appeal to a Civil Service Commission, including trial-type procedures and right to back pay, if reinstated. However, all of these rights, especially the evidenciary hearings, would occur only after discharge. The plaintiff, Kennedy, upon notice that he was being charged with certain offenses, requested a full evidenciary hearing before dismissal; when this was refused he filed suit in federal court. He won in the lower federal courts, but the government appealed to the Supreme Court.

The Supreme Court reversed, based on their ruling in *Roth*. The most interesting detail about this case was that the plurality of opinions in the name of the Court by Justice Rehnquist extended *Roth* logically and held that, if the state could substantively limit the extent of the entitlement, which in this case was the right not to be fired except for due cause by the statute, it could adopt procedural limitations as well. Ironically, the concurring opinion of Justice Powell, and the dissenting opinion (which covered six justices in all), found that, in the case of state-granted substantive rights, as opposed to constitutionally granted substantive rights, the provisions concerning procedures could be distinguished from this substantive right itself, with a constitutional basis to the procedures once they were held to apply.

This case is of interest because it apparently undercuts the validity of *Roth* to a certain degree; if *Roth*'s logic was followed consistently, Justice Rehnquist's position would be the correct one, and the series of cases cited by Justice Douglas in dissent in *Roth*, including *Goldberg* v. *Kelly*, concerning a welfare recipient's right to procedural due process before termination, would be totally inconsistent with the *Roth* doctrine and should be overruled. Since the Court apparently does not wish to overrule *Goldberg*, the system becomes a crazy quilt in which certain types of statutory-created government entitlements have accompanying rights of procedural due process which must be afforded before the entitlement is taken away, while others have either no rights of procedural due process or rights to procedural due process only after they are taken away.

This obviously means that the Court, while talking about the nature of the interest being determinative, is really talking about the weight of

28. 416 U.S. 134 (1974).

the interest. No real reason should cause the right to welfare benefits to be considered of a different nature than the right to continued government employment. As a class, welfare recipients stand in the same position to government employers as teachers; yet, from the combination of the opinions, obviously welfare recipients are afforded a much higher level of procedural due process than teachers. The Court may really be implying that because welfare recipients have fewer resources to fall back upon than teachers, to take away their rights might condemn them to near starvation, whereas dismissing a highly educated teacher might have a lesser impact, especially if the teacher is in a position to collect unemployment insurance or to get another job. To argue with the Supreme Court concerning the economic prospects of dismissed junior teachers is not feasible; nevertheless, the Court should not eliminate entire classes of persons from entitlement to due process on the false ground that an unexplained dismissal is not a real hardship. If the Court really wants to reimpose the right-privilege doctrine, which denies constitutional rights because of a power relationship, then it should state the doctrine in those terms. To characterize the denial in the terms it has is simply intellectual dishonesty.

At this point the Court apparently has boxed itself into such a corner that it either is not going to accept any more cases in the area for some time, or, if it does, will make individual determination as to the weight of the particular interest involved, and not try to reconcile the *Arnett* and *Roth* cases. Logically, either the Rehnquist plurality opinion in *Arnett* or the Douglas dissenting opinion in *Roth* is the "real law," depending on individual problems. While, obviously, I favor the Douglas position without question, nevertheless, taking the conservative or Rehnquist view of rights of procedural due process, which holds that if a state can substantively limit the extent of entitlement it should also be able to adopt procedural limitations, the view is, within its own terms, logical. However, this obviously is a restatement of the discredited right-privilege theory, and if the Supreme Court has found that that theory cannot apply to substantive rights, I cannot see how it can logically be applied to rights of procedural due process.

Unfortunately, the United States Supreme Court did make that decision in *Bishop* v. *Wood*.[29] In *Bishop* v. *Wood*, a North Carolina policeman was fined on the basis of a mistake, or libelous charges. The Supreme Court, in addition to limiting access to federal courts, held that a state cannot only provide the basis of the entitlement, that is, tenure or per-

29. 426 U.S. 341 (1976).

manent employment, but can also provide the remedy, or fail to provide a remedy.

This holding was precisely what I feared would be the problem in *Arnett*; that is, a limited constitutional right of due process is impossible. While the majority opinion in *Bishop* v. *Wood* was devastating to public employees, since the *Arnett* position at least guaranteed procedural process rights to a certain class of public employees, *Arnett* had a basic logical inconsistency which the Court found and upon which it based its ruling.

This logical inconsistency was as follows: If a government employer is allowed to do anything it pleases to nonpermanent employees, but can only dismiss permanent employees after affording them procedural due process and a determination of who is and who is not a permanent employee, the governmental employer will not want to continue the employment of persons found to be somewhat difficult to work with, since once that person is granted the equivalent of tenure, his dismissal becomes more difficult. If a dismissal is judged to be arbitrary after a given period of time is passed in the duration of employment, it should also be judged arbitrary if the dismissal was for the same reasons before that period of time. This was the basic inconsistency; any court subsequently faced with it would probably have ruled against the *Arnett* position. Unfortunately, the present, more conservative Court simply reached the conclusion to the detriment of public employees; since no reason could be given why postpermanent employee status should give rise to different rights than prepermanent status, it held that all employees should be treated the same. That is, the same procedural rights should apply to all or none; since the state has a right to determine who is and who is not a permanent employee, it should therefore also have the similar right to determine the extent procedural due process is to be afforded its employees. A more liberal Court, faced with the same inconsistency, would have simply decided the other way, that since no reason could be given why post- and prepermanent status employees should be treated differently, all employees would be entitled to full procedural due process.

The issue in *Bishop* v. *Wood* differed from *Arnett*; *Arnett* did not question whether the employee should be entitled to any procedural due process, but rather stated that it could be given before or after dismissal. The question of which due process is the adequate one is an entirely different issue from whether or not any due process should be given at all. Under *Arnett*, federal employees are entitled to at least postdismissal due process.

After *Bishop* v. *Wood*, challenges to nonconstitutionally related dismissals must be based entirely upon the grounds of procedure set out by the employer, that is, whether the employer complies with his own procedures. While the federal government was not a party to *Bishop* v. *Wood*, the majority opinion indicated that, if the federal government chooses to limit the existing rights of employees to procedural due process, by statute or regulation, federal courts would be powerless to overturn such change on constitutional grounds. Likewise, state actions can only be challenged on state law grounds.

The Supreme Court minority has no one to blame but itself. In 1972, before Justice Douglas's retirement, the ostensibly liberal majority of Justices Douglas, Brennan, Stewart, White, and Marshall could have given a much more expansive ruling on procedural due process in *Roth* and *Sindermann* which would have guaranteed it to all employees, except possibly in cases of those under limited probationary periods. Instead, the Court engaged in a game of legal hairsplitting, attempting to make distinctions between property rights, no property rights, permanent employee status, and nonpermanent employee status, to the point at which the constitutional basis of procedural due process was so undercut that a conservative Court, as in *Bishop*, could decide that if half of the constitutional basis of procedural due process is to be cut away, all of it should go; that is exactly what has, in fact, happened.

I strongly suspect that *Bishop* v. *Wood* will be severely undercut over the next few years, if not completely overruled. But, in the meantime, numerous public employees are going to undergo a great deal of suffering as a result of these decisions.

Chapter 7

Public Employee Unions

Part of the popular image of public employees today undoubtedly involves a militant public employee union. Whether a strike of municipal employees in San Francisco, a strike of public doctors in California, teacher strikes around the country, or policemen and firemen staging slowdowns, the image remains the same.

This image is grossly misleading; not only is the majority of public employees not unionized, but the effectiveness and capabilities of different public employee unions varies greatly over the entire spectrum of state and federal employment.

However, before the discussion of rights and wrongs of public employee unions is attempted, I think it should be halted at the beginning, because the question of public employee labor law is a study of law entirely to itself and could not be included and discussed adequately in anything short of a second book. Some questions which should be covered in the general area of public employee labor law are such matters as the right to strike, bargaining, the enforceability of bargaining contracts, the obligation to bargain, remedies short of striking such as arbitration; and included within all of these questions is an examination of how different jurisdictions throughout the country react to the particular problems. Obviously, this is too large a question for this book.

However, since this book is most concerned about the role of the individual employee and the forces and pressures asserted against him, some very important questions concerning public employee labor law do exist in the context of how public employee law relates to the individual employee.

Two problems in particular should be examined: first, the right of a public employee to belong to a union; and second, the rights the public employee has if he is dissatisfied with the representation given to him by the union. In focusing on these questions, I specifically exclude the question of whether or not a public employee can be dismissed for engaging in some form of collective action, such as a strike, slowdown or work stoppage, because any answer would involve the whole question of the scope of union activity in greater detail than would be warranted in this study. Within the limits set forth, however, such issues as the right to strike will be tangentially touched upon insofar as they apply to the public employee's relationship with his union and/or employer.

The Right to Be Organized

The right of the public employee to become a member of a collective unit should be distinguished immediately from the right of the employee to engage in actions against his employer as a member of that unit. In discussing the question of joining the unit, the reader should immediately recognize that the employee is not necessarily joining a union affiliated with a recognized national labor organization. A group of public employees organized on their own initiative into a loose association, which need not even be called a union, would be sufficient for purposes of asserting in one form or another rights and grievances against their public employer. The nature of the association's affiliation is not the object of concern, but rather the existence of the association.

At the outset the legal basis for a public employee joining a public employee organization which has, as its goal, representation of the employee's interests in the working relationship with his public employer should be recognized as differing from that of employee organizations in private industry. Since 1935, all employer-employee relationships in the private sector have been governed by a series of federal labor laws which not only give private employees the right to form organizations and engage in collective action, but also spell out the various limits of action both by the union against the employer and the employer against the union.[1] The same is not true with regard to public employment, because

1. The original labor law was the National Labor Relations Act of 1935, better known as the Wagner Act. In 1947 it was amended by the Labor Management Relations Act, or the Taft-Hartley Act. Both acts are now legally called Chapter 7, 29 U.S.C. In addition, the Labor Management Reporting and Disclosure Act, 29 U.S.C. 411 et seq., covers internal policies of unions.

federal labor legislation specifically excludes public employees from coverage (except postal employees)[2] and, while some states have their own legislation in the area of public employment permitting public employees to bargain collectively, public labor organizations in many ways operate in a legal vacuum.[3]

Because of this legal vacuum, other legal doctrines designed to enable public employees to form collective associations without fear of immediate dismissal or blackballing from public employment were necessary; they were found in the Constitution.

The constitutional basis allowing public employees to join employment organizations equivalent to private labor unions is based on the same doctrine used to protect civil rights organizations in the South from being required to disclose to state authorities a list of their members. In civil rights cases the Supreme Court enunciated a doctrine that the First Amendment in effect spun off, as a part of the Fourteenth Amendment concept of liberty, a right to freedom of association which is an integral part of the freedoms of speech and assembly. In the first of these cases, *NAACP v. Alabama, ex rel. Patterson*,[4] Mr. Justice Harlan stated this doctrine most effectively:

> Effective advocacy of both public and private points of view, particularly controversial ones, is undeniably enhanced by group association, as this court has more than once recognized by remarking upon the close nexus between the freedoms of speech and assembly. [Cite omitted.] It is beyond debate that freedom to engage in association for the advancement of beliefs and ideas is an inseparable aspect of the "liberty" assured by the due process clause of the Fourteenth Amendment, which embraces freedom of speech. . . . Of course, it is immaterial whether the beliefs sought to be advanced by association pertain to political, economic, religious or cultural matters, and state

---

2. There is a form of labor law for federal agencies. Under Executive Order 10958 of 1962, a federal executive branch agency must accord "exclusive recognition" to a union selected as representative by a majority of the employees in the appropriate unit. Under this order, these unions can bargain collectively with the agency with administrative remedies provided if the agency refuses to bargain in good faith. However, the one exception to the exclusion of public employees from coverage of the National Labor Laws is the Postal Service. Under the Postal Reorganization Act, 39 U.S.C. §1209(a), all provision of the national labor law, except the right to strike, applies to the relationship between the new Postal Service Corporation and the employee unions. The specific exclusion of public employees is found in 27 U.S.C. §152.

3. For a comprehensive list of these statutes, see *American Jurisprudence* §1191–94. Specific statutes will be referred to as needed.

4. 357 U.S. 449 (1958); see also Shelton v. Tucker, 364 U.S. 479 (1960); NAACP v. Button, 371 U.S. 415 (1963); NAACP v. Alabama ex rel. Flowers, 377 U.S. 288.

action which may have the effect of curtailing the freedom to associate is subject to the closest scrutiny.[5]

This language is the bedrock upon which the right of public employees to form and belong to labor organizations is based.

The fact that the Supreme Court ruled in favor of associations such as the NAACP and similar organizations does not mean that, as of that moment, all public employee organizations suddenly found that they could organize without any resistance or difficulty whatsoever. Just as in any other line of work a lot of people did not "get the word," or if they did get it they refused to believe it; thus, throughout the 1960s, public employees fought for the right to form, or the constitutional right to join, employee organizations.

A typical case of the period, one considered by many legal authorities to have the greatest precedential value although not a United States Supreme Court decision, is the case of *Atkins* v. *The City of Charlotte*.[6] North Carolina had a law prohibiting public employees in any governmental body in the state of North Carolina, whether at the state or local level, from becoming a member of a trade or labor union.[7] This law was all-inclusive and allowed for no exceptions. Members of the Charlotte Fire Department sought to become affiliated with the National Association of Fire Fighters; to that end they sought recognition from the city of Charlotte for their organizational activities. The city of Charlotte refused to accept them as a union because of the provisions of the state statute. The employees, joined by the national union, went to federal court to have the statute invalidated. They argued that the statute on its face was abridgement of the First Amendment rights of freedom of speech and assembly, and the Fourteenth Amendment right of the freedom of association. The federal court agreed with them and declared that the North Carolina statute was unconstitutional on its face, citing *NAACP* v. *Alabama, ex rel. Patterson* as the controlling law. The language used by the court in discussing the specific problems of the firemen seems to operate for public employees anywhere; this is highly significant. The court held:

> We would make the same distinction here. It matters not we think whether the firemen of the city of Charlotte meet under the auspices

5. 357 U.S. at 460.

6. 296 F. Supp. 1068 (W.D. N.C. 1969). See also American Federation of State, County and Municipal Employees v. Woodward, 406 F.2d 137 (8th Cir. 1969), and McLaughlin v. Tilendis, 398 F.2d 287 (7th Cir. 1968), which held in cases arising in Nebraska and Illinois that public employees have a right to unionize.

7. N.C. Gen. Stat. §95–98 (1965).

of the intervenor [the National Association of Fire Fighters] national labor union, but whether the proposed concerted action, if any, endangers valid state interests. We think that there is no valid state interest in denying the firemen the right to organize a labor union—whether local or national in scope. It is beyond argument that a single individual cannot negotiate on an equal basis with an employer who hires hundreds of people. Recognition of this fact is a basis of labor-management relations in this county. Charlotte concedes in its brief that the right of public employees to join labor unions is becoming increasingly recognized (with the exception of policemen and firemen) and even admits that collective bargaining might be beneficial in many situations in the case of municipal firemen. It is said that fire departments are necessary because individual firemen must be ready to respond instantly and without question to the orders of a superior and that such military discipline may well mean the difference between saving human life and property and failure. . . .[8]

The court went on to hold that the mere fact that the state was afraid of possible strikes does not give it the right to prevent employees from joining organizations. However, and this is important, the court was unwilling to go any further, holding that while a right to strike may exist, no constitutional right to bargain collectively is extant.[9] In this, the court upheld another part of the statute which constituted a ban on governmental organizations in the state of North Carolina from entering into collective bargaining agreements with labor unions. In view of recent Supreme Court cases establishing the "entitlement doctrine," the present Court is not likely to rule that states have a constitutional obligation to bargain with public employee organizations because, a priori, if there is no constitutional right to bargain collectively, there is certainly no constitutional right to strike, since collective bargaining is the activity most akin to First Amendment speech, while a strike is akin to action, which is much less protected under the First Amendment.

However, a somewhat more liberal Court may possibly find a statute similar to North Carolina's, which absolutely found collective bargaining unconstitutional, to be a violation of the employees' right of association. This would probably be the limit of the law. Such a rule would allow local jurisdictions who wished to bargain to do so (political considerations often play a considerable role in such a decision); it would not require unwilling jurisdictions to do so or allow employee job action for refusal to bargain.

Finally, a law requiring bargaining with state imposed sanctions on

8. 296 F. Supp. at 1075.
9. 296 F. Supp. at 1076–77.

reluctant local governments would have to be valid because, if the original Wagner Act requiring private employees to enter into bargaining under penalty of sanction was constitutional, certainly a law requiring local governments, which are in effect creatures of the state, to bargain would be equally valid. All the state is really doing is obligating itself and its subdivisions to bargain.

If no constitutional right exists for public employee labor unions to require their public employees to engage in collective bargaining with them, while strict prohibitions do prevent employee labor unions from striking, what good are employee unions to public employees? Why would they wish to enter them in the absence of any specific statutory right of collective bargaining?

Public employees might desire to belong to unions for many reasons, even without the unions' ability to engage in the type of activities private labor unions can engage in. First of all, most states and the federal government have some form of grievance procedures concerning individual employees, and one major function that public employee unions do for their members is assist them with the processing of their individual grievances.

Often the best time to stop an action by an employer against its employee which might result in the loss of the job or suspension is before anything takes place. When differences arise between a supervisor and his employee based partly on personality differences, a public employer may attempt to trump up a charge against the employee to have him dismissed or otherwise reprimanded. The employee is often helpless against this action until it is too late, the action has already been taken, and all that remains is grievance procedures and, perhaps, court. This is an expensive and often ineffective remedy. The existence of a labor organization which has the funds to hire counsel or coordinate different activities for the members can, however, often reach a higher supervisor before the job action is taken, preventing such unfair acts from occurring. This is not collective bargaining, but rather assisting an employee in taking advantage of rights given under grievance procedures.

Second, of course, unions can assert political pressure on governing bodies. If such pressure does not necessarily lead to collective bargaining agreements, it could certainly lead to the enactment of laws or ordinances which improve the lot of the public employees, such as the institution of a state-wide grievance machinery or even a different way of insuring that persons appointed to different organizations are not antilabor. In view of *Bishop* v. *Wood*, this may become very important.

Finally, of course, labor unions can financially assist an employee who has suffered job action and needs to process his grievance or file suit, since the cost of legal action is often prohibitive. The latter point is especially true with regard to the various teacher organizations, especially the National Education Association (NEA), which has a legal defense fund to pay the cost of litigation of members fired for unconstitutional or quasi-unconstitutional reasons.[10] This defense fund, while not accepting all cases of teachers dismissed for allegedly illegal reasons, nevertheless has participated in many cases, and its existence is one of the major inducements for teachers to join the organization, even in areas in which laws similar to those of North Carolina, prohibiting collective bargaining between teacher organizations and boards of education, are in effect.[11] Likewise, knowledge that a public employee union would support individual employees subject to job action, thus forcing the local or state governmental agencies to engage in expensive litigation, is a strong factor in preventing actions against individual employees.

In short, the mere fact that collective action may be prohibited, whether at the level of collective bargaining or even striking, does not mean that public employee unions could not serve a function for an individual employee. Quite the contrary is true; employee organizations, whether affiliated with a national organization or not, can provide representation in grievance proceedings and court actions. In many cases, this legal function is the most important one for the employee, since salary scales are often set by state law and cannot be changed in view of budget problems.

Indeed, the areas possessing the strongest laws against collective bargaining by public employees are also the areas in which the necessity for collective action may be the greatest, because any state which is so anti-union that it prohibits collective bargaining by public employees often has negative attitudes towards public employees in general and their rights. When public employees find themselves subject to arbitrary action on a continuing basis, the formation of a union may well be the only way to have grievances, including those not involving salary levels, resolved. Often the employee seeking to form a collective association, whether or

10. The NEA and its various state and local affiliates have an extremely strong legal defense fund and the capability to respond to almost any legitimate complaint of a member teacher and to prosecute the complaint to the highest courts. Indeed, Mt. Healthy Board of Education v. Doyle, a recent Supreme Court case, had NEA participation.

11. Vernon's Tex. Civ. Stats. Act. 5154c §1. The Virginia Supreme Court recently held that it was against public policy for a municipality to enter into a collective bargaining agreement with a public employee union. A California court even held that an agreement agreed to as the basis for ending an illegal strike was illegal since the consideration for the agreement was invalid. Grasko v. Los Angeles City Board of Education, 31 Cal. App. 3d 290, 107 Cal. Rptr. 334.

not one affiliated with a national association, is most vulnerable to retaliatory action by the state, and thus most in need of constitutional protection.

The *Atkins* case, previously discussed, exemplifies another major trend in law. Certain types of public employees, never previously organized or attempting to assert their rights in a collective manner, are beginning to do so now, and are doing so very often in areas, such as North Carolina, in which the laws are strongly against bargaining. While teachers have traditionally been organized, policemen, firemen, prison guards, state police, and others have traditionally been unorganized. Yet the present trend is for many of these groups to begin to assert their rights as employees, rather than regarding themselves as enforcing agents of the state who carry with them a certain measure of sovereignty.

For example, within the last year a large group of state policemen in Virginia formed what they called an informal organization. While they never referred to this organization as a union, obviously that is what they have, and the head of the Virginia State Police became literally apoplectic over the idea. Likewise, such previously pliant groups of employees as prison guards are beginning to assert their rights against departments of correction.

Thus, an anomalous situation exists with regard to public employee unions. Public employees doubtlessly have a constitutional right to form and join unions; but the same right does not extend to activities of the union in a collective sense, such as bargaining for wages or job conditions which affect all the members of the employee group. The legal question involved in collective action by employee unions is beyond the scope of this book. I have only raised it to differentiate between the type of action employee unions can take on a collective basis and the type of action they can take on an individual basis. Since this book is concerned with the individual employee and his rights as an employee, nothing further will be said about collective action.

However, since the individual employee is of concern, and since his right to belong to a labor organization has been discussed, the next question is, if an employee becomes a member of a public employee labor organization, what rights does he have, in the context of the labor organization, either to protest the action of his union or to protest if he feels that the union and the employer are engaged in collaborative efforts which work against his interest? An easy answer would have the employee quit the union, but that is really begging the question; when a labor organization is present, and when it is permitted to act, it acts for all employees, whether or not they are union members. Thus the problem here is different. Indeed, the problem of disassociation is really the other side of the coin from the problem of association. The problem of association arises with regard to the individual employee in areas which frown upon labor organizations; the problem of disassociation arises primarily in areas in which the labor organization is allowed to function as a labor organization in collaboration with or working with the governing bodies. Thus the next problem to be explored is the role of the individual employee when his adversary is not only the public employer, but the union as well.

The Employee and the Union

The legal relationship between an individual and his labor union, whether a public or a private union, is an exceedingly complex relationship, in some ways one of the most complex relationships in law. Unlike most relationships, with a basis in some concept of contract obligation, in which the rights and duties of the parties to the agreement are delineated so that a dissatisfied party may or may not leave the relationship if certain conditions are not met, the labor union relationship is quite different.

Even in status relationships, such as marriage, given acts can lead to a dissolution of the association, even if the procedure is somewhat difficult. However, in labor law nothing is that easy, because labor law features a tripartite relationship, as opposed to a dual relationship; that is, the relationship exists between the employer, the employee, and the union, and the different areas of the relationship are sometimes difficult to delineate. First of all, when a representation agreement exists in a given work situation, all employees, whether or not actual members of the employee organization, are covered by the terms of the agreement. Second, during the period of an agreement, no individual member or members of the organization can abrogate the terms of the agreement. Finally, once a labor organization is established, it has its own legal basis, in that the labor organization need not act by common consent of members, but may act in its own right, and such acts, unless specifically required to be ratified by the membership (such as a strike vote in the case of private labor unions), have the force of law.[12]

Thus, the complexity of the situation concerning the employee and his labor union can be seen, although the employee should not be assumed to be as helpless before his union as he is before his employer. While

12. In effect Congress has created a "common law" for labor-management relationships, with the use of elections as the basis of approval. See United Steelworkers of America v. Warrior and Gulf Navigation, 363 U.S. 574 (1963).

certainly limits are placed on an employee's ability to act, they are by no means total, and while the relationships between a labor union and workers in the private sector and public employees seem different, they actually involve the same legal relationship. An attempt to delineate for public employees the scope of the problem is possible, therefore, through an examination of how the relationship has evolved in private unions, since the law is too new in the public section to do more than speculate as to its applicability.

I can delineate three areas in which the labor union and individual employees may be in conflict. They are: (1) the right to be represented; (2) the right of the individual member to disassociate himself from actions of the union; and (3) the right of the individual employee to challenge the actions of his union which would be in contravention of the employee-union relationship.

The Right to Be Represented

The first of the three areas of union-public employees relationships concerns the right of the employee to be represented. As stated previously, one of the complexities of labor law relationships is that the existence of a labor agreement covers all persons within the subject area of the agreement, whether or not they are members of a union. This law is settled in the area of private labor relations, in that dissident members of an employment body have no right to disregard the terms of the employment agreement, other than to seek changes in the terms of the agreement when they expire, to seek deunionization after the period of the agreement expires through the procedures of the National Labor Relations Board, or to change the membership of the union officials after the period of their term of office changes.

The opposite problem of a union refusing to represent a group of employees has been resolved in that, just as employees have no power to negate the existence of an agreement because of the total representation requirement, no union has the power to exclude employees from coverage. The area of most concern, of course, has been exclusion for racial reasons. In the past, especially in certain kinds of craft unions such as railroads, the agreement covered all employees except blacks; the Supreme Court has held that the union is required to protect the equal interest of all members of the craft, even if the union constitutionally prohibits blacks from joining.[13] The question of whether or not a union could

13. Steele v. Louisville & Nashville Railroad Co., 323 U.S. 192 (1944); Brotherhood of Railway Trainmen v. Howard, 343 U.S. 768 (1952); Syres v. Oil Workers International Union, 350 U.S. 892 (1956).

prohibit persons from joining because of their race, religion, or color is a different legal issue, one which has obviously been answered in the negative by the Civil Rights Act of 1964. The fact that many unions are notorious in their attempts to exclude blacks from membership does not in any way change the legal position.

However, in the area of public employment law, several different problems arise, problems not found in private labor laws regarding the question of right and obligation of representation. As stated previously, the terms of the National Labor Relations Act do not apply to public employment, so that legal safeguards for and against minority members of the craft or of the union are not applicable as such. In private employee relations law, when a union has been voted in a given work unit, all members of that unit, whether or not members of the union, are covered by the collective bargaining agreement. They receive benefits of any contract negotiation including wages, working conditions, and grievance machinery. At the same time, they also suffer the same penalties of those belonging to the union, such as going on strike and being subject to layoffs based on a union-negotiated seniority list. In addition, because public employee labor law is not recognized by the national labor relations laws, the possibility is present that when a government employer acts through a public employee union, officially or unofficially, and whether or not the action is recognized by state law, the action would nevertheless not constitute private labor law in the contract sense, but state action in a constitutional sense.

A precedent holds that when a governmental body acts indirectly through a private agency, and the private agency engages in practices which would be illegal or unconstitutional if engaged in by the government, the private agency becomes a state body for purposes of enforcing constitutional rights. The classic case concerns a restaurant leased in a public parking garage in Wilmington, Delaware. The restaurant refused to serve blacks. The Supreme Court held that, since the state government could not refuse to serve blacks if it ran the restaurant, it could not avoid the constitutional requirements by simply leasing space in the public facility to a private organization.[14]

This case and others held that when a private person is exercising "powers traditionally exclusively reserved to the state, the exercise is

14. "State action" is a special legal concept used to apply the provisions of the Fourteenth Amendment to activities of state governments which are quasi-public. See Evans v. Newton, 382 U.S. 296 (1966), will deeding land to city for park specified white only; Burton v. Wilmington Parking Authority, 365 U.S. 715 (1961), restaurant in public parking garage refused to serve blacks; Shelly v. Kraemer, 334 U.S. 1 (1948), court enforcement of restrictive covenants prohibited.

subject to the Fourteenth Amendment"; in this context "state" indicates any government, as opposed to a form of political organization.

While no cases concerning the use of state action doctrine with regard to public employee law exist at present, the use of the doctrine should possibly be something that individuals who have complaints with their public employee union should bear in mind, both pro and con. While such matters as racial, religious, or sex discrimination in representation would be prohibited whether public employment law relationships were considered private or public matters, since it is prohibited both by the Constitution and by statute, other areas are not so clear and could require some legal legerdemain.

One major difference, of course, between public and private employment law is that because no national legal sanction requirement forces public bodies to engage in labor collective bargaining with public employees as in the private sector, if an employee organizes his fellow public employees, while they may be constitutionally protected from dismissal at the time of joining the union, the public employer is under no obligation to recognize the existence of the union and bargain with it. Problems arise when the governmental body recognizes the existence of the union and seeks to bargain with it as a private organization. What, under those circumstances, are the rights of dissident public employees, or those who would seek to upset the terms of the collective bargaining agreement on the grounds that it is not legally enforceable?

The major legal problems concerning the right of representation of the public employee come in two parts. The first is the right not to be represented by the union; the second is whether or not the terms of the collective bargaining agreement can be legally challenged by an employer.

In private labor law one of the traditional rights of labor unions is to be able to bargain with employers to obtain an agreement that employment at a given plant is contingent upon the employee joining the union after a certain period, which usually expires thirty to sixty days after hiring.[15] In addition, the employer assists the union by checking off (subtracting) union dues from the employee's pay and turning the money over to the union. While an exempting provision in the National Labor Relations Law exists to allow states to pass so-called right to work provisions,[16] which allow the state to prohibit this type of contractual agree-

---

15. This is the so-called union shop permitted by section 8(a)(3) of the National Labor Relations Act (29 U.S.C. §158 (a)(3)).

16. Section 14(b) of the Labor Management Relations Act (29 U.S.C. §164(b)) provides that "nothing in the act shall be construed as authorizing the execution of application of agreements requiring membership in a labor organization as a condition

ment, in these approximately thirty-six states, this type of contract arrangement is the prevailing norm in many industries: An individual employee can object to such a situation in public areas if for no other reason than the lack of a national law which allows the union shop-type of situation found in private employment.[17] In the absence of legal compulsion, however, a governmental body is extremely unlikely to give up an amount of power to a union to include the equivalent of a union shop provision.[18]

The second problem, one which will be discussed only in passing, since it concerns general labor law more than individual rights but which should be recognized, is a situation in which the state challenges the terms of a collective bargaining agreement signed by a political subdivision of the state. This question has suddenly become extremely important in Virginia, where a number of school districts around the state have entered into collective bargaining agreements with various teacher organizations, and the governor of the state has instructed the attorney general to file suit to challenge the binding effect of these agreements, since Virginia has a law similar to North Carolina's prohibiting collective bargaining by public employees. A lower court upheld the agreement, but the Virginia Supreme Court has reversed holding such agreements to be in violation of public policy.[19]

The Right Not to Be Identified with Union Actions

Another area involving the individual employee and his union is one that, while limited in scope, is nevertheless a problem that often manifests itself most acutely on the individual level and has ramifications similar to the problems discussed in regard to the employee and his First Amendment rights. This is the right of a public employee who is a member of a public employee union to disassociate himself from the official

of employment in any state or territory in which such execution or application is prohibited by state or territorial law." Such an exemption is needed because without it such state laws would be "preempted" by the federal laws.

17. The various types of shop are as follows: closed shop, in which the union can refuse to permit a person to work without its approval; union shop, in which all employees must join the union after a certain period of time; and agency shop, which requires nonunion employees to pay certain fees to the representative union as a condition of employment, to pay for the union's expenses in connection with the enforcement of the collective bargaining agreements.

18. Some jurisdictions permit check off arrangements; Conn. Gen. Stats. §7–477; Rev. Code of Wash. §41.56.110.

19. The Commonwealth v. Arlington County Board 217 Va. 558 (1977).

policies of the union, and in the process be free from obligations to support such programs.

In the course of labor relations, a dissident union member has only limited remedies if he is dissatisfied with the activities of the union in regard to actual bargaining with the employer. This is not necessarily true when unions are engaging in activities not directly affecting the bargaining process with their employer. At issue here are the political and quasi-political activities of the union, although ironically in the public employment field such activities may have more relevance to bargaining than they would in the private sector.

Labor unions in this country constitute, as an entity, a major political force, in that unions as institutions cannot only supply large amounts of money, but also manpower to the political parties and candidates that they favor.[20] Since unions are funded primarily, if not exclusively, by dues paid by the members of the union, funds spent by the union in support of a political candidate or a political position can be directly traced to union dues; computation can determine fairly exactly, on a pro rata basis, how much each member has actually contributed individually to a given expenditure for a political purpose.

Since this union activity (that is, collective bargaining and the managing of the collective bargaining agreement) is not specifically covered by the National Labor Relations Act, the subversion of the individual member's interest to the union management agreement would not necessarily be present with regard to such expenditures. Thus, if a dissident member wishes to disassociate himself from this type of union activity and demands a pro rata refund of his dues used for this purpose, can he in fact collect?

The Supreme Court had to face this question directly in the case of *International Association of Machinists* v. *Street*,[21] in which a group of dissident employees challenged the action of the union on the grounds that "money each was compelled to pay to hold his job was in substantial part used to finance campaigns of candidates for federal and state offices whom we oppose and promote the propagation of political and economic doctrines, concepts and ideologies with which we disagree."[22] The challenge was made both on constitutional and statutory grounds, and the United States Supreme Court, in a six to three decision, upheld the position of the dissident employees.

20. See Harry Wellington and Ralph K. Winters, *The Unions and the Cities* (Washington, D.C.: Brookings Institution, 1971).

21. 367 U.S. 740. See also Railway Employees Dept. v. Hanson, 351 U.S. 225 (1956).

22. 367 U.S. at 744.

Justice Brennan, writing for a plurality, construed the National Labor Relations Act as having the primary purpose of allowing dues to be checked off from the rest so as to "force employees to share the cost of negotiation and administering collective agreements, and the cost of the adjustment and settlement of dispute." He found that this purpose was not intended to "provide the unions with a means of forcing employees, over their objections, to support a political cause which they oppose." The remedy, he found, was not to enjoin enforcement of union shop agreements, but either to prohibit the expenditures of that portion of the union funds representing the contributions of the dissident employees, or give them a refund of their dues; both solutions he found constitutionally satisfactory.[23]

The concurring opinions of Justices Douglas and Black reached the same conclusion as Justice Brennan's, but based it on constitutional rights of the First Amendment, rather than statutory interpretation. However, one factor common to all the majority was that the reason a union member could assert this right was not only because it was beyond the scope of bargaining, but because, under National Labor Relations Law, a union shop presents an element of coercion, since the employee is required to join the union.

Because of this aspect of coercion, the question of whether or not the *Street* decision would be applicable to public employment is an interesting one. If the Brennan opinion, that the basis of the *Street* ruling was (1) coercion and (2) the statutory interpretation is accepted, in the absence of both statutory authorization for bargaining and coercion to join a public employee union, the logic of the *Street* case could not be extended to cover public employee unions, and the only alternative would be for the employee to leave the union, since his job is not dependent upon belonging to it.

However, this may be asking a great deal of the employee because, if the union is engaged in bargaining and grievance procedures, by leaving the union the employee may possibly waive his rights to be represented in grievance procedures and other types of personnel matters. (If the union is both unrecognized and does not engage in bargaining, it would be a voluntary organization like any other voluntary organization, and a member would lose no state recognized rights.)

In the context of a recognized union, the doctrine of state action previously discussed may well come into play. The dissident public employee, by using the state action doctrine, may claim that a recognized public employee union becomes clothed with state action when it acts

23. 367 U.S. at 764, 770, 774.

as a union. Thus the members of the union, while not able to assert National Labor Relations Law as such, may, in the absence of any other specific legislation covering public employees, assert constitutional provisions which can be used to protect their rights in this context.

The rights in question, of course, are First Amendment rights, and the argument for the assertion of rights is that the public employee union only exists because of its relationship to the public employer, that its funds are derived solely because of the public employment, and, because it would not exist but for the employment, it is in effect quasi-public; in such situations its functions are, in effect, limited to involvement with the public employer. Therefore, when the public employee union engages in partisan political activity using union funds, those members of the union objecting to the position of the union can claim that it causes its members to be considered advocates of that position, and that they have a right to either enjoin the use of funds in an amount which represents their pro rata share of the dissident employees dues, or get a refund.

Ironically, the public employee union may be able to successfully assert that, because the limitations on the right to strike amount to almost a total prohibition, the only sanctions a union can bring to bear on public employers who do not negotiate with the union or with whom the union has a dispute over terms of employment is to bring political pressure upon those persons, either through lobbying with other branches of the government or by trying to put into office persons more sympathetic to the union view. While, of course, private unions would make the same claim, nevertheless, with the array of weapons they have available to assert their economic interest, this becomes somewhat superfluous. However, as stated before, since the public union has no such legal weapons, and since use of such weapons is a violation of the law, the political action would tend to be a legitimate, if not the sole, source of legal pressure which can be brought by the union to assert its position against a reluctant or antagonistic public employer.

Once the union is allowed to assert this particular provision, the dissident employee is almost barred from challenging the union position; no court will want to get into the question of whether or not a given candidate is pro- or anti-labor, since this is a political and not a legal question. Only if the candidate or the cause being supported by the public union's funds can be shown to be far afield of any legitimate union interest can a public employee be able to make a challenge.

I cannot state how the courts would react to this question simply because no law presently exists on the issue, and different courts in different areas might react differently, eventually leading to a Supreme Court decision. The real question is whether or not, in the context of public employment, contributions to political activities and candidates become more of a union activity than would be found in the context of private labor law. I believe that this is more of a legitimate union activity, and as such the *Street* doctrine would not be as readily applicable to public labor unions as to unions in the private sector.

Democracy in a Union

Another aspect of the union member's ability to disassociate himself from or to challenge the position of his union concerns the whole area of democracy in the union. As a result of the hearings of the Senate committee on labor racketeering in the late 1950s, Congress passed the Labor Management Reporting and Disclosure Act of 1959, commonly known as the Landrum-Griffin Act. Among other things, this act guaranteed to members of unions a form of First Amendment rights within the context of union organizations.[24]

However, this act applies strictly to unions in the private sector and as such would have no direct applicability to public employee unions. But whether or not the problems which led to the passing of the Landrum-Griffin Act exist in public employee unions is irrelevant, because the potential for problems exists just as much in the public sector as it does in the private sector.

To set the record straight, to the best of my knowledge, unions in the public area, especially teachers' unions and those associated with the American Federation of State, Local and Municipal Employees Union, are militantly democratic in their actions, as are most, but not necessarily all, private sector unions. However, with the rapid growth of public employee unions, an assumption that the leaders-to-be in the area of public unionism would not take on many of the traits of some of the more arbitrary leaders in the private sector is not warranted. Thus similar problems are presented to public employees who wish to have their views expressed in the internal machinery of their union.

While Congress, of course, has the power to legislate in this area and to extend Landrum-Griffin to public employees, and indeed bills have been submitted to do so, in the absence of such legislation the dissident public union member would only be left with the attempt to show that

24. 29 U.S.C. §411(a)(1) and (2) guarantees that: every member of any labor organization shall have the right to meet and assemble freely with other members; to express any views, etc., at meetings of labor organizations as to union elections; to nominate and/or vote for candidates for union election; to be disciplined only according to the union's own rules, which must be approved by the secretary of labor.

the action of the union is really somehow state action rather than private action, and thus covered by the Constitution, especially the due process clause. However, unlike the previous areas discussed, the internal union mechanism may well be considered an aspect of public employee unions that is not state action but strictly private action, in that within the context of its own affairs, barring such matters as racketeering, a public employee union is completely insulated against charges by its membership that it is acting in an unconstitutional manner. I think that all public employees who belong to unions should be aware of the inapplicability of the Landrum-Griffin Act to their particular situation; in the absence of state legislation giving them that right, they should be particularly vigilant about the actions of their leadership, especially since most public employee union constitutions have within them basic democratic principles. Employees should therefore become familiar with these principles and be prepared to act within the context of their own union, rather than assume that an outside agency or court would be able to interfere on their behalf.

Union's Failure to Protect Members' Rights

The final area which should be discussed in this chapter concerns the problem of union failure to protect the union member's interest, or what the union member perceives to be his interest, in disputes between the member and his employer. This problem usually arises in two different contexts, although they are, to some degree, somewhat interchangeable. These are the failure of the union to process an employee's grievance as required under a union-management agreement or, in the absence of an agreement, action by the union in collaboration with the employer for the purpose of punishing a union member.[25]

If one area could be said to constitute the "litmus test" of a union's true interest in the well-being of its members, it is in the area of grievance processing. Indeed, in my experience dealing with union members in the private sector, their chief complaint with their union leadership is not over the adequacy of negotiated benefits or questions of internal

25. The National Labor Relations Acts impose upon unions the duty of fair representation, and the member may sue under 29 U.S.C. §185(a) for violation of those contracts. However, the concept of lack of fair representation has been narrowed almost to the point where it is meaningless. See Ford Motor Co. v. Huffman, 345 U.S. 330 (1958); Vaca v. Sipes, 386 U.S. 171 (1967).

union policy, but rather whether or not the union leadership is willing to go to bat for them when they have a grievance over an enforcement of contract provision.

In the private sector, if a union fails to properly process an employee's grievance, the failure to so constitutes a breach of its duty of fair representation. However, the definition of breach is limited to actions on the union's part which are either arbitrary, discriminatory, or in bad faith. In such circumstances the employee may sue the union or the union and the employer if an element of collusion is present, although as a matter of practicalities in many areas the courts have made it difficult for employees to show breach of duty and prove actual bad faith.

Indeed, some, if not complete, control over the grievance machinery must be allowed the union; otherwise, if an aggrieved employee resorted to the courts for every incident in which he felt the union was not properly protesting his grievance, the situation could become rampant. Thus the union has some requirement to screen out frivolous complaints. However, this, like everything else, can be overdone. The power to screen is also the power to deny. Many times employees who, for one reason or another, ran afoul of union officials or are considered by their employers to be troublemakers found that their grievances, while legitimate, were not properly processed by the union if it did not wish to upset its arrangements with the employer. Some remedy is necessary; indeed, the "troublemaker" often finds himself subject to arbitrary action by the employer in its desire to rid itself of this particular employee, thus making the situation a vicious circle.

If the same situation occurred in a case of public employment, the public employee might be on stronger legal footing with regard to his rights against his union and employer than his private counterpart. A union member thus aggrieved could have the choice of either going into federal court to sue under some form of due process of law, claiming that the union, acting in conjunction with the public employer to deny a resolution of grievance, was acting as a form of state action, or, in the alternative, could bring in a state court, claiming that a contract exists between the union and its members (especially in the absence of formal state recognition of the public union), in which the union has agreed to undertake representation of the employee with regard to grievance procedures in return for the employee's dues. While, again, an element of bad faith would have to be shown since the union has a right to screen out frivolous complaints under any doctrine of law, nevertheless, the public employee would probably not find himself shut out from legal remedy in such situations.

Conclusion

This chapter has attempted to examine the role played by unions vis-à-vis the individual public employee. Much of the discussion has had to be somewhat speculative, because public employee unions are relatively new; even unions organized for some time are only now beginning to assert themselves in a traditional union form as opposed to a pre-existing, voluntary type of organization. In many ways the development of public unions parallels the history of private unions. During the years they lacked recognition, they acted as a kind of voluntary organization; when they finally were recognized, they played a heroic role in the 1930s. Finally, after they became well established, many of the problems that developed were not between the union and the employer, but between the union and its individual members, because the institutional interest of the union was in many ways similar to that of the corporation or business they were ostensibly opposing. A community of interest tended to exist between the management of the union and the management of the corporation, rather than between the union and its members.

Similar situations may be developing in the public sector. For years all public unions tended to be voluntary organizations without any real role to play in the employment process. Now, in many areas of state law they are recognized as legitimate bargaining agents. Constitutionally their right to recruit members and the rights of employees to join the union are protected; even in the absence of bargaining they are functioning as a pressure group for their members, or as representatives in the grievance procedures. However, because the relationships between public unions and employees tends to be harmonious at this time, apart from disagreements over basic policy found in any democratic organization, once the unions become institutionalized in the way of private unions, they may begin to assert institutional rights against the interests of their own members. Since public employees do not have the same legal relationships that the unions of private employees do, they may find themselves again subjected to arbitrary action.

Epilogue

The purpose of this book has not been merely to summarize the state of the law as it pertains to the public employment relationship, nor simply to list the cases a lawyer representing a public employee would need to analyze regarding a particular factual problem.

Rather, the purpose of this book has been to give the public employee and his lawyer an understanding of the employee's legal status vis-à-vis the employer, to enable the employee to be cognizant of the risks his actions might entail to his job situation, the type of actions the employer may take against the employee, and the methods and procedures under which these actions can be taken.

In many areas of life, the law follows and, in effect, incorporates the accepted methods of behavior practiced by participants in a given area. This is especially true in daily business activities, in which the common business practice is the determining factor in a legal dispute and, in effect, a court generally acts more as arbiter than imposer of law. However, the public employment relationship is the opposite. Here practice follows the law, and the employer and employee look to the courts or the legislature for guidance, rather than the courts looking to the parties of the employment relationship for guidance.

Thus, because the parties look to the courts, any understanding of the employment relationship has to be based on an understanding of the law; and in order to understand the law both current cases and the legal theory underpinning these decisions must be studied.

What I have attempted to do is explain the legal theories behind the law, how they developed and where they may go, and provide the employee strategies that he can follow to avoid finding himself out of a job because he did not understand the law or had a mistaken impression as to the protection afforded by the law in a given action.

If any one theme runs through this book, it is that given the present state of the law (unlike the 1960s when the Warren court was in full force), an employee should be cautioned that he acts at his own peril if he seeks to engage in activities that have not been given constitutional sanction in the past. While this does not mean that an employee must bury his beliefs in order to continue employment, or that all court cases would necessarily go against the employee, nevertheless, at the present time an element of risk extends to all assertions of constitutional rights by the employee unless clear precedent—in a similar or exact situation upholding such activity—exists. This is true whether or not the activity is speech related.

This book seeks to enable the employee wishing to engage in apparently constitutionally protected activities to tailor such speech or activities so that they will come within the terms of an existing precedent. If he acts with caution and knowledge, an employee can be just as effective without running any risks or having a job action taken against him.

The return of legal theory to a time predating the Warren court has, in effect, bottomed out; President Carter perhaps will have the opportunity to appoint justices to the Supreme Court and judges in other lower federal courts more sympathetic to the ideals of the Constitution. A shift of one or two justices could allow a new doctrine extending procedural due process to all public employees, or allow a theory of the First Amendment which would provide a presumption of validity to any speech, or reverse *Bishop* v. *Wood*, which denied aspects of due process, and reopen federal courts to public employees challenging the procedural basis of their dismissal.

This, of course, is in the future; at present the public employee, faced with *Bishop* v. *Wood*, the *Roth* case, or any other cases previously discussed would find himself in deep trouble unless actions are fine-tuned to comport with a narrow interpretation of the law. This is what this book hopes to do; if it is successful, public employees will be able to preserve both their constitutional rights and their jobs.

Selected Reading

The following constitutes not an exhaustive list of all books and law review articles used as references or sources in this book, but rather a selective group of books and law review articles of broad appeal that would be very helpful to the lay person in understanding many of the legal concepts in this book.

Books

Barth, Alan. *The Loyalty of Free Men.* New York: Viking Press, 1951.

Bowers, Claude G. *The Party Battles of the Jackson Period.* Boston: Houghton Mifflin, 1972.

Brown, Ralph Jr. *Loyalty and Security.* New Haven, Conn.: Yale University Press, 1958.

Chafee, Zechariah. *The Blessings of Liberty.* Philadelphia: J. B. Lippincott, 1976.

Emerson, Thomas I. *The System of Freedom of Expression.* New York: Random House, 1970.

Goodman, Walter. *The Committee.* New York: Farrar, Straus and Giroux, 1968.

Joughin, Louis, ed. *Academic Freedom and Tenure.* Madison: University of Wisconsin Press, 1969.

McWilliams, Carey. *Witch Hunt: The Revival of Heresy.* Boston: Little, Brown, 1950.

Moorehead, Alan. *The Traitors*. Rev. ed. New York: Harper & Row, 1963.
O'Neill, Robert M. *The Price of Dependency*. New York: E. P. Dutton, 1970.
Reitmann, Alan, ed. *The Price of Liberty*. New York: W. W. Norton, 1961.
Stern, Phillip. *The Oppenheimer Case: Security on Trial*. New York: Harper &
   Row, 1969.
Ten Broek, Jacobus. *Equal under the Law*. New York: Macmillan, 1965.
Ungar, Sanford. *The Papers and the Papers*. New York: E. P. Dutton, 1972.
Wellington, Harry H., and Winter, Ralph K. *The Unions and the Cities*. Wash-
   ington, D.C.: Brookings Institution, 1971.

Law Reviews

Powell, Thomas Reed. "The Right to Work for the State," 16 *Columbia Law
   Review* 99 (1916).
Reich, Charles. "The New Property," 73 *Yale Law Review* 733 (1964).
Van Alstyne, W. W. "The Constitutional Rights of Teachers and Professors,"
   Duke Law Review 841 (1970).
———. "The Demise of the Right-Privilege Distinction in Constitutional Law,"
   81 *Harvard Law Review* 1439 (1968).

Index

Academic freedom: acquired right, 231; constitutional right, 100; danger to, in investigative programs, 191–92

Adler v. *Board of Education*, 28, 199–200

Administrative necessity doctrine, 36; use of, 93–96

Alcoholic consumption. *See* Drinking

Aldinger v. *Howard*, 46–47

Alien and Sedition Acts, 196

Alternatives to lawsuits: grievance procedures, 257; procedural due process, 234

American Association of University Professors, 112 n.54; 113 n.56

American Civil Liberties Union: concerned about Supreme Court trend, 69 n.51; Northern California Chapter of, 191

American Federation of State, Local and Municipal Employees Union, 255

Ancillary jurisdiction, 47

Anonymous information: immunity for publisher of, 91; as proof, 75–79; sanctions on employees for supplying, 91–92

Army-McCarthy hearings, 166, 193

Arnett v. *Kennedy*, 44–45, 220; contradicted by *Bishop* v. *Wood*, 49–50; just

cause standard upheld in, 44–45, 140–41; logical inconsistency of, 237; procedural limitations to due process in, 220–21, 235

Ascertainable deleterious effects, 65

Association, right to: limited by loyalty-security order, 28–29, 174; limited by specific intent, 208; for public employees, 163–65, 241–42

Associations, public employee. *See* Unions, public employee

Atkins v. *The City of Charlotte*, 242–43

"Badge of infamy," 201

Baggett v. *Bullitt*, 205–7

Bailey v. *Richardson*, 175–77; anonymous charges in, 28; use of informants in, 75, 76, 166

Baird v. *State Bar*, 210

Balancing test: between First Amendment rights and governmental interests, 83–85; effect of, on national security issues, 90; use of, 67, 131, 133, 155–56, 157, 211–12

Barron v. *Baltimore*, 26

Beilan v. *Board of Education*, 202, 203

Beliefs, right to, 163–65; limited by loyalty-security order, 174